1329

D0795120

RETHINKING C
PRACT...

Developing transformative
neighbourhoods

Gabriel Chanan and Colin Miller

With a foreword by Alan Twelvetrees

First published in Great Britain in 2013 by

The Policy Press
University of Bristol
Fourth Floor
Beacon House
Queen's Road
Bristol BS8 1QU, UK
t: +44 (0)117 331 4054
f: +44 (0)117 331 4093
tpp-info@bristol.ac.uk
www.policypress.co.uk

North American office:

The Policy Press
c/o The University of Chicago Press
1427 East 60th Street
Chicago, IL 60637, USA
t: +1 773 702 7700
f: +1 773-702-9756
e:sales@press.uchicago.edu
www.press.uchicago.edu

© The Policy Press 2013

British Library Cataloguing in Publication Data
A catalogue record for this book is available from the British Library.

Library of Congress Cataloging-in-Publication Data
A catalog record for this book has been requested.

ISBN 978 1 44730 009 0 (paperback)
ISBN 978 1 44730 010 6 (hardcover)

The right of Gabriel Chanan and Colin Miller to be identified as authors of this work has been asserted by
them in accordance with the 1988 Copyright, Designs and Patents Act.

The Policy Press uses environmentally responsible print partners.

Cover design by Qube Design Associates, Bristol
Front cover: photograph kindly supplied by Jupiter Images
Printed and bound in Great Britain by Hobbs, Southampton
The Policy Press uses environmentally responsible print partners

Contents

List of tables, figures and boxes v

Foreword by Alan Twelvetrees vii

one Introduction 1

two National policy on community involvement – the historical journey 17

three Community practice and the state 35

four What happens in communities 49

five Towards neighbourhood strategy 77

six Building partnership 99

seven Different perspectives 117

eight Outcomes and evidence 133

nine Conclusion – strategy for community practice 155

References 173

Index 181

List of tables, figures and boxes

Tables

4.1   Total number of listed third sector organisations in selected local   63
        authority areas

6.1   Internal and external perspectives of a neighbourhood partnership   104

6.2   The C2 seven step model   105

6.3   Skills for community practice coordination   107

7.1   Complementary actions of residents and services   129

7.2   Impact and difficulty grid   130

8.1   Six outcomes model from *The Community Development Challenge*   140

8.2   Community strength indicators from the England Local Government   143
        Performance Framework 2007–10

8.3   Selected findings from the National Survey of Third Sector Organisations   146

8.4   Components of evaluation and performance management   151

9.1   Six points of divergence in community development models   164

9.2   Key factors in community practice strategy   165

Figures

4.1   Functions of community groups   56

4.2   Levels of involvement in a community   65

4.3   Four stages in community groups   70

4.4   Picturing interaction   73

5.1   The Egan Wheel   79

5.2   Building the creative space between communities and public agencies   96

6.1   Neighbourhood as interlocking systems   101

8.1   Example of an LSP 'family'   137

9.1   The policy chain   156

Boxes

4.1   Blyth Valley, Northumberland: A district-wide community development   49
        strategy

4.2   Southwark: A two-year project   50

4.3   Wrexham Maelor Community Project, 1986–92   51

4.4   Ashton, Tameside: Reclaiming the neighbourhood   51

4.5   Townstal Community Partnership   52

5.1   Negotiating together instead of getting lost in the system   81

5.2   Organisational development in the community sector   81

5.3   Travellers' access to public services   82

Foreword

My first thought on reading this book was that the two authors should meet the leaders of the three main political parties in the UK in order to explain their vision and to seek to have aspects of it incorporated in governance and service provision. Gabriel Chanan and Colin Miller envisage a significantly different way of managing the welfare state from the one we now have. Modern industrialised countries in Europe have developed extremely complex services which are provided by professionals. Anybody working on the ground knows that, in many cases, due to the specific circumstances of those in need, a particular service may badly miss its target. Or the supposed beneficiaries must jump through many hoops if they wish to get that particular benefit, which is a huge disincentive.

The vision of the authors is of a society where, based on the neighbourhood, there is a team of professionals, who basically do two things. On the one hand, such professionals specialise in delivering their particular service, whether it is social care, education, environmental improvement, health, housing, policing or any other. On the other hand, they liaise both with each other and with community groups, in order to assist those groups to be effective and also to ensure that local knowledge is applied to ensure that service delivery is more effective.

Such a task may at first sight seem Herculean, but would actually be the wider implementation of what is already done in patches by good community work. Chanan and Miller point to many examples of service professionals working both together and with neighbourhoods to make such improvements. And when it works, as it certainly can, and as they show, the benefits can be enormous. The time has come for this perspective to be mainstreamed and not to remain the 'start, stop, start' phenomenon it mostly is, relying on the hard work and vision of a few innovators, who eventually move on or are unable to continue obtaining funding. If there could be political progress on this front (and it is obviously a huge 'if') the next step is for Chanan and Miller, with others, to begin to work out how appropriate training, structural arrangements and other supports could be provided in order for that vision gradually to be implemented. It would cost money (particularly difficult today, of course) but service improvements would certainly ensue and probably there would be savings too.

Those reading this book who know much about community work/development (the two terms are used differently by different people, and often interchanged) will also know of the neo-Marxist theoretical underpinnings of some of those in the field and writing about it. In various discussions about community work with friends and colleagues of this persuasion I have sometimes asked how their practice differs from what could be called pragmatic community development practice such as mine. After much discussion, it turns out that, in reality, our work would not differ much at all, except in the sense that all workers have slightly different styles, which are influenced by many things, but probably not, in the main, by their politics. I emphasise this because Chanan and Miller present strong arguments which, in my view, show that what can be called the Marxist tradition in community work is largely a distraction, certainly passionately felt, but masking a sparsity of practical strategy. I write this with some feeling because, as a young community work lecturer in the 1970s, I had to cope with some very left-wing students who sought to realise that vision *in their community work jobs*. I always thought that such a hope had no basis in reality (which is not to say that such a political vision, in itself, is invalid). In reality, community work is about 'putting the manure on the rhubarb', without which such a plant will scarcely survive. To achieve real improvements in local conditions you have to work with community members on issues both which are meaningful to them and in relation to which you are likely to have some success. However, this does also involve making ultimately moral judgements as to which groups you will work with and which issues you will help them take up.

Having made the above points, I readily acknowledge that some community work writers and thinkers who started out with an extremely left-wing vision and hope in relation to the outcomes of their community work have modified that vision in their community development practice to take account of the 'real world' in which we live. I respect such people hugely.

The practical wisdom and theoretical underpinnings of effective community development intervention in (mostly disadvantaged) communities is extremely rich; it is also a world-wide phenomenon, with, often, very different 'flavours' in different countries. It would be disastrous if the potentially emerging occupation of 'community practice', which Chanan and Miller point to, ignored this storehouse of knowledge of theory and practice, whatever its origins. From 30 years' experience of many aspects of the community work field, including in some other countries besides the UK, I would testify that it is extremely difficult to do well. If community practice does emerge as a new variant, it is vital that it doesn't re-invent the wheel, and that it draws on this rich tradition.

I cannot finish without a mention of Gabriel Chanan, a colleague and friend for many years at the Community Development Foundation (CDF). Readers who are familiar with the history of community work and, more particularly, the principal books, articles and other publications about it over the last 20 years, will recognise Gabriel's huge contribution, though this has mainly been in closely argued and evidenced reports for Government and papers for CDF, on the need to evidence the positive effects of community work intervention and indicating the criteria on which such intervention should be evaluated and quantified. As Colin Miller and he make clear here, a bit of an arctic winter has settled over community development in England, though less so in the other countries within the UK and Ireland. It is important, therefore, that many of these ideas resurface here and will be seen now by a much wider audience. Such ideas are crucially important to the development of our democracy and will, I hope, be carefully and thoroughly read by a much wider range of practitioners and policy makers.

I wish Gabriel, Colin and others who take up this mantle of seeking to bring community practice into the mainstream, all success.

Alan Twelvetrees

Alan has been a community worker, community work lecturer, and Director, Wales, for the Community Development Foundation. He has written 10 books in this field and is now a freelance consultant.

ONE

Introduction

In this chapter we explain what we understand community practice to be and why it is increasingly vital to local governance and the delivery of public services. We describe the rise of community involvement as an issue in public policy, leading to the need for community practice, and identify key components, such as neighbourhoods and community groups. We ask whether conditions in disadvantaged neighbourhoods could be transformed by more coordinated community practice; and if so, whether this change should be led by the community development occupation. Anticipating the discussion in the following chapters of this book, we flag up the need for a new synthesis of policy, experience, concepts and skills to meet this challenge.

What is community practice?

Community practice means the ways in which the staff of public services, or those involved in voluntary organisations or other local initiatives, reach out to support local residents, by working together to improve conditions and to help them gain greater control over the forces that control their lives. Whether undertaken by community workers, housing officers, health workers, teachers, police officers, social workers, youth workers or others, community practice is action over and above the delivery of the service alone. It goes beyond consultation, though that is where it may begin. Residents are treated not as passive consumers of services but as active collaborators. The more intensive forms of community practice, notably community development, boost the long-term internal strengths of local and other types of community: increasing people's ability to support each other and to work together on common issues; helping them to influence service change; giving a stronger voice to those with least power; and so making democracy more meaningful and effective.[1]

Residents themselves are the main actors in the neighbourhood, but what we are concerned with here is the role of those people who provide services to those residents from outside the community itself. If these people also happen to be residents of the neighbourhood concerned, they may play a dual role of activist and service provider.

Some community practice is driven simply by front-line workers' natural responsiveness to people's needs; some by organisations' policies; and some by appeals or criticism from local residents or groups. In different agencies it might be called, for example, community engagement or involvement, neighbourhood policing, patient and public involvement, or support for a bigger role for the local third sector or social enterprises. Regeneration of disadvantaged areas has been a particular driver. Whatever the vehicle, democratic regimes worldwide have increasingly recognised that government by consent demands a general ethos of collaboration with citizens achieved through working with local and other forms of community.

Although tens of thousands of public agency workers in the UK have carried out community practice to some degree, and millions of residents have benefited from it, it is not widely understood, because it is dispersed, and differently defined from one field to another. Most social policies include some narrative about engaging with communities, but in many cases this is mere flavouring. In some policies the commitment is more practical, but community engagement is interpreted as just being about consultation and public relations. Where involvement is understood as an active component of delivery, it is may be seen as a matter of technique in that professional field alone, rather than a means of joining up with all services in the area in order to strengthen community life as a whole.

An exception to this somewhat random picture is the concentrated form of community practice: community development (CD). Within community development there is a long tradition of practice, theory and debate about how people, working together, can overcome the structural factors which generate poverty, inequality and disadvantage.[2] But there are few community development workers compared with the number of staff of the major public agencies. And despite its long track record – and worldwide presence – community development is often in a weak position. This is particularly the case in England in the 2010s; less so in Scotland, Wales and Northern Ireland.

Community development also has an ambivalent relationship to the wider, looser field of community practice as a whole. On one hand, community development has helped to create community practice, and has a great store of experience and skills which could help that practice to become more effective. On the other hand many community development advocates have misgivings about the effects of their work being absorbed into conventional service objectives. They are uneasy about fitting their aims into state services, which they may regard as reinforcing rather than alleviating disadvantage.

One of the recurring themes in this book, therefore, is the relationship between community development and the rest of community practice: can community development, a small (and in England now reduced) field, lead and raise the level of organisation of the much larger but more amorphous field of community practice? How might community development itself need to change if it were to try to take on this role? On the other hand, how would community practice fare without leadership from community development? Would it remain weak and spasmodic, or even disappear altogether under service cutbacks? Or would it be freer to develop an alternative identity of its own?

One way or another, there is a need for new strategy in this area. As public services reel under the impact of global economic turmoil, bringing greater need but reduced resources, it is vital that they find more effective ways to manage their relationship with the local populations which depend on them, and which also, as citizens, ultimately govern them. This need is manifest in England, which is our primary focus and limitation in this book, though the same dilemmas appear in different forms in all countries. The pressures of austerity threaten to squeeze out the space for innovation in public services just at the time when it is needed most. Community practice will only flourish if it can demonstrate that it can both help to make public services more effective and economic, and also reinvigorate local democracy in the face of increasing challenge.

The community involvement trajectory

Until the global recession struck in 2008, efforts to increase local community involvement in public services and local democracy in the UK appeared to be on an unstoppable trajectory of growth. Over the preceding 20 to 30 years there had been a gradually expanding history of user involvement in local services concerning housing, health, regeneration, education, policing, environment and other public issues.

The momentum had come from both 'below' and 'above'. Social movements, campaigning organisations and community groups put pressure on governments and local authorities for better services, increased human rights and reductions in poverty. Governments in turn looked for ways to enable people to feel that they had a stake in decisions made about local conditions and service reform. Community 'involvement', 'engagement' and at times 'empowerment' became policy objectives, intertwined with delivery of services. Even if some of this was cosmetic, it provided opportunities for genuine advance. A scattered occupation of community workers emerged, funded insecurely by various, often short-term, government and local government schemes, and initiatives from voluntary sector and philanthropic bodies. Gradually, many other public service workers also began to incorporate elements of community work into their roles.

In this book we review the emergence of community practice in both its more intensive and dispersed forms, and make the case for combining them into a systematic approach to improving quality of life through action at neighbourhood level. The action would equally concern, and intertwine with, communities of interest and identity. We illustrate what community practice has achieved, show why it is an essential instrument to help meet the current challenges facing society, analyse what has stood in its the way, and draw together a framework for local strategy to implement it. Many elements of the strategy will be familiar to public and voluntary bodies from existing or past practice but we believe the overall synthesis is new.

Our aim is to show how and why community practice should become universal, and what changes this requires from common past practice. But this is far too ambitious a project to be achieved simply by our efforts here. We see this book as just one contribution to a widespread movement created by many more people than we could possibly acknowledge. We are conscious of limitations of several kinds, including perhaps our gender outlook. Women's experience and ways of networking are crucial to community life. If we have a propensity to deal more with structural factors and strategic issues than with personal relationships and the dilemmas of practice on the ground, perhaps nevertheless this is a valid contribution in a field where – in our judgement – the strategic side has often been too weak. We deal more with policy and strategy than with community practice as a social movement, but readily acknowledge that without the social movement policy and strategy would never have come onto the agenda.

The book is far from being a complete prescription for transforming neighbourhoods, if such a thing is possible. We concentrate on the central issue of how to move from a long history of fragmentary and short-term community practice to a framework for comprehensive neighbourhood partnership between a wide spread of local residents and the full array of public services. There are some important elements of neighbourhood development which we touch on but do not feel able to do justice to, such as the role of the private sector, the impact of climate change, the importance of gender and ethnicity, and variations in experience across different nations. All these need deeper investigation, and integration into strategy. But we believe that our central framework has a degree of universal validity, and that if it is understood and put in place, it will be easier to work out how other elements can also be advanced.

From one-way provision to co-production

Historically, in the early stages of mass provision of public services, users of the services were largely seen as passive beneficiaries. This is still the dominant ethos of most services, but over the past 20 to 30 years a more sophisticated model of the relation between public services and their users has emerged. In this model, service providers not only anticipate but encourage and seek to collaborate with users. They recognise that the service they are providing works best when the beneficiaries both hold it to account and complement it with their own activities. The health service cannot make the population healthy if people lead unhealthy lifestyles. Housing authorities and social landlords cannot manage their stock well unless there are effective tenants' associations to liaise with. Schools cannot get the best out of their pupils unless parents are also active in their children's education. Protection of the local environment, decisions on local planning, transport and leisure, sports and cultural amenities depend on residents' vigilance, feedback, influence and at times protests, as well as on the local council.

Lately this model has been called 'co-production':

> Co-production means delivering public services in an equal and reciprocal relationship between professionals, people using services, their families and their neighbours. Where activities are co-produced in this way, both services and neighbourhoods become far more effective agents of change.[3]

In a comprehensive strategy, community involvement and co-production would be practised across all public services in a locality and coordinated by neighbourhood partnerships led jointly by residents and providers. In most localities, however, community involvement in public services is still very spasmodic. It is also suffering from the recent cuts in resources. Yet involvement is even more vital in conditions of austerity. If councils, schools, health agencies, police, social services and all the other agencies on which we depend are to retain the confidence and cooperation of the public, they need to be able to ensure that people feel that they are fairly treated, feel involved in agencies' decisions, understand the agencies' dilemmas, and willingly cooperate with those agencies to make society work. Creating an ethos of collaboration is one of the basic objectives of community practice. However, when people are struggling with poverty and multiple disadvantage, a pervasive feeling of disempowerment needs to be overcome if they are to be able to take an active part in local affairs.

The neighbourhood focus

Not everyone wants to be or need be involved in local affairs, but there is plenty of appetite for involvement in most places.[4] As a means of improving local conditions, involvement is more crucial in some places than others. Advantage and disadvantage are clustered in different localities: life expectancy can vary by 10 years between different neighbourhoods in the same city. Poor neighbourhoods are both a result of disadvantage and a cause of it. Community practice is particularly important where needs are greatest. But it is also important in the 'average' places where many people live, and where disadvantage is scattered less obviously but just as painfully.

There are also other reasons why the neighbourhood – or another similar–sized area such as an estate, village or scattered rural settlement – is a crucial level for practical change. At this level – say on average amongst populations between 5,000 and 15,000 – people encounter each other face to face, sharing amenities, schools, shops, places of worship; they receive the same services; and some join together in social clubs, sports clubs, youth clubs, day centres and environmental campaigns. This is the same community that the public agencies are serving. Yet each service tends to try to engage with it separately. Could a more coordinated, cross-sectoral, interactive form of engagement transform life in disadvantaged neighbourhoods?

'Transform' is an ambitious word, and we hesitated before using it in the subtitle for this book. But we judged it preferable to err on the side of vision and optimism rather than accommodate too readily to the limitations which currently exist. For whatever happens during the rest of the 21st century there is undoubtedly a need for change in the way we run our society. Economic pressures demand that public services yield maximum cost-benefit, and the imperative of social harmony – if not simple social justice – demands that rampant inequality is overcome. Equally, environmental pressures are likely to impel far-reaching changes in lifestyle, both at governmental and personal levels.[5] In all these areas, action at neighbourhood level is a critical lever. It should therefore aim not just to ameliorate but to transform.

Neighbourhood partnerships of one kind or another are already widespread but often fragile. In focusing on them as a key vehicle for local solutions we are, at one level, merely seeking to reinforce a relatively well known instrument. But many partnerships are much less effective than they need to be. Our aim is to put them on a firmer footing both theoretically and practically, focusing in particular on three aspects:

- First, taking a comprehensive view of community activity in the neighbourhood, mapping all groups and activities, not just concentrating on a particular community project.
- Secondly, mobilising all existing and latent community practice from across the public and voluntary services, not just relying on a small and often temporary community development input.
- Thirdly, applying objective criteria of effectiveness and improvement both in community strengths and in material conditions, not only subjective impressions of core activists.

But all this must also be tempered by awareness of the limitations of neighbourhoods: that the residents of a neighbourhood or area do not necessarily amount to a unified community; that people have, and need, allegiances outside the neighbourhood; that neighbourhoods can sometimes be too tightly identified with one community to the exclusion of others, exacerbating conflict rather than healing it.[6]

The book is addressed to policy makers, programme planners, managers, project leaders and trainers. But it is addressed equally to activists in communities and to practitioners at the front line, since these are the people who, ultimately, must make community practice happen – and who often see the need for it most clearly.

The basic unit: the community group

The role of local community groups is fundamental to the whole question of community involvement and practice. Community activity is about people doing things together, and as soon as people do such things over a period of time, meeting repeatedly, they begin to take on some sort of group existence. Groups with a long-term existence are the basic vehicles of community activity. They are also the clearest evidence that community activity is taking place. Collectively they can be described as the community sector, and they form the largest part of the voluntary sector. Other parts of the voluntary sector are professionally run charities and social enterprises. There are also a variety of national voluntary organisations which consist largely of autonomous or semi-autonomous local branches staffed mainly by volunteers. Many of these are in effect local community groups.

The line between different types of voluntary and community organisation may sometimes be difficult to draw, but it is the condition of the mass of smaller community groups which is the surest indication of the strength or weakness of community life in a particular place.

Social policies both local and national often invoke community involvement without appearing to understand how fundamental community groups are to the life of a community. After all, many are small and very low profile. Some of the groups themselves may not be aware of others in the same neighbourhood, and the majority of residents may not even know that some of them exist. Even community development theory and guidance, whilst assuming the importance of community groups, often has little to say about their combined effectiveness across a neighbourhood.

This is not to say that everyone is involved in groups, or that such groups are the only expression of community life. Beyond the identifiable groups in a given locality are hundreds of networks of friends, extended families, acquaintances and workmates.[7]

The visible groups may not be representative of majority interest and opinion. Yet such groups embody the commitment of those residents who are most active, most dedicated to a particular interest or most determined to improve local conditions. Without these groups and networks, public agencies and services would have few footholds for sustained dialogue and interaction with local residents. A long-term community involvement strategy would place a high value on them, helping them grow in size, inclusiveness and effectiveness, and helping them to be more aware of themselves as a sector and to interact more productively with the public agencies, without ever equating them with the entire community.

Emergence of community practice

Since the second world war, governments of different complexions have created a variety of community involvement policies and projects to stimulate or accommodate participation and meet challenge halfway. As a result, numerous front-line public service workers have increasingly been expected not only to carry out their expert service but also to engage in dialogue and collaboration with users. This might, for example, involve organising consultations with local residents; attending residents' meetings to discuss local issues; supporting community groups; negotiating with community representatives on local committees; or planning joint projects with community organisations. Whereas social work mainly addresses individuals or households on problematic personal issues, community practice engages with a group of residents on collective issues such as the conditions and opportunities in the neighbourhood, the delivery of local public services or participation in local democracy. There is sometimes a bridge from social work to community practice, when residents realise – with new hope – that what seemed to them to be a personal problem is an issue faced by the community as a whole.

The purposes of community involvement policies are multiple. On the one hand there are reasons of principle promoted by politicians and community development workers: everyone is entitled to an equal share in society's goods; people in disadvantaged situations should have more influence over the services they rely on; and vigorous democracy demands an active citizenship. Perhaps more compelling, however, are managerial reasons of state: disadvantaged neighbourhoods are difficult to manage, threatening to erupt in frustration; young people with poor prospects and few positive role models are vulnerable to drugs and crime because they feel they have no stake in the wider society; areas where few people are in paid work become ghettoes of despair; disadvantaged areas are more dependent on public services, putting pressure on resources; improvement in services needs pressure from users; and services which elicit cooperation and voluntary help are cheaper to run.

The growth of these policies did not emanate from a long-term plan but came as a spasmodic, gradually increasing response to problems of ensuring effectiveness in the management of localities and delivery of services. Housing departments and social landlords found it easier to manage estates if there were credible tenants' associations. Police found it easier to control crime if residents talked to them and kept watch. Residents in poorer areas were more likely to cooperate with regeneration projects if they had been involved in the planning. The spread of community practice was not the product of a unified theory or policy but of a growing awareness amongst policy makers and public service agencies that post-industrial society was characterised by a decline in organic communities and an increase in isolation and anomie, and that this posed problems for public order and consent, relations between governments and citizens, and the effectiveness of public services.

Involvement can be interpreted weakly or strongly. Weaker versions are more common. Many public agencies regard consulting their users as sufficient. Consultation itself has weaker and stronger versions.[8] Questionnaires distributed to all households in a locality usually have very low response rates. Citizens' panels and deliberative inquiries, where people have a chance to go into greater depth on a local issue, produce more meaningful results, but are only likely to involve a more highly motivated fraction of the population.

The term 'community practice' was first coined by Butcher et al in 1993[9] to recognise the fact that the purpose of strengthening or engaging with local communities was becoming increasingly widespread in public service jobs, spreading way beyond the limited pool of those known as community development workers, though with little coordination or guidance. This was during the Conservative government of John Major. The first book to focus exclusively on community practice was concerned by 'an increasing number of posts at policy-making and managerial levels with a brief to develop and implement community policies ... At the same time the role of the generalist paid professional community worker has continued to decline.'[10]

Most of these jobs would not be described as community development roles: the involvement element was only part of their job, and the perspective on involvement tended to be at the top-down end of the spectrum. But there were very many more people working in these roles than there were community development workers, so the collective impact of their involvement activity was potentially much greater.

Growth and setback

Whilst the spread of community practice was more practical than ideological, it was reflected in policy in different ways by different governments. The Conservative government of the early 1990s generated an increasing variety of community-oriented public service roles, notably through the Single Regeneration Budget (SRB) in England, which 'top sliced' budgets of five government departments to fund a programme focussed on disadvantaged neighbourhoods. The programme grew rapidly, from around 100 local schemes in the first year to over 1,100 concurrent projects in its sixth year. And as its volume grew, so too did the community practice element within it (see Chapter Two).

After a hesitant start, this growth in community practice multiplied under New Labour. Although the government wastefully curtailed SRB in 1998, it soon replaced it with Neighbourhood Renewal and a variety of other community-oriented local schemes. Even more far-reaching, it later extended the principles of these 'area-based initiatives' (focused on priority neighbourhoods) into the governance framework for local authorities as a whole. Furthermore, it complemented this by embedding requirements to 'engage with the community' in most of the separate public services. Finally in 2008 it passed into law a duty for public services to involve the community in their decision making.[11]

The 'Duty to Involve' hardly had time to bed down, however, before the policy climate was drastically altered by a series of challenges: changes of Labour government leadership, the onset of recession, a crisis of confidence over MPs' honesty following the expenses scandal, and eventually the general election of 2010 and the public service cuts which began in 2011. In this maelstrom the incoming Coalition government's repeal of the Duty to Involve and decommissioning of community development organisations escaped any serious public attention.

Clearly the reasons behind the growth of community practice did not disappear just because of the recession in and after 2008. In many ways they became even more pressing. But there was, in England, a loss of vision and momentum regarding community involvement. And decline in community involvement is likely to have accelerated after the Coalition government came to power in 2010, despite the 'big society' theme which has purported to boost it. The big society policy appears to suggest that the solution is for communities to provide more services for themselves instead of relying on state provision. But the signs are that community groups and community practice did not grow but rather shrank in 2010–12.[12] This would not be known from the big society policy itself, since it began with no baseline, being promoted as if it were a wholly new idea.[13] The sustained and renewed trajectory of community development in Scotland, Wales and Northern Ireland, and the failure of the big society idea to take hold in those nations[14] provide interesting contrasts with England at this time.

All this poses some stark questions about the role of community involvement in 21st century society: is it only in effect a luxury, an aspiration that can only be pursued in a benevolent economic and ideological climate? Or is it something that is even more vital in times of austerity when disadvantage is increasing? What kind of community strengthening can take place in conditions of austerity? If it is vital, does it grow spontaneously amongst residents, or does it have to be stimulated by the use of community practice techniques by professionals working amongst them? If community practice is an essential instrument, how can its cost be justified when mainstream services themselves are under-resourced? Does greater involvement mean greater demand on limited resources, or is involvement itself a resource that can alleviate pressure on demand? And what strategy can advance it under these conditions?

Can neighbourhoods be transformed?

Under whatever government, we believe that the key stepping stone to synergy between communities and services is coordination of community practice across whole neighbourhoods or similar-sized areas such as villages, parishes, estates or small towns. How far this is possible is critically affected by whether favourable conditions exist in government, local government and other public agencies, at strategic and managerial levels as well as at the front line. But it needs to be pursued even if conditions are not favourable.

The historical evidence for the feasibility of major change in neighbourhoods is not encouraging. Disadvantaged neighbourhoods persist for generations, even with recurrent input of special resources and programmes. Some of the causes are quite clear. People with less money go to, or stay in, the places where they can afford to live, which are liable to be those seen as less desirable. Public housing is built on land that is cheaper because it is less well located and less well served by communications. Concentrations of people with less money to spend result in fewer amenities and shops, and postcode discrimination by banks and insurance companies. Community involvement alone is unlikely to be able to overcome all these and other obstacles to prosperity.

What we mean by 'transformative neighbourhoods' are not places which completely change their character but neighbourhoods which make it easier for people to transform the conditions of their lives: to build wider friendship networks; to create new activities and facilities around them; to connect better with areas of economic opportunity; to overcome poverty and disadvantage; to create a more ecologically sustainable lifestyle; and to exercise a more meaningful local democracy. What we do not know, because both community development and other community practice have generally been so spasmodic, is *how far* neighbourhoods could potentially be transformed; how much further than we have seen in the past. And how much further again if community practice strategies in disadvantaged neighbourhoods were better integrated with wider economic revival strategies in cities and regions.

A variety of whole-neighbourhood approaches have been tried over the past generation. There have been some striking go-it-alone examples like Balsall Heath in Birmingham,[15] the Beacon estate in Falmouth[16] and the whole city of Seattle in the USA;[17] there has been Community Led Planning in rural areas;[18] and there have been major government programmes in selected areas across the country such as the Single Regeneration Budget and Neighbourhood Renewal. We will draw on sources such as these in seeking to construct a rationale and framework which we believe would take us a major step further on the erratic historical journey towards the best possible community practice outcomes compatible with real-world conditions.

Can community development lead?

We have said that community practice is to some extent an expansion of a relatively little known discipline with a history of several generations: community development (CD). Community development workers and champions have played a significant supporting role in the spread of community practice by promoting their principles and campaigning for community-oriented policies for the past 20 years. At the same time they have often become uneasy about the dilution of their discipline into weaker forms, and incorporation of their methods into mainstream public services, seeing these as being responsible for some of the top-down control of people's lives which they felt they were fighting against.

The line between community development workers and other community practitioners might be hard to draw in some cases. What might distinguish the community development workers would be their long-term relationship with a number of community groups and networks, helping them develop, grow and become more influential. They emphasise the bottom-up approach, taking their cue from local residents' declared concerns. Other community practitioners, being tied in to particular agencies and departments, may be more concerned with getting local people to engage with their specialist issue from the top down, be it housing, health, safety or any other. These practitioners would also be likely to have less time to engage in depth with the development of community groups through many stages, and would be more likely to engage in dialogue with groups that are already well-organised and articulate.

We see community development as part of community practice – a particularly concentrated part, with potentially much experience and theory to offer to the wider network of practitioners. We therefore use the term community practice to span both the top-down and bottom-up approaches. The two perspectives are not always as distinct as the labels would suggest, and need to be used together in order to give as wide a range of help to communities as possible.

However, when public service agencies turn to community development exponents as a source of expertise and frameworks for new areas of community practice, they often receive a somewhat ambivalent response. Community development sometimes has a tendency to hold itself apart from government, local authorities and public services. It might be said that community engagement by public service agencies is not true community development; that to be authentic, community practice needs to be 'generic' – it needs to put itself at the service of the community without preconceptions as to what issues the community might want to take up. And in answer to questions about how to define objectives, how to measure results and how long it would take to obtain them, it is likely to be said that true community development is about process, not product; that the process is very long; and that the important thing is not measurement but values such as equality and anti-discrimination, social justice, collective action, community empowerment, and working and learning together.[19]

But how are the values to be injected into reality if not through an accumulation of practical gains? And how is progress towards a major cumulative effect to be recognised if it is not measured objectively against local conditions?

In disadvantaged neighbourhoods, small practical achievements may provide vital improvements in quality of life for a number of residents, and may lead on to greater improvements. For those few residents at the core of the action, these changes may entail personally transformative experiences. So in a patchy way community development does empower a number of residents, or at least reduces their sense of being disempowered. But if we want this experience to extend to the majority of the local population, community development workers would need to work closely with all other community practitioners and offer them a linking framework and attractive leadership to boost their combined impact.

We see the current condition of modern society and economy as demanding a shift from a situation in which community development has been rather isolated and embattled to one which deploys a comprehensive approach to the development of localities, coordinating the whole range of community practice and co-production with the whole range of public authorities and services. This requires some rethinking both of community development and other forms of community practice.

We do not claim to have a complete model for reform, and some of what we say may be found provocative by other schools of thought in this field, but in the interests of constructive debate we put forward what we see as the best direction of travel. Whether they agree with our view or not, we owe a substantial debt to numerous people who, through practice or theory, have advanced the cause of community involvement and development over the past 30 years and more.

Terminological ground-clearing

Before going into further depth about the possibility of a more comprehensive solution, it is as well to summarise our understanding of the cluster of key terms needed in this debate, which often sound confusingly similar. What are the key differences between 'community practice', 'community development', 'community involvement' and other terms that crop up in this field of action?

The key points, in short, are these: 'community development' is a discipline with at least 50 years' continuous history in the UK. Practitioners have usually seen its role as helping people in neighbourhoods or other types of community, especially people facing multiple disadvantages, to gain greater control over the conditions of their lives, combating poverty and increasing equality. Community development has therefore been a recourse for government, local government, other public agencies and voluntary organisations when they have wanted to increase community involvement.

'Community practice' is a term that was introduced in Britain in the mid-1990s to describe the use of community involvement and empowerment techniques by a much wider range of workers across the public and voluntary services, often as part of another job. Two books in particular developed the concept;[20] but with or without this terminology, it is now widely recognised that many front-line occupations are concerned with stimulating community involvement of one kind or another. Community development specialists argue about whether this is a genuine extension of their practice or a dangerous dilution.

We are concerned throughout this book with both of these fields and their interaction. Broadly we see community practice as the wider field, at least in terms of volume, since it involves many more practitioners – possibly as many as 10 or 20 times the number who would claim to be community development workers.

We see community development as a more intensive, dedicated, articulated form of community practice. We therefore use the term community practice to indicate the entire field *including* community development, and the term community development when we want to focus specifically on the dedicated core of specialists.

We use the term 'community involvement' to mean the involvement of local residents in local governance, public services and development. Community involvement, therefore, is a broad part of the *aims and results* of community practice and development. 'Community engagement' is a narrower term usually meaning the engagement of residents in a *particular* public service or initiative.

It should also be recognised that the term 'community work' covers a wide range of work done in local communities. This term is therefore an alternative to community practice and is in effect used in that way in Alan Twelvetrees' seminal book of that name.[21]

We use the term 'community practitioner' for anyone who is doing some form of community practice, whether full or part time as a community development worker, whether as an aspect of another job, or whether as a neighbourhood manager or coordinator. As our concept unfolds, it will become clear that the neighbourhood coordination level is particularly important as the centre of a network of the other community practitioners and public service front-line workers.

We are sparing in our use of the term 'community' on its own. It is generally used in social policy to mean the whole nexus of relationships between people who either live in a particular place (geographical communities) or share a common culture, ethnicity or identity (communities of interest or identity). Both these are fundamental to our concerns, but the word community is too imprecise to be heavily relied on in strategy or evaluation. Changes in community strengths, engagement, development and practice should be measured in terms of specific populations and places rather than 'communities'.

Towards a new synthesis

The issue of how citizens can be involved in the governance and development of their own localities and society will not go away. The situation demands a new response: a new understanding of community practice which can facilitate a new kind of partnership between state and citizens across the board. We address this question through the chapters which follow.

Chapter Two looks at the history and growth of community involvement and its facilitation, and the faltering in that growth in England since 2008. In Chapter Three, the relationship between community practice and the state is examined. We look back at some of the theory on which community development was based and which continues to influence community practice. In the remaining chapters we look more closely at what can be done now. Chapter Four considers what happens on the ground in community groups and networks, in localities and particularly across whole neighbourhoods. Here we also re-examine the nature of community groups in the light of ideas from other disciplines.

Chapter Five considers factors that must be taken into account in working towards an enduring strategy for community involvement: why the neighbourhood, not the community, is the fundamental unit for strategy; some precedents and models for neighbourhood strategy; how community groups should be supported; the role of communities of interest; the economic context and austerity; and whether complexity theory adds to our understanding.

Chapter Six looks at how neighbourhood partnerships can be built; the role of teamwork and leadership; the value of an independent coordinator; power and pitfalls; and whether the big society concept helps.

Two extended stories in Chapter Seven show how neighbourhood development can be approached from different perspectives, each having some similarities and some limitations.

Chapter Eight addresses the questions of evidence and impact: What is the evidence of effects of community practice? Why is solid evidence in this field so sparse, and how can it be improved? Some major advances were made under New Labour: we re-examine these and assess how some of these and other elements can be pulled together and further improved.

Finally, Chapter Nine reprises key points from the main thread of the narrative and provides a template of the essential components for new strategy to create transformative neighbourhoods through community practice.

Notes

[1] This is primarily a UK definition. The term community practice has a longer history in the US, associated particularly with social work, though it has also expanded over time to link with other fields. See *Journal of Community Practice*, www.acosa.org/jcpwhat.html.

[2] There is an extensive community development literature going back many decades. For a recent short overview see Gilchrist and Taylor (2011). For an approach through the perspective of recent policy contexts see Taylor (2011). For international comparisons see Campfens (1997).

[3] NESTA (2012), p 5.

[4] 67 per cent of people in England feel that people in their neighbourhood pull together to improve the area – see CLG (2011c), chapter 2.

[5] Heinberg (2011), chapters 6–7.

[6] Gaffikin and Morrissey (2011).

[7] Gilchrist (2009).

[8] Jones and Gammel (2009).

[9] Butcher et al (1993).

[10] Banks et al (2003), p 9.

[11] Pitchford, Archer and Ramsden (2009).

[12] Bowen and Keogh (2011); Crawley and Watkin (2011); Boffey (2012).

[13] Chanan and Miller (2010).

[14] For information on community development and related issues in these nations see the websites of some of the leading organisations and networks: www.scdc.org.uk (Scottish CD Centre); www.communitydevelopmentalliancescotland.org; www.communityplaces. info (Northern Ireland); www.cdcymru.org (Wales).

[15] Atkinson (2004).

[16] www.healthcomplexity.net

[17] Diers (2004).

[18] www.communityledplanning.co.uk

[19] From the *Community Development National Occupational Standards*: www.fcdl.org.uk/NOS.

[20] Banks et al (2003); Butcher et al (2007).

[21] Twelvetrees (2008).

TWO

National policy on community involvement – the historical journey

How did community involvement gradually become a virtually obligatory part of the narrative of the various branches of social policy? How did it begin to acquire practical substance? And why did it nevertheless remain largely dispersed and unclear? This chapter traces the growth of community involvement in the UK through some major landmarks of social policy from the late 1960s onwards. It shows how involvement grew in breadth and volume, and reached a relatively high point of universality and coherence prior to the onset of recession in 2008, when it was beset by new obstacles.

The journey so far

By 2008 community practice appeared to be on the threshold of becoming a norm across most public services in the UK. Then in quick succession came global economic turmoil, a more-than-usually acute crisis of loss of trust in Parliament triggered by the MPs' expenses scandal, a change of government, the onset of public service cuts, and further waves of economic instability.

In seeking to establish where community practice stands now, we need to look back at what lessons may learnt from how it grew over the preceding few decades. This would include factors which held it back, and what obstacles it would need to overcome if it were to fulfil the role it appeared to be reaching for before the setbacks of recent years.

The idea that residents need to be actively involved in improvements to their neighbourhoods may seem common sense but was not at first part of the ethos of the welfare state. It emerged, however, in a number of different policy areas over the second half of the 20th century. Immediately after the second world war the overwhelming priorities for the reconstruction effort were jobs, housing and health. Once the postwar economy had got into gear, and Prime Minister Harold Macmillan (1957–63) was telling the nation that they had 'never had it so good', policy attention began to focus more on areas that had been left behind by the postwar recovery.

Schemes to regenerate disadvantaged areas were a main incubator of community involvement policy. One early landmark was the Community Development Project (CDP, 1968–73). This consisted of 12 concentrated projects in disadvantaged local areas, launched by the Labour Government of Harold Wilson. The aim was to test out ways of overcoming poverty by strengthening the ability of local communities to organise themselves and put pressure on public services to improve local conditions.

The methods were then supposed to be adopted into mainstream social policies and applied wherever they were needed. Perhaps unsurprisingly in the climate of the times, several of the projects took on a radical left-wing colouring and gave the impression of viewing themselves as a Marxist vanguard. They were gradually closed down during the 1970s, under the Conservative government of Edward Heath. The return of Labour under Wilson and then Callaghan (1974–79) did not see their revival. But they left a legacy, on the one hand, of illuminating fieldwork experience and on the other, for many practitioners, of a conviction that a capitalist state would by definition be hostile to community development.

Although the term 'community practice' had not yet been born, the practice itself was already emerging in a number of fields.[1] Community development by name was also invested in by a number of local authorities during the 1970s, irrespective of the decline of the CDP, albeit without such overtly radical programmes.

The Urban Programme, which ran from 1969 to the mid 1980s, included a wide variety of community projects. Their focus was on employment, education, housing and health. But evaluation of these projects had little to say about community involvement as a distinct factor in the modest success shown on these 'hard' issues.[2]

Assessing the impact of urban policy from 1980 to 1990,[3] Brian Robson found a moderate degree of success in terms of economic criteria and benefits for disadvantaged localities, but a widening gap between the most and least disadvantaged residents. He concluded that there was a need for much more resident involvement:

> Benefits appear to have had as much or more effect on the broader surrounding areas as on the targeted areas themselves … (This) adds force to the need to develop effective linkages between policy targeted at areas and the disadvantaged residents living in those areas … (There is) scope to capitalise on the place-loyalty of local communities … Effective coalitions within localities … require long-term collaborative partnerships … Local communities need to be given opportunities to play roles in such coalitions.[4]

The City Challenge incubator

Robson's analysis influenced the design of City Challenge (1992–98), championed by Michael Heseltine as Minister for Environment under the premierships of Margaret Thatcher and John Major. The challenge element was addressed to local authorities, on the quality of their regeneration plans, their ability to attract private sector partners, and their ability to involve local residents. A review by MacFarlane explained:

> Left to themselves, developers (in both the private and public sectors) have produced poorly conceived, poorly designed, poorly built environments, and have shown no awareness of the interrelationships between economic, housing and social policies. Local people are being introduced into the development process because, as the intended beneficiaries ... they have the greatest stake in the future of the area, and they know from experience the range of issues.[5]

City Challenge was a substantial concentration of resources on a small number of deprived areas. Each of 31 partnerships received £37.5m over five years. The aims included promoting successful partnerships of public, private and voluntary bodies and local communities; and developing capacity within the targeted neighbourhoods for self-sustaining regeneration and self help. 'Players saw it as an improvement on previous regeneration initiatives particularly ... because of community and private sector involvement.'[6]

There was by this time a considerable history of other attempts to involve communities in public policy, particularly around tenant participation and local authority decentralisation experiments. And in the background was the European poverty programme of the early 1990s, which made participation a high priority – but failed to link it to community groups. Forty-one projects were carried out across the then 12 countries of the EU, but only four of the projects discovered the essential connection with local voluntary and community organisations: '(Most) projects felt that the direct participation of target groups ... was problematic' but one reported that 'the decision to work with local associations was the key which opened the door to involving target groups'.[7]

City Challenge was seen as better value for money than preceding schemes such as the Urban Programme (1969–80) for several reasons. First, it was competitive rather than allocated purely on the basis of local need, and thus allowed government to select what it judged to be the best-designed projects. Secondly, the government grant was used to lever in additional money from private sector investors such as property companies who would rebuild an estate, shopping centre or amenity and make a long term profit from rents or sales. Third, but unaudited, was the value of a higher level of participation by local residents.

Two years into City Challenge, an independent evaluation found 'a growing involvement of local communities in project implementation ... (but) it is patchy ... it takes time for communities to get organised and ... it requires a commitment to openness, flexibility and innovation by all partners (which is often lacking)'.[8] The evaluators feared that 'under the existing evaluation criteria none of the advantages of community involvement ... will be adequately assessed' (p 39).

Despite this timely alert, the prediction was borne out. The issue of community involvement was barely visible in the final evaluation of City Challenge, despite the fact that it had been named as one of the basic objectives of the scheme.[9] This is an example of a syndrome that recurs up to the present day: the assumption by most ministers, civil servants and academic evaluators that community action, and the community practice that supports it, is there simply to help achieve other objectives, and it is not seen as an objective with its own intrinsic value.

The Single Regeneration Budget breakthrough

Seen as a success, but limited to its 31 small areas, City Challenge was used as a model for the Single Regeneration Budget, launched in 1994. This was a much wider scheme, allocating smaller but still significant grants to, eventually, over a thousand local projects. Despite its erratic history, the message about community involvement was getting through. Projects were supposed to 'involve the community in setting up and running these programmes'; intended beneficiaries were expected to 'have a continuing say in the management, development and implementation of the scheme'.[10] What was not so well understood was that communities were not unified bodies which could simply carry out these roles once they were allowed to do so. They consisted, particularly in disadvantaged areas, of numbers of people with very varying degrees of connection and interest, and many of them under great stress from difficult conditions. Motivation and capacity to participate needed to be built.

In the Single Regeneration Budget (SRB) in the 1990s community involvement was at first, as in City Challenge, mainly a loose exhortation rather than part of the structure of criteria, outputs and budgets. Using its previously largely dormant quango status within government, the Community Development Foundation negotiated a successively stronger community involvement element in the annual rounds of SRB from its inception in 1994 onwards, and supplemented this with guidance to project designers and implementers.[11] The fifth of the annual rounds momentously introduced capacity building of the community sector as a virtually obligatory output, with guidance that it could deploy up to 10 per cent of the government grant.[12]

SRB grew to well over 1,000 local schemes. A government grant in excess of £20m was received by 5 per cent of schemes; 42 per cent of schemes received between £1m and £5m each; and a further 18 per cent received up to £0.5m each. The total government expenditure on SRB of £5.7bn attracted over £20bn in private sector investment.[13]

Almost half of the schemes sought to regenerate a relatively small local area, consisting of a number of wards, covering around 10,000 people. A further 20 per cent overall concentrated on an entire local authority district, covering up to around 100,000 people. Over two thirds of all schemes were set to run for five years or more, half of these for seven years. The lead partner was usually the local authority, but the voluntary sector was usually well represented and occasionally in a leading role. Some partnerships included separate representation from the voluntary sector and the community sector or local residents.[14]

Having a strong foothold in a large national scheme yielded much greater resources for community practice than having the entire budget of much smaller schemes. If even 5 per cent of SRB's £5.7bn was supporting community involvement, that amounted to £285m – much more than any dedicated community development programme had ever commanded.

This was an enormous breakthrough for the principle of participation. It led to the release of funding for thousands of local community groups and for workers to support them. It thereby put the local community sector on the map as an important player in local negotiations. Practice still varied greatly between those local public authorities which welcomed this ethos, and had been looking for ways to resource it, and others for which it appeared as simply another government requirement which they had to meet. Over the short life of SRB, however, great strides were made in understanding the local value of building participation, and this experience began to flow into the different policy silos.

The Community Development Foundation lever

Community-oriented programmes from the late 1960s onwards had gradually generated a recognisable occupation of 'community worker'. This occupation gradually acquired its own organisations and voice. Parallel developments were taking place in other countries: community development was a global movement, though very uneven from one place to another. From the 1970s onwards, community development organisations in Britain urged local and national policy-makers to incorporate community development into publicly funded programmes. But it was difficult to get serious attention for community development in the policy process.

A change to this pattern was the gradually increasing role of the Community Development Foundation (CDF) in strengthening the position of community involvement in regeneration programmes. In an unusual example of organisational change driven from below, CDF had emerged from a very different organisation. The Young Volunteer Force Foundation (YVFF) had been created as a non departmental public body (a quango) by the Wilson government in 1968 to mobilise young people at risk in disadvantaged areas and channel them towards useful forms of volunteering such as helping older people in their communities. YVFF was initially attached to the Department of Education and later to the Home Office. A variety of local projects attracted young people through drop-in centres and coffee bars, engaging them in discussion to see how their energies could be guided.

The feedback within the Foundation from its field projects was that engaging with young people on an open agenda showed that their problems were part of a more complex set of problems experienced by their whole communities.[15] The fieldworkers' remit was widened and their experience eventually led to the organisation changing its name to the Community Projects Foundation in 1978. It then took on a rolling programme of substantial local community-based projects, each in collaboration with a local authority and other local partners, on areas such as housing, employment, safety and health as well as youth issues.[16]

Further analysis of the widened fieldwork experience led the organisation to change its name again in the late 1980s, becoming the CDF. By this unusual evolutionary route, the government once again had an official community development advisory body for the first time since the CDP, albeit with a more cautious profile.

Between its origin in 1968 (as YVFF) and 1990, CDF delivered about 80 major local projects distributed across England, Wales and Scotland.[17] Most projects were three to five years in length and consisted in a local team of four or five full-time staff working with residents and local authorities on an agreed programme of priorities for improving conditions in disadvantaged neighbourhoods. This gave the organisation a solid base for seeking to inform government policy on communities, as it did increasingly in the 1990s and 2000s. CDF's ground-level projects gradually dwindled after 1990 but were replaced by indirect support for wider networks of independent local community groups.

Being accountable to government through a trust, CDF did not represent community fieldworkers. Other networks took this role to one degree or another: the Association of Community Workers; the Federation for Community Development Learning; and the Community Development Exchange. At various times these small bodies worked together in uneasy alliance with each other and with CDF. Scotland, Wales and Northern Ireland also had their own facilitating networks, as did some other countries, and there were fragile networks of international information exchange.

Equally important as the release of resources was the implicit establishment of the principle that participation was an objective outcome, parallel to the much better known outcomes of jobs, housing, health, education and reduction of crime. The SRB system was based on a menu of local outputs, such as new houses built, jobs created, anti-crime initiatives carried out, school attainments improved. To fit into the scheme, community participation had to be framed in a similar way. CDF entered into dialogue with the controlling department[18] and negotiated the inclusion of 'capacity building schemes supported' in the output menu and budget framework. This bland phrase meant very little outside the context. In context, however, it released many millions of pounds for community work and community groups providing a wide variety of help to local residents.

The greater challenge that had implicitly been posed, however, was the challenge of demonstrating benefits: if participation was so important, what did it consist of? How were you to know when it was taking place? And what verifiable difference did it make to people's lives and to the delivery of public services? These questions would become critical in the New Labour period, with its emphasis on 'evidence-based policy'.

At this earlier point, however, the emphasis was mainly on explaining what community involvement was and how to do it. During the SRB period, the Department of Environment produced guidance which played a significant role in moving community involvement from aspiration to practice in regeneration schemes. *Involving Communities in Urban and Rural Regeneration*[19] addressed both the underlying philosophy of involvement and the practicalities. Drawing on a now growing literature in the field, it defined principles of involvement and how to implement them by stages, from building partnerships, through involvement in the bid process, design and management of projects, to monitoring and forward strategies, and how to work with particular sections of the community. The revised edition, in 1997, added guidance on involving ethnic minorities, faith communities and young people.

At the same time, CDF's supplementary guidance emphasised that increasing people's involvement 'upwards' into development plans would depend on first increasing their involvement 'outwards' into general community activity: 'A strategy for strengthening communities should … address first and foremost people's ability to relate to *each other.*'[20] It recommended maintaining clear distinctions between:

- activity which represents the community, as users and controllers;
- activity which the community freely chooses to do (or to stop doing) for itself, eg mutual aid; and
- activity which bids to deliver some part of the public services by taking on a contract and the systematic accountability that goes with it. (p 19)

It had taken many years before policy-makers began to accept that participation was an outcome in its own right, not just a lubricant to other objectives. This was a vital step in gaining recognition for the importance of community development and practice. Without a name for a visible outcome, community involvement had been treated merely as feelgood rhetoric, an attribute of the voluntary sector, or an occasional method to assist other occupations. The theory of social capital which emerged from the mid 1990s[21] was helpful in providing language for the *product* of community involvement and development, though it had little to say about the process. It would take more years before the community development field, which mostly emphasised process and *not* product, was prepared to make use of the new language of social capital, including measurement, and to build up objective evidence of outcomes.

New Labour

Soon after its accession to power after 18 years of Conservative rule, New Labour set up a unit in the Cabinet Office to pull together the best ideas it could find on every topic that might have a bearing on social exclusion. The 18 'Policy Action Teams' (PATs) on social exclusion would soon lead to the National Strategy for Neighbourhood Renewal, an extensive programme to overcome disadvantage.

An influential working party in the first period was the Urban Task Force,[22] which paved the way for Neighbourhood Renewal. The working party set out a vision for urban regeneration and recommended piloting different models of neighbourhood management that would give local people a stake in the decision-making process.

Participation was to be closely linked with flexibility of aims:

> There will be complete flexibility on what programmes can cover; bodies such as housing associations, the private sector and voluntary organisations will be given the chance to lead regeneration programmes, and the very local focus will allow communities to identify closely with the programme and be actively involved. ... Partnerships will be expected to involve the whole community throughout the process, secure their participation, listen to and act on their views and gain their support. Experience shows that solutions which are imposed on a community rather than developed with them won't deliver lasting change. (p 2)

However, when the full strategy for Neighbourhood Renewal emerged, flexibility gave way to a system of required targets on employment, health, housing, safety and education. The principle of involvement suffered some 'constructive demotion' by the dominance of the high-profile targets, not being seen as a factor requiring its own equally explicit target.

It is striking, in policy documents over several decades, how community involvement is at first loudly trumpeted, and then, when the policy is turned into a practical programme, thrust back into the penumbra. This may be because of an instinct on the part of politicians and civil servants to retain top-down control. But equally disheartening is a disinclination on the part of many community enthusiasts to adopt instruments for making involvement definable and measurable in ways comparable to the conventional issues, so that it has a better chance of taking its place alongside them in public understanding and policy planning.

Part of the problem is that community involvement can be justified in so many different ways that it has no clear single policy 'address' to promote it. A report from the Office of the Deputy Prime Minister in 2003[23] found that government endorsed community involvement for these six key purposes, all exemplified in the 2000 Urban White Paper,[24] yet that these were never brought together into a unified concept:

A. Involvement is people's right.
B. Involvement overcomes alienation and exclusion.
C. Involvement makes the community stronger in itself.
D. Involvement maximises the effectiveness of services and resources.
E. Involvement helps 'join up' different contributions to development.
F. Involvement helps sustainability.

These purposes could be summarised as reflecting an essential triangle of mutually enhancing objectives which should form the basis of community practice strategy and measurement but should never be reduced to each other:

- Involvement as part of *governance* (A, E, F).
- Involvement as part of *social capital* (B, C).
- Involvement as part of *service delivery* (D).

Neighbourhood Renewal, Community Strategies and Local Strategic Partnerships

The Urban White Paper of 2000 was followed by guidance on Community Strategies and Local Strategic Partnerships (LSPs), and the Neighbourhood Renewal action plan.[25] The aim of community strategies was stated as being to enhance the quality of life of local communities and contribute to the achievement of sustainable development in the UK.[26] The National Strategy for Neighbourhood Renewal was announced as marking the beginning of a new approach to turning round the most deprived communities. Neighbourhood decline was attributed to economic change, the disappearance of old industries, joblessness, family breakdown, the decline of social housing and 'ever greater concentration of vulnerable people in poor neighbourhoods ... Government policies have not been good enough at tackling these issues and sometimes they have been part of the problem ... Government failed to harness the knowledge and energy of local people or empower them to develop their own solutions' (p 7).

The strategy aimed to initiate a long-term process to ensure that within 10 to 20 years, no-one would be seriously disadvantaged by where they lived. There were three key dimensions: new policies, funding and targets; better local co-ordination and community empowerment; and national and regional support (p 8). There followed what became known as the 'floor targets', ie minimum levels that had to be attained even in the most disadvantaged areas, in work and enterprise, crime, education and skills, health, housing and physical environment. ('Whitehall departments will be judged for the first time on the areas where they are doing worst rather than on the national average' (pp 9–10).)

It would perhaps have been naïve to expect government to enact literally its initial promise of 'complete flexibility' in programmes 'acting on the community's views'. This rhetoric flattered disadvantaged communities as if they had all the answers. This may have sounded like heaven to traditional community development enthusiasts but it may also have been patronising and unrealistic. Communities need to be listened to but also face hard work in forging their own collective views through dialogue. A snapshot of community views from an articulate minority in a meeting or consultation is better than nothing, but it is not necessarily a balanced or well-worked-out view of what the whole community needs or wants. The most isolated, marginalised and housebound people may be unheard even in the community development process.

Public services exist for good reasons, forged historically by pressure from many different communities, and the issues they address are important in every community. The weakness of Neighbourhood Renewal regarding community involvement was not its insistence on prescribed issues or floor targets; it was the failure to give community involvement equal status with the other issues and establish targets for it alongside them. The possibility of doing so would have been accelerated if community enthusiasts had given more attention to describing the effects of community involvement in terms of verifiable outcomes. This was quite feasible, as was shown a few years later in the establishment of the national indicators for Local Area Agreements, which are discussed further in Chapter Eight.

Nevertheless there were a wide variety of mechanisms for empowering communities as part of Neighbourhood Renewal: Local Strategic Partnerships (LSPs); Neighbourhood Management Pathfinders ('someone visibly taking responsibility at the sharp end'); a Community Empowerment Fund to help communities participate in LSPs; and Community Chests 'to fund local small grant schemes so that communities can run their own projects' (p 10).

Resources were targeted at the 88 local authorities containing the most deprived neighbourhoods, but the principles were commended to all local authorities and over the following five years extended to them. Most Neighbourhood Renewal funding was still concentrated in deprived areas but, for the first time, regeneration – and community involvement with it – were treated in principle as universal issues.

An agenda of 105 'government commitments to help realise this long-term vision' was assembled (p 61ff). These covered the local economy, health, housing, crime, education and community involvement. Twelve of the 105 commitments were directly relevant to community involvement:

* Community Development Venture Fund (Commitment 7).
* Innovation fund, to support community and voluntary organisations linking people with employment (Commitment 23).
* Establishment of 6,000 UK online centres. Every deprived area to have at least one accessible, community-based facility (Commitment 43).
* A small fund to enable local authorities to boost tenant participation (Commitment 70).
* Neighbourhood Renewal strategies and LSPs to be judged by government regional offices partly on the degree of resident involvement (Commitment 84).
* Requirement on LSPs to seek out as well as welcome resident involvement (Commitment 89).
* Community Empowerment Fund (Commitment 90).[27]
* Support for faith organisations (Commitment 91).
* A community task force to advise the Neighbourhood Renewal Unit (NRU) on how communities' priorities and needs can best be met (Commitment 92).
* Community Chests (Commitment 93).[28]

- Simplified access to funding for community groups (Commitment 94).
- Clear responsibility to ensure that neighbourhood renewal benefits ethnic minorities (Commitment 98).

Despite the failure to establish a community involvement 'floor target', these amounted to by far the most concerted effort by government yet seen to turn community involvement aspirations into concrete reality. Pointers to how to put these into practice were more cryptic, and focussed mainly on the visible pinnacle of involvement, the Local Strategic Partnership:

> Community involvement is a complex process and to do it well would include at least the following steps:
>
> - outreach, especially to excluded communities, to make them aware they have the chance to express their views and influence service providers;
> - facilitation to pull together the community's views and procedures for choosing community members of the LSPs;
> - participation of community members in sufficient numbers on the LSP, for which they might need training and other forms of support (e.g. pre-meetings, briefings); and
> - Government Office action if an LSP did not engage with the community appropriately and does not take sufficient account of community views. (p 52)

None of this, however, prevented a continuing pattern of erratic recognition and neglect of community involvement in government thinking. The Urban White Paper's own implementation plan[29] appeared to forget community involvement all over again. Some civil servants, one imagines, fail to register that community involvement is a real factor, and regard the rhetoric about it as simply that, not as a component which needs to be a solid part of programme design. But politicians who approve such programmes need to be more alert to combating this erosion process.

The Neighbourhood Renewal strategy articulated a crucial distinction between two purposes which are often confused both in government and non-government literature:

> There are two quite different ways in which people working in community and voluntary sector groups might be involved in a Local Strategic Partnership. The first category relates to their role in providing services for their own members and for other local people, and the second category relates to their role in speaking for local people. (Annex C, paras 13–14)

Ten years later confusion of these two quite different community functions – two of the three points in our irreducible triangle above – would become a feature of the Coalition government's big society.

Between 2000 and 2008 the ambitious programme flagged up in the Urban White Paper was rolled out with great energy, if a degree of confusion. It led at first to an unmanageable proliferation of local development schemes and partnerships; and then to a rationalisation of schemes in each locality under a coordinating umbrella, the Local Strategic Partnership (LSP). There was a growing policy emphasis on community involvement, signalled by the renaming of the Office of the Deputy Prime Minister as the Department for Communities and Local Government in 2006. This was shortly followed by the establishment of a Community Empowerment Division in the department, which had the task of negotiating an element of empowerment into all policy streams impacting on localities.

It would be difficult to give a single definition of what was meant by empowerment. Prendergast[30] argues incisively that the concept was deeply confused, conflating different issues about participation and democracy: 'The two aims of service improvement and tackling disengagement have been lumped together and given one all-encompassing solution, community empowerment, largely conceived in participatory terms' (p 16). She considers that this conflation exacerbated mistrust between elected members – local councillors – and unelected and unaccountable community 'representatives'. Her solution is for the participative agenda to be vested in neighbourhood, parish and town councils, formally elected and accountable to their constituents but much closer to them than local authorities (p 28). It should be acknowledged, she says, 'that governing is complex and demanding and that the appetite for deeper forms of participation is limited, and (we) should not rest hopes on a participatory model that requires too great a burden of commitment by the citizen' (p 34). But this important critique tends to undervalue the intrinsic dimension of participation – participation in one's own community, with increase in social capital as a direct outcome.

Maturity, divergence and disruption

One of the first acts of the New Labour government in 1997 had been to devolve a wide range of domestic policies to Scotland and Wales. Together with the unique history of Northern Ireland, this meant that the policies for community involvement, already somewhat different, diverged even more in the four nations of the British Isles during the next 15 years. Some links however were maintained by practitioner networks across the four nations, and also with the Republic of Ireland, though interchange has become more difficult following the onset of public service cuts in 2010.

In the last few years of its administration, New Labour's public services and local government reform came together in a more coherent way, with clearer but fewer targets, including prominent community indicators (see Chapter Eight).

The various programmes of the National Strategy for Neighbourhood Renewal were maturing into a coordinated system. There were also new streams of policy thinking which aimed to take a more rounded view of local development and services. 'Total Place' experiments, for example, sought to map all the public service costs going into an area, both in order to make them more efficient and to save money by combining some functions. However they did not include assessment of private assets or the productive force of local communities themselves, such as the condition of the local community sector.

A complementary idea of 'empowering the front line'[31] emerged briefly, too late to take root. The idea originated partly in the private sector, where management theory stressed that staff who interacted directly with customers should be seen as a main source of information on what customers want, but that recognised that they were rarely listened to, because they were low down in the company hierarchy. However, the report only scratched the surface of its own concept: it tended to assume that the key point was for managers to listen to ideas coming up to them before making their next set of top-down decisions. It is a concept which needs to be reshaped to extend to direct collaboration between service users to improve a service at the point of delivery.

In 2008 there was a loss of momentum in policy on community involvement. The onset of the financial crisis coincided with other factors which had rapid side effects: change of leadership and Ministerial reshuffle in the Labour government; abandonment of the original design of Neighbourhood Renewal; and the closure of the so-called Empowerment Unit in the Department of Communities and Local Government. Less than two years later the New Labour administration had given way to the Conservative–LibDem Coalition government. Despite the new government's big society theme, charities, community groups and community practitioners alike were soon staggering under the effect of cuts in public service budgets. Investment in regeneration shrank from £11bn to £3bn. The framework for community involvement in local authorities that had been built up by New Labour was disbanded. As part of a 'bonfire of the quangos', the Coalition Government ended the CDF's governmental role, and withdrew most of what had only ever been modest support to the other CD national organisations. CDF reshaped itself as a social enterprise and secured government contracts under big society policy. But national support for community development in England was largely eroded.

The decimation of community development, however, was not total across the UK. Leading bodies in Wales, Northern Ireland and Scotland pursued positive ways forward, as did a number of individual local authorities in England. More widely there was still a widespread if patchy legacy of experience and understanding of community practice within public authorities, stemming from the preceding decade of development.

Coalition government: from New Labour to big society[32]

The decline of policy on community practice in England is of particular interest because it followed a period of exceptional opportunity and influence. What went wrong? Why did community practice not become irreversibly embedded in public policy? Were policy-makers resistant to a real increase in community power? Were community development enthusiasts resistant to integration in public policy because they believed that this would neutralise their underlying radical agenda? Or was community development unable to convert its 'youthful' radicalism into mature strategy and wider forms of practice?

Even before the decline in community practice had fully come to light, the deceptively similar concept of 'big society' gained currency as a personal commitment of Coalition Prime Minister David Cameron, even against misgivings in his own party. Big society appeared to promise new opportunities for community groups and a wave of community organisers to help them. But community organisers were to be funded only on the stringiest of shoestrings. Paucity of funding was commended as a virtue as it would keep the organisers independent of the state. And the promise of 5,000 community organisers *over the lifetime of the Parliament*, ie 1,000 a year, was substantially fewer than the number of community development workers who were already losing their jobs.

The big society theme provided little protection against a decimation of support for community groups, community practice jobs and community development organisations. And even more swingeing, though barely noticed by the media, was the ending of the Local Area Agreement (LAA) system in England, in which, for the first time, the objective of strengthening local communities had been firmly embedded in local policy alongside the traditional 'hard' issues of housing, education, employment, health and safety. Without the LAA framework and funding, local authorities have been free to keep or drop their Local Strategic Partnerships. Some have gone one way, some the other, and there is no national overview.

In retrospect it can be seen that increasing understanding of the way in which issues interact at very local level had led to gradually more sophisticated approaches to regeneration during the 1980s and 1990s. A degree of continuity is discernible under both the Conservative and Labour governments, despite some major breaks. The breaks are sometimes artificial, in the sense that a new government tends to close down a programme purely because it is associated with the previous government, and then invents one that is similar. This is a very wasteful process, often losing years of momentum. New Labour's main Neighbourhood Renewal programme, for instance, was not in practice very different from the previous Conservative government's Single Regeneration Budget.

The Coalition government's big society, however, was a more fundamental break. Within a year it became apparent that the idea functioned in practice largely as a smokescreen for service cuts, even if it was genuinely believed in by the PM and some of his allies. There was no vision of dynamic collaboration between communities and the public sector, only of the voluntary sector or local communities taking over declining public services. Commentators looked for the essence of the concept but it was more of a ragbag of issues linked simply by the fact that they all had some voluntary element.[33]

Big society rhetoric was, however, writ large in the Coalition government's Localism agenda.[34] There were gleams of empowerment for ordinary citizens here, but the bulk of the plan was about local authorities and the farming out of public services. The authorities would, on the one hand, have greater flexibility in some areas, but on the other hand would be under pressure to sell off assets and parts of services to local community organisations. The splendid phrase 'Empowering communities to do things their way' was focused just on the siting of new developments, local authority flexibility and, once again, community groups' right to buy 'threatened' assets. In one policy paper 'empowering communities' is defined as 'giving councils and neighbourhoods more power to take decisions and shape their areas'.[35] In an accompanying paper, empowering communities is explained as: 'Those who think they can do better will have the right to bid for public contracts and take over the use of community assets.'[36]

The idea that local people who are dissatisfied with the running of a public asset would see themselves as empowered by having to *buy* it and run it themselves in order to put it right is dubious. There are successful examples but these are exceptions rather than a basis for a general policy. Why should local residents have to buy an asset for which they have already paid, through their rates and taxes? And how would the community as a whole be empowered by the sale of an asset which belongs to all of them, to an organisation which consists of only a fraction of them? There were disturbing moral and perhaps even legal questions here.

In the long run big society may come to be seen less as a new beginning than as an ending – the end of a 40-year trajectory of community involvement initiatives which started as a scattering of projects in the 1960s, were embedded in major regeneration programmes in the 1980s and 1990s, and were reshaped into a universal system intended to drive permanent improvement in all local authorities in the 2000s. Within this carrier wave, community involvement had begun as a small seed, graduated into being a standard background component and eventually came to be seen as fundamental and central, shortly before being dispersed by the events of 2008 and after.

Footholds for the future

Where does this leave community practice? A legacy of experience and understanding of community involvement is still widely if unevenly spread throughout public services and local government. The experience of the past 40 years is also reflected in a rich literature of analysis, guidance and evaluation, and we build on that here.

Ironically, in the aftermath of its 2010 defeat, the Labour Party made very little of the remarkable strides which it had made in building community involvement, perhaps because it was nervous about trumpeting any achievements of the New Labour period for fear of appearing backward-looking and 'not learning the lessons of its rejection by the British public'. But it would be superficial to regard community involvement as the heritage of one political party. Despite deciding in 1998 to phase out the Conservatives' Single Regeneration Budget (SRB), New Labour in fact built substantially on experience from that scheme. SRB had in turn built on area-based initiatives previously carried out by both Labour and Conservative administrations. Also despite their general Euroscepticism, the Conservatives had both drawn on and influenced European regeneration programmes for disadvantaged areas in the 1980s. The Liberal Democrats had also championed local participation for many years, and implemented imaginative policies on it within local authorities which they controlled. It is hard to believe that the rewarding experience and manifest benefits of collaboration between communities and public services will not eventually reassert themselves throughout social policy.

Notes

[1] Banks et al (2003).

[2] Thomson et al (2006).

[3] Robson et al (1994).

[4] Ibid, Summary, pp x–xiv.

[5] MacFarlane (1993).

[6] KPMG (1998) p 3.

[7] Animation and Research (1994), pp 160–1.

[8] MacFarlane, op cit, p 37.

[9] KPMG, op cit.

[10] DoE (1995).

[11] CDF (1997a).

[12] DETR (1998b).

[13] Thomson et al (2006).

[14] Tyler and Rhodes (2007).

[15] Allinson (1978).

[16] CPF (1982).

[17] NI, like Scotland and Wales, was represented on CDF's trustee board, but it was not seen as appropriate for an England-based organisation to run local projects there.

—

[18] DETR, later DTLR, ODPM and CLG.

[19] DETR (1995, revised 1997).

[20] Chanan et al (2000), p 16.

[21] For example in the work of Robert Putnam, such as Putnam (2000).

[22] Rogers of Riverside (1999).

[23] Chanan (2003).

[24] DETR (2000a).

[25] Social Exclusion Unit (2001).

[26] DETR (2000b).

[27] Neighbourhood Renewal Unit (2001a).

[28] Neighbourhood Renewal Unit (2001b).

[29] DETR (2000a).

[30] Prendergast (2008).

[31] HM Treasury (2009).

[32] We use 'big society' without capitals as we understand it to be a general idea linking a number of initiatives rather than a firm programme.

[33] See Chanan and Miller (2010).

[34] CLG (2010).

[35] Office for Civil Society (2010a).

[36] Office for Civil Society (2010b).

THREE

Community practice and the state

State support has been a key driver of community practice, yet the relationship between practitioners and state agencies has often been uneasy. This chapter traces a debilitating fuzziness in community development theory to an unresolved tension between a vein of radicalist rhetoric in community development and the actual conditions and role of the occupation; and argues that a genuinely progressive solution would ally community practice vigorously with the great heritage of public services and actually existing democracy, despite their imperfections.

The problem of scale

For community involvement to flourish, it is necessary to have favourable policies at three levels: national, local and neighbourhood. We use 'neighbourhood' as a generic term for the very local – around 5,000 to 15,000 people. This might equally be a village, cluster of villages, estate or scattered settlement. In the UK one must make a distinction between 'local' and 'very local', or neighbourhood, since 'local' is often used in policy documents to mean 'local authority level', which can be anything from around 100,000 to 250,000 or more. This is a very different scale and perspective from that of the neighbourhood. In the Local Government Association's recommendations on 'place-based budgets',[1] for example, 'place' is mostly equated with a city or county.

Involvement is rooted in very local relationships and can develop from the bottom up, but without a receptive culture at higher levels it soon hits a brick wall. National, regional and large local policies and programmes for community practice are a vital form of support. In the nature of large-scale policy planning it is not easy to accommodate varied local inputs, yet these are the authentic expression of residents' wishes at very local level. So community practitioners, whose purpose is to support community influence on decisions and development, find themselves in the midst of a natural tension. Equally, large-scale policy making is susceptible to manipulation by powerful and wealthy interests – interests which may exacerbate inequalities at local level. Yet community practitioners who support very local groups are largely employed or supported by the state. What is the most productive way to navigate these conflicting perspectives and pressures?

It can be tempting for community practitioners to see the role of the state as inherently oppressive of disadvantaged communities. This posture is widespread in the history of community development. But this fails to see that the state is the framework in which tensions between more and less powerful forces have to be fought out, where territory can be won for the forces of equality. This chapter looks at the nature of these tensions and suggests the most constructive approach to dealing with them.

Provision and participation

One of the main factors which led to the growth of community practice (or community work[2]) was the gradual realisation, in the latter part of the 20th century, that expansion in the provision of public services was not in itself enough to eliminate poverty and create an equal society.

When public services were first established, the overriding consideration was provision itself: houses, schools, hospitals, benefits, pensions. Once a form of welfare state had become the norm, questions of quality, equity and effectiveness came to the fore. Why did delivery of services often seem to be poorest in areas that needed them most? Why did the gap between rich and poor continue to grow, even if there was less absolute poverty? Why did some people appear to become dependent on services to the extent that it sapped their initiative?

There have also always been dilemmas about cost, which in turn evoke questions about taxation: do the public services use the public purse to maximum effect? Can the costs of provision be contained as expectations continually rise? How can productivity and effectiveness of public services be improved in the absence of the supposedly efficient 'market discipline' of the private sector?

The Conservative governments of 1979–97 devised Compulsory Competitive Tendering to try to break what they saw as public service sinecures, and expose them to market competition. The New Labour government of 1997–2010 replaced this firstly with Best Value inspection and then, increasingly, with stimulus to community involvement:

> Citizens and communities want a bigger say in the services they receive and in shaping the places where they live. The best councils and councillors already work closely with citizens and communities. We want this to be the case everywhere – for people to be given more control over their lives; consulted and involved in running services … and enabled to call local agencies to account if services fail to meet their needs … One of the guiding principles of this Government is that no-one should be disadvantaged by where they live. So local authorities and other local agencies must reach out to citizens who are disadvantaged, and support marginalised or socially excluded communities to have their say. They must ensure that services evolve to reflect their needs as well as those of more vocal citizens.[3]

This could be called the reformist stream of community involvement theory. A more interactive relationship between services and their users seemed to offer promise of alleviating inequality. One of the reasons why services were often better in more affluent areas was that wealthier people were readier and

—

better equipped to demand quality. They would more willingly and confidently complain to authorities, form pressure groups or serve as councillors or school governors. Perhaps if poorer people were encouraged to do the same, they too could get better results.

Another factor in local quality of services was that people with secure jobs and more income automatically 'co-produced' the services they drew on. They boosted their children's education at home, they took more care of their health, and they owned and improved their housing. All these resulted in better life chances. Perhaps spreading more community activity, clubs and organisations in less well-off areas could help to supply some of the benefits seen in better-off areas through encouragement and local initiatives.

The crystallisation of community development

There was also, however, another, more drastic theory about the shortcomings of the services in disadvantaged areas. This was a radical critique of the services as being essentially flawed because they were part of a fundamentally divisive capitalist state. This belief emerged particularly in the 1960s and 1970s, but also continues. It was said that the public services had not really been designed to achieve equality but rather to produce a compliant workforce, buying off dissent with a minimal safety net of provision whilst imposing social control. Capitalist society as a whole was the *source* of poverty and inequality, so it was futile to look to it to solve them.

Both the reformist and radicalist streams of thinking contributed to the emergence of the community development movement, and later influenced community engagement and practice at large. However, the unresolved mixture of radicalism and reformism resulted in a fuzzy community development culture which had difficulty in transmitting clear messages to sponsors, policy makers and even communities. As a result, public agencies variously used community development but kept it on a short leash. Experimental or innovative projects were commissioned to demonstrate participative methods, with the stated intention that if successful they should be mainstreamed into standard practice. They were often judged to be successful but instead of being mainstreamed, they were simply followed by further 'experimental' projects.

Meanwhile as each of the major public services grew, participative methods gained footholds in housing, social services, youth work and a number of other professions. But participation was mostly brought in as an afterthought to mainstream practice, for limited times in limited places. The voluntary sector had a more participative ethos in general but only the community development profession consistently treated participation as a top priority issue. But community development projects were generally small scale, short-term and the lessons rarely applied more widely.

This ambivalent relationship between community development and main services continued long after the 1960s and 1970s and to some extent filtered into the ethos of community practice as a whole. If community practice is to become a universal aspect of public services, the relationship between community practice and the state must be clarified.

Community development as an occupation

For a movement which tends to see itself as progressive, community development has paid relatively little attention to defending or advancing the position of its workers. There have been only three surveys of community workers across England in the past 50 years, two of them being across the UK. The first was in 1984.[4] It defined community workers as 'paid staff whose primary responsibility is to develop groups in the community whose members experience and wish to tackle needs, disadvantages or inequality'. Arguably this definition was unnecessarily limiting since many community groups, even in disadvantaged areas, define their goals in terms of interests, enjoyment and aspirations rather than deficits, as the later 'asset based community development' movement argues.[5]

By surveying local authorities and a variety of voluntary organisations, the 1984 survey found 5,365 community workers across the UK plus 291 community work managers. Seventy per cent of the workers were in England. Two fifths of them were employed in the statutory sector and three fifths in the voluntary sector, but the latter were also mainly funded by government and local government. Thirteen per cent were from ethnic minority groups, and the number of men and women was roughly equal. Fifty per cent of the workers had no specific qualifications for this work. Part-time workers were included, but not volunteers. The authors of the survey thought for various reasons that the total number of community workers and managers given was probably an underestimate, though not a huge one.

The second and third surveys, in 2002 and 2009, were carried out in a different way. Possibly reflecting distrust of state agencies and conventional statistics, there was no approach to employers, and community workers were not defined as a profession. The defining characteristic was not employment but agreement with a specific set of values. Contact was made with respondents through community development organisations and networks. Almost 3,000 responses were obtained to the 2002 survey[6] but as they had been obtained simply by sending out word through networks, it was not possible to assess how many such workers there might have been in total, especially how many paid workers, though responses suggested these were the majority. Given the increase in community-oriented programmes in the period, it is likely that there were considerably more paid community workers than indicated by the survey.

The third survey[7] found its respondents in a similar way, by 'making the questionnaire available to the sector'. This 2009 survey was carried out in England only. It recorded 900 responses but obtained more in-depth information from respondents about their roles and views and how they spent their time. Most respondents were in paid jobs. Only 27 per cent of time was spent working directly with community groups. Twenty per cent of respondents were from black or ethnic minority communities. Interestingly, a quarter of volunteers had previously been paid community development workers and 42 per cent of paid workers had previously been volunteers.

The national surveys both confirm and reinforce the extreme patchiness of community development provision. Given the idiosyncratic way the responses were collected in the second and third surveys, it is difficult to compare numbers across the surveys. A much smaller study of six local areas in England in 2006[8] set out to calculate the amount of paid work being done to directly support community groups in six contrasting local areas, irrespective of the name of the job. A rough national estimate based on the areas studied suggested that across the UK there were then the equivalent of 20,000 full-time workers carrying out this function (many doing so during part of their time alongside other work). Examples of the worker titles were: Outreach and Development Worker; Small Grants Worker; Neighbourhood Renewal Worker; URBAN II (European programme) Officer; Resident Involvement Officer; Partnership Director; Community Resource Team; Area Worker; Housing Neighbourhood Manager; Community Regeneration Manager; Advice Worker; Multi-Lingual Advocacy Worker; Community Education Worker; Tenant Participation Officer; and Community Association Worker. Most of these kinds of role would count as community practice rather than community development, even though many were full time. They lend weight to the impression that whilst community practice was spreading in an organic way, community development organisations may have been losing touch with wider forms of community practice.

State use of community practice

Most community practice jobs, including those called community development, exist because government and local government creates or supports them through policy decisions, programmes and funding. Yet much community development theory and debate reads as if the aims of community work and the aims of the state were antithetical. Is this adversarial posture integral to the identity and purpose of community practice as a whole? Does it help or hinder the most productive use of community practice for the benefit of communities?

The Taylor study in 2006[9] estimated that 70 per cent of community practitioners were funded by the state: 45 per cent worked in public authorities and another 25 per cent in voluntary or community organisations receiving a local authority or state grant. Others were funded by housing associations, voluntary organisations, philanthropic trusts or the social responsibility departments of big companies. In England, numbers have declined since then but the mixture of employing bodies is likely to be similar. The extent of paid community practice is therefore due to predominant but not exclusive reliance on the state.

Volunteering and community activity, by contrast, is done for one's neighbours, for good causes, to give something back to the community or to campaign for improvements in conditions affecting a neighbourhood or a particular section of the population. All this by definition is not directed by or carried out for the state, but for people or for society as a whole.

Voluntary community action and paid community work may sometimes be doing similar things but accountability makes a critical difference. Volunteers are accountable firstly to their own motivation and secondly to any organisation or group to which they voluntarily hold themselves accountable. Paid workers are accountable to an employer, whether it be a voluntary, statutory or private organisation. The employing or funding organisation, particularly if it is a statutory one, using public funds, will naturally want the worker to do things which are not being done by activists and volunteers. There would be no paid community work if there was not a need for it, over and above what people do spontaneously for themselves and each other. Community practice is therefore a professional role which helps people to be active in their community and to achieve improvements which they would be unable to achieve on their own, either because of the burdens of disadvantage or the unresponsiveness of public agencies. It is different from the role of activists, even though some experienced activists may carry out the professional role in a voluntary capacity.

Many people who become community practitioners do so because they are motivated by experience of living or working in disadvantaged communities. They want to fight on behalf of those communities against whatever holds them down, and will do so either as activists or, if the opportunity arises, as paid workers. So they may start as voluntary activists but later become paid professionals. In this sense community work can be seen as a social movement rather than a job. From this perspective voluntary motivation is more important than professional remit.

From the policy perspective, however, community work is something which the state and its agencies need in order to make public services work effectively, to invigorate local democracy and to minimise poverty and inequality. As a state commitment, this needs to be managed and audited for maximum effectiveness. Every paid community worker represents an opportunity cost in terms of one less teacher, nurse, social worker or police officer. State agencies therefore seek to manage their community workers by objectives, outcomes and evidence, in the same way as other services are managed. But to the community worker who is 'on the side of the community' this can feel like top-down bureaucratic control and interference, particularly if the worker sees the state as the source of inequality.

A schizoid tradition – or a skilled balancing act?

The heritage which community practice draws from community development can therefore be somewhat conflicted about its relation to the state. Part of the tradition sees itself as embodying a radical critique of the state.[10] Here we call this 'radicalist', rather than radical, as we have doubts about whether it really does go to the root of the problem. Others see community practice as a means of development within rather than against the state. Chantal Mouffe argues[11] that democracy depends on recognising that inequalities have to be permanently fought against even though they cannot ever be wholly resolved.

Dealing with tension is therefore an endemic part of community practice. There are several kinds of tension that may arise and can be confused with one another. There is a natural tension at times between management and front-line workers in every field, and some of the stress in community work is simply that. Other tension arises from the natural difference between the lived experience of residents and the working experience of service providers. People are naturally inclined to be critical of services. Community practice is particularly important in disadvantaged areas, and residents there may be under multiple forms of stress – lack of employment, high crime, poor health, poor environment. These are not the fault of public services, but the local public agencies are often first in the firing line for any discontent. Community practice needs to support issues taken up by residents, and finds itself at times involved in positions critical of other public services. And residents may be critical of the local political leadership. There is inescapable tension in representative democracy, in that elected administrations, local or national, inevitably reflect the bias of the section of the population which most voted for them, even though their commitment is to govern for, and be accountable to, the whole of the society.

Ability to navigate these tensions is necessary to community practice. This is different from seeing the state and all its machinery as 'the enemy'. Since the state belongs to everyone there is no *fundamental* antagonism between the aims of the state and the aims of community practice. If the state is identified *en bloc* with a class faction, there will appear to be just such a fundamental antagonism. And if the state *is* synonymous with a class faction, as in dictatorships, then there will indeed be a fundamental antagonism. But in such cases there is no room for community practice and development, only community resistance.[12]

Radicalist theory holds that the state and its agencies are themselves the primary source of the poverty and inequality that community work is fighting against. If this is the case then tension is not only unavoidable but irremediable. There can be no successful community practice under such conditions. If you see the state as a monolithic structure with an overall single purpose such as defending capitalism it is easy to attribute all shortcomings to it. But in a state which already has a functioning democracy there is no guarantee that a revolution would improve the democratic function. It might destroy it. Or, after a good deal of turmoil, it might simply reinstate it in the current condition of tension.

It is more realistic to see the state in a democratic society as a mechanism for decision making which must respond to different, often conflicting, opinions and interests, and this view will reveal more options for change. To be sure the rich and powerful have great and unfair advantages in this process. But in a democratic state, flawed as it may be, it is open to the citizenry as a whole to seek to use the state and its instruments to redress the balance. Democracy is about striving constantly to establish equity between all interests. Working for this is a never-ending job, and community practice is a key part of this process.

The dilemma of how to operate in this environment is made more visible and acute by the historic shift which has been taking place from community development to community practice. So long as we were concerned only with community development workers, who form a tiny proportion of all public service workers, the question of their possibly antagonistic attitude to the state could simmer away on the margins without resolution, as it had done for several decades. Community practice, however, is potentially an element in the work of all public service workers. The question of their relationship to the state has to be better understood and managed, since the workforce concerned *is* a substantial part of the state. As austerity and globalisation eat away at the fabric of public services, community practitioners need to be clear that they are performing a public service alongside the other services, are part of them and are committed to defending and improving them.

If community work was only a movement of social protest, governments would never employ community workers. Repressive governments would stamp on it and permissive ones would tolerate it, but no government would deliberately allocate tax revenues to provide it. Community work as a paid occupation arises because national and local governments develop a sophisticated view about how public services and democracy work best. They realise that in order to meet citizens' needs without creating dependency, and to do so with maximum economy and effectiveness, one of the components that is universally needed is a participative ethos in which users' voices are heard, their influence is effective and co-production is facilitated.

The ambivalent effects of radicalism

The divergence between radicalist and reformist community development has a long ancestry and still affects community practice now, even for those who are unaware of this history. On the one hand, radicalist theory has little influence on practical local strategies precisely because it does not concern itself much with local tactical details. On the other hand it has appeal through its egalitarian sentiments and political analysis. However, it is questionable whether that influence is constructive or demoralising. It may boost practitioners' values and create passion for change but at the same time make them feel uneasy about collaborating creatively with other public services. It may lead to a feeling of inauthenticity, as if they should be 'on the side of the community' and therefore *against* the state.

What might be called radicalist utopianism has a dampening effect on strategy by transmitting the feeling that it is not worth trying for large-scale impact within the existing state. Ironically it may therefore impede the emergence of widespread community practice as a norm in state services.

Some theorists tend to look back on the 1960s and early 1970s as almost a golden age of community development when its radical commitment was loud and clear. In fact, the classic sources for the period exhibit as much confusion about the situation then as now. An influential tract was the memorably titled *In and Against the State* (IAAS).[13] Authorship was wittily attributed to the London Edinburgh Weekend Return Group, because they held their discussions on the Intercity train. IAAS was disillusioned with participation:

> For as long as we can remember, the question of the transition to socialism has been polarised between two positions: on one hand gradualism, on the other 'the seizure of state power'. But … this debate is sterile. The obvious lack of possibilities for reform, coupled with our eye-opening experiences of 'participation', have disabused us of hopes in gradualism. There is no way that society can be transformed through institutions that have been developed precisely to take away our power. … On the other hand … a new society cannot, either, be built in a single moment… We were trying to pose some alternative to these two unhelpful approaches. It hinges on the idea of *opposition* … the only realistic socialist practice is that of *building a culture of opposition*. (pp 130–2, their emphasis)

The 'culture of opposition' was to apply to public services as much as to capitalist enterprises. The fact that the public services were the part of the state that had been won by workers' struggle – the social wage – made no difference:

> Labour councils just as much as Tory councils are experienced by most people as the enemy, as the oppressor, as the body that won't provide decent housing or repair what exists, that keeps children out of nurseries and refuses to pay decent wages to its workers … we are the ones who will be expected to cope as living standards fall and nurseries, hospitals and old people's homes close down. (p 139)

Yet the single practical example of 'fighting back' was about the way in which a group of women prevented the threatened *closure* of a clinic. The women's collective action was of course applauded – 'they were a real grass roots group, angry, unpredictable and uncontrollable'. There was no reflection on the fact that their aim was to restore an agency of the state which they highly valued: 'It was a beautiful place – friendly, non-authoritarian.' Was this an 'institution that had been developed precisely to take away our power'? Unconsciously, it was an excellent example – not for the would-be revolutionaries' case, but rather for protecting and enhancing the valuable aspects of the state.

The book is riven through with this contradiction. It assumes the existence of all sorts of benefits from 'the state', and urges fighting to protect them when they are threatened, but never admits that they were any good to start with. The health service, for example, 'obscures capitalism's guilt for our ill-health' (p 131). The whole argument is an extended illustration of Woody Allen's quip on people's attitude to life: 'The food in this restaurant is terrible. And the portions are so small.'

Naturally, with this attitude the authors and their sympathisers were not about to recruit to their cause large sections of the working class, many of whom could remember living in far worse housing in the 1930s and 1940s, being jobless, with no national health service, and leaving school at 14. But radicalists did leave a longstanding mark on the ethos of community development, in three ways: first in a general 'culture of opposition'; secondly in an underlying unease at being state employees or dependent on state funding; and thirdly in conceiving their projects in isolation from other state services. This heritage has cast a long shadow even amidst a generation that knows little of its origin, and has to some extent seeped into community practice at large.

Although this position tends to be found most overtly in older literature, it continues through to the present. Radicalist passion still seems to lead to an isolationist attitude in which community development is seen as the sole authentic instrument of social equality and progress:

> The community work objective is to address poverty, social exclusion and inequality … It is a key pathway from poverty and stands in contrast to other approaches such as relying on income transfers through the social welfare system, approaches that are vulnerable to political whim – if social welfare is increased the poverty rate decreases, if welfare rates are decreased poverty increases.[14]

A constructive approach would assert that community practice is an essential *complement* to other progressive policies, not in competition with them; that these policies will not work properly without it; that community practice extracts maximum value from them. But to get this message across one must first acknowledge the value of the other progressive policies – the positive parts of the imperfect state.

Fuzzy orthodoxy

This history left a distinct mark on the occupational ethos of community development, which still filters through into community practice. For veterans of the radicalism of the 1960s and 1970s there was a long-term legacy of hope deferred. They saw community development as an embryo of revolution but also saw that if they wanted funding to do this work pending the revolution they would need to compromise in their rhetoric. But there was little fundamental rethinking of the relationship between community development and the state. This stream of theory signals its position by calling itself 'critical', but it is only critical of the state and its agencies, not in analysing its own practice.

As postwar capitalism and democracy continued through their many unpredictable twists and turns, practical community development produced pragmatically an increasingly wide range of low-profile beneficial local effects, participation and small local gains whilst still mostly remaining a fringe practice, with some important exceptions. To accommodate to, and take advantage of, this piecemeal but gradually widening landscape of small-scale opportunities, community development advocates developed a form of narrative which melded together the radicalist and progressivist sources, but without resolving their conflicts and contradictions. A certain fuzziness entered the narrative of funding bids, project descriptions and reports. Thus was born a style of community development justification which mixed high ideals with sometimes baffling rhetoric and jargon. Instead of clear attainable objectives, community development offered 'process not product'. And in more than a few places community development acquired a reputation for being hostile towards local authority councillors and officials, as if a commitment to the interests of the local community necessitated a degree of distrust towards those who administered their localities.

This fuzzy community development culture does not deny that progress in localities is possible – otherwise what would be the point of doing community work at all – but avoids the question of how such progress could be scaled up and integrated into state provision. It is particularly vague on measuring impact. There is a disconnection between identifying the conditions which make community practice necessary, such as poverty, disempowerment, bureaucracy, exploitation and poor local governance, and the question of whether community practice can be shown to alleviate these conditions. Conventional statistics and information are used to show the extent of poverty and inequality as a baseline to secure backing for local projects, but statistical measurement is regarded as suspect when questions of measuring community development effects themselves are raised. Community development is largely evaluated by what it feels like to take part in the process.

The statistics on poverty and inequality apply, of course, to the whole of the relevant population, eg a neighbourhood of 10,000 people. It is obvious to anyone close to community action that the numbers of people directly involved – community activists – are a small minority of the relevant population. Practitioners work with handfuls of people. How can the work of one or two community development workers, working with two or three community groups of a few dozen people each, make an impact on the poverty and inequality of a neighbourhood of 10,000 people? There are answers, leading to neighbourhood-wide strategies enlisting a range of community practitioners from different occupations. But this question is not posed in radicalist literature.

This divergence between reformist and radicalist approaches results in something of a tug of war between different mindsets in the psychology of the community practitioner. The radicalist position results in a mindset which feels isolated, embattled, sees few or no allies in the local social and political landscape, and deals with public institutions from a position of suspicion and mistrust. Is it surprising that this style of practice is in return regarded with mistrust by many local politicians and public agencies? This is disempowering of practitioners themselves. It pulls the rug from under their feet – tells them that whatever they do they are up against a monolithic inequality-reproducing state machine, in which all the public services except themselves are suspect.

Reformist community practice lacks, as yet, a fully articulated theory. This needs to be drawn together from a number of sources, and we would hope this book is a contribution towards it. It needs to take a long historical view, seeing how industrial and post-industrial states have benefited from successive waves of struggle by the labour movement and liberal and progressive interests. The state is, amongst other things, the repository of important gains made by previous phases of progressive struggle. These gains include the universal franchise, freedom of association and the press, freedom of conscience and religion, the universal public services and welfare benefits – the whole heritage of the social wage. Progressive community practice should situate itself in a positive relation to these, seeing itself as a catalyst to protect and improve them, make them work more fully and help them meet the aspirations of local communities.

This results in a style of practice which, whilst seeing the limitations and mistakes of public service bureaucracies, approaches other public service workers, local councillors and officials as potential allies. It cherishes the gains made through benefits and services, and the opportunities provided by even a very imperfect democracy.

Democracy needs community practice but does not guarantee it

If democracy is the worst political system except for all the others, it is also the system in which communities can at least struggle to be heard and in which community practice can flourish. This is not because capitalism 'itself' promotes community practice, merely that the association with democracy and individual liberty prevents capitalist society from suppressing it. The capitalist dynamic as such does not ensure community practice any more than it promotes trade unionism, the rights of women and minorities, or a conscientious environmental movement. Most of the best things in capitalist society other than productivity itself are created in some degree of criticism of the great economic engine of the system and actually conserve it by combating its inherent excesses. Out of correctives to the present wild instability of capitalism, political regimes may arise which not only stabilise and discipline capitalism to some degree but which use community practice in a more fundamental way, to ensure the health of civil society at the roots.

Accommodating to this reality does not mean giving up the need to resist oppression and struggle for equality. John Abbott[15] shows that the nearer a society gets to total repression, the less room there is for community development and the greater the necessity for resistance and possibly revolution. But a revolution does not in itself guarantee the instituting of community development values any more than capitalism does. Either reform or revolution can only lead to conditions favourable to community practice if they lead to improved participative as well as representative democracy.

The collapse of Soviet Communism revealed how completely antithetical that system had been to any kind of real citizen participation. 'Community groups' in Eastern Europe were in effect cells under the control of the party, to ensure compliance, conformism and surveillance – the exact opposite of the community development concept. To many observers this had been clear for decades, but the lesson became inescapable after the collapse of the USSR. This also revealed that, in the absence of free environmental campaigning groups, pollution in the Soviet realm had been unchecked. In the West, environmental whistleblowers and campaigners had trodden a long hard road over 50 years from being regarded as outlandish cranks to having serious policy influence. In the Soviet and Chinese realms there had not even been that possibility. It is only because of the West's gradual learning on environmental issues that the empires of the East have also had to, and been able to, begin to incorporate these lessons. It is terrifying to think how little would be known about the state of our environment if democratic societies had not allowed 'cranky' groups to develop their case.

The Soviet and Chinese regimes were built originally on popular ideals and local groups. Once in power, however, not only did they not foster the grass roots of collective action but they destroyed trust at a micro level. These kinds of society are the last that would tolerate, let alone promote, community development. This was illustrated, if it needed illustrating, by the upsurge of genuine community and voluntary groups in all their rainbow variety immediately on the collapse of each of the soviet regimes, as people seized back the initiative in their neighbourhoods.

This underlined the fact that genuinely independent community groups are not only suppressed in doctrinaire societies of the left (and by definition of the right) but are in reality a characteristic product of liberal, progressive democratic societies, even with all the shortcomings of actually existing democracy. Whatever the upheavals that may confront us over the next generation, if community practice is to fulfil its mission as part of the solution, it needs to be clear about its allegiance to democracy, pluralism and the open society.

The role of community practice is more limited than envisaged by the utopian dreams of 1960s community development but precisely by defining its limits we reveal what a huge and essential job there is to be done. Where the 20th century saw the creation of public services providing health services, education, social services, pensions and benefits after a century of campaigning, the coming years should see community practice turn from a vague movement into a universal aspect of public service.

Bringing the vision down to earth enables us to see community practice as part of the great historical movement towards creating a form of modern state that is democratic in detail as well as in outward form, and public services that are responsive and human. This will lead to much greater achievement than the scattering of improvised projects which has been the dominant pattern since the 1960s, but these projects should be credited with having valiantly carried the flame of participative practice through a long trail of obstacles and misunderstanding.

Notes

[1] Local Government Association (2010).

[2] Community work is the overall term used by Alan Twelvetrees in his classic handbook: Twelvetrees (2008).

[3] CLG (2006).

[4] Francis et al (1984).

[5] Foot and Hopkins (2010).

[6] Glen et al (2004).

[7] Sender et al (2010).

[8] Taylor (2006).

[9] Ibid.

[10] Eg Ledwith (2005).

[11] Mouffe (2005).

[12] Abbott (1996).

[13] Mitchell et al (1979).

[14] *Working for Change* (2010).

[15] Abbott, op cit.

FOUR

What happens in communities

Turning from policy and theory to actuality, this chapter begins with five short examples of what successful community practice can achieve. It then examines in some depth the basic building blocks of community life, especially community groups, which are curiously under-examined, even in community development literature. The conditions which enable groups to flourish are identified, though it should not be assumed that they necessarily represent the whole community. The chapter then focuses on the neglected question of whether it matters how many community groups there are in a given neighbourhood, and it is shown that this is crucial to the amount of activity, the effectiveness of networking and the potential for neighbourhood-wide strategy, including the impact on the uninvolved majority of residents. The discussion borrows from organisation theory to throw light on how community groups work, and concludes with an illustration of the mixture of levels across which practitioners need to operate in order to achieve a concrete gain for the community.

What good looks like

Before a strategy to strengthen community life can be drafted, it is necessary to understand what goes on in communities, with and without the help of community practice. It is as well to begin with some brief pictures of what successful strengthening of community life looks like, to illustrate what is being aimed for. There is of course no single perfect model but Boxes 4.1 to 4.5 show different types of achievement. These are drawn mainly from community development literature, but they also show the kinds of objective which coordinated community practice could aim for.

Whilst there are thousands of examples of community projects, there are relatively few which both take a whole-neighbourhood approach and whose results have been measured and published.

> ## Box 4.1: Blyth Valley, Northumberland: A district-wide community development strategy[1]
>
> Blyth Valley achieved a remarkable turn-around of conditions and morale between 1995 and 2005. Following a period of shocks resulting from high unemployment, poor conditions and the deaths of a number of young people through drug abuse, the Council reshaped itself as 'a community based council'. Though only a district council with limited resources, it took a holistic view of the needs of the locality, and invested £1m out of its £10m budget in

community development, drawing in complementary resources from other authorities. Twenty workers were employed to build up the capacity of the community in terms of its own socially productive activities and its engagement with the Council and other authorities. In parallel, the Council built up a 'hub and spoke' network of 25 community centres, at least one in each ward, as a focus for the development process. The aim was to increase the capacity of the community both to solve its own problems and to draw in extra resources.

The result over 10 years was a doubling of the number of voluntary and community organisations from approximately 300 to 600, with a corresponding doubling of volunteers. The danger of Blyth becoming a stigmatised area after industrial decline and emergence of major social problems was averted. It changed from a low housing demand area to an area with demand for new housing and consequent investment by property companies, bringing further money into the area. The Council used the Section 106 housing receipts to create further community amenities, whilst the growth in the voluntary and community sector also enabled it to bring in an extra £6.5m from external sources.

The 20 community workers were distributed across a number of thematic areas dealing with the main social issues, thus enabling the community to get maximum benefit not only from this council but from other providers – the County Council, police authority, Primary Care Trust and others. Key staff were trained in the principles of community development which they then cascaded both through the authority and wider partnerships.

ODPM (2005a)

Box 4.2: Southwark: A two-year project

A small project was run by two Council workers to improve life and community involvement in a disadvantaged neighbourhood over a period of two years. The work succeeded in establishing four new residents' groups, a neighbourhood watch scheme, a newsletter, an area forum, a park improvement plan, a summer playscheme and a youth club. A baseline-and-results study of residents' feelings about the locality was carried out for the council by independent consultants OPM and showed the following results:

- the number of residents saying they felt settled in the area increased by 13% compared with 3% for the borough as a whole;
- the proportion who said they enjoyed being out and about in the area increased by 17% compared with 4% for the borough as a whole;
- the proportion who felt the area was improving increased by 12%;
- the proportion wanting to get involved in local events increased by 10%.

Southwark, London Borough of (2000), Appendix 1

Box 4.3: Wrexham Maelor Community Project, 1986–92

This was one of an extensive programme of local development projects which the Community Development Foundation carried out in the 1980s and 1990s. Covering a large disadvantaged area of the town, the six-year project deployed a staff of eight workers to assist local residents to analyse the impact of unemployment, help to develop new community organisations, strengthen existing ones and help them to negotiate with the authorities to improve conditions or service delivery on issues like housing, environment, education and amenities.

Over seven years, 25 new community organisations were started and seven more intensively assisted; 190 people were intensively involved in the development process, 591 regularly involved as volunteers, 1,550 involved less intensively and 16,000 benefited from the services provided by the organisations. Assessments of the organisations' effectiveness were made on these criteria:

• members' self-help;
• development of individuals' capabilities;
• delivery of services to others;
• participation by the wider community;
• fundraising;
• influence on authorities;
• stimulating other local development;
• influence on local policies.

Bell (1992)

Box 4.4: Ashton, Tameside: Reclaiming the neighbourhood

The Ashton regeneration area in Tameside consisted of blocks of terrace housing with gaps between them which had become degraded, vandalised and unsafe, to the extent that residents now largely stayed within their own homes and there was little community interaction. Council community workers brought tenants together to look for solutions, which led to a widespread demand for 'alley-gating' at a time when this was a new and little-known option. This would need the consent of every resident in the relevant block. The workers located enthusiasts in each block and supported them in mobilising their neighbours and negotiating with the council and police for the installation of gates controlled by residents and the reclamation and improvement of the common areas. The scheme gave residents a new feeling of control over their territory. There was a dramatic reduction of crime in these formerly vulnerable areas, and the newly protected spaces were turned into safe areas for play and leisure. Residents volunteered to take their turn in keeping watch on the areas, and there was a huge increase in resident interaction and volunteering, visibly building social capital. Within a short time there were five residents' associations where there had been none before.

ODPM (2005a)

Box 4.5: Townstal Community Partnership

Townstal is an estate of about 4,000 people on the edge of Dartmouth, at the top of a long hill which isolates it from the main town. Most of the public services are located in the main town and difficult to access from the estate. Unlike much of Dartmouth, Townstal suffers from extensive disadvantage in terms of health, income, education and children in need.

The intervention in Townstal began in 2009 through contact with a police inspector who had seen the effects of the 'C2' Beacon project in Falmouth. NHS Devon became a major partner. The project became one of three local pilots of the Health Empowerment Leverage Project using the C2 method.

Townstal Community Partnership (TCP) was set up as a resident-led, multi-agency partnership in July 2009. Initial anger at neglect of the estate by public services gradually changed into optimism and collaboration. A major breakthrough was the partnership's collaboration with South Hams District Council on the refurbishment of the only open green space on the estate, which had long been derelict. Local children were involved in redesigning the park and took part in the official opening. Residents took on warden duties. The involvement process created a strong sense of residents' ownership and protection of the amenity. The park rapidly became a constant hub of activity. More people spent more time in the open, and there was more social activity and networking.

Achievements in TCP's second year included:

- Getting an NHS dentist located on the estate for the first time.
- A variety of residents' concerns resolved through multi-agency action.
- The police working with the local housing associations tackled crime and antisocial behaviour more swiftly.
- Better responsiveness of the housing associations on repairs and maintenance, and a better relationship with tenants.
- Reduction of speeding traffic, better parking and reduced litter.
- Increase in social and leisure activities and festivals.
- A major change of atmosphere in the estate.

Devon PCT used the experience of the Townstal project as a model to apply elsewhere in the County.

Health Empowerment Leverage Project (2012)

Though diverse in other ways, these examples share two features which make them unusual: they are about the life of the neighbourhood as a whole, and the outcomes were documented. Most community practice, and even most community development, is more fragmentary. Systematic recording of results against baselines and simple quantitative analysis are even rarer. (The way in which evaluation could be improved is discussed in Chapters Eight and Nine.)

Behind each of the summaries lies a history of detailed development, the drawing together of many local interests, overcoming scepticism and previous disappointments, building relationships and jointly tackling deep-rooted problems. The special contribution of community practice, as distinct from the delivery of main services, is to mobilise constructive energies from within the troubled community itself, to unlock the creativity of service providers and to create space for flexible or unconventional solutions.

But how do you work with a community, as opposed to simply a large number of individuals?

Fundamental building blocks: community groups

The continuous detailed life of a community cannot be observed directly. It consists in the thousands of conversations and interactions that happen in the course of a day, month or year. When residents choose to do something together over a period of time, they tend to come together as some sort of group or network.

The very term 'community group' is open to misunderstanding and leads to much dialogue at cross purposes. The kind of groups discussed in this book are independent, self-created and self-managing organisations, however small. They are often wholly voluntary, with no paid staff. A small proportion may have acquired sufficient funding to employ one or two staff, and an even smaller number may have grown into local agencies in their own right. The mass of small groups are part of the voluntary sector – indeed, the largest part – but it won't do simply to call them voluntary or third sector organisations, because those terms also cover large professionally run charities and social enterprises, and these are not necessarily based in or governed by the neighbourhoods they serve.

Professionally run charities and social enterprises are vital to society but perform different functions from community groups. The large charities and nonprofit organisations run specialist social services or campaign nationally on social issues. The small community groups build the inner strength and reciprocity of communities and are the principal footholds for local participation. Ironically, it is the community groups which are voluntary in every sense, whilst the large voluntary organisations are directed by paid staff.

The contrast is not always easy to see, because there are some organisations which skilfully straddle both roles. There are also some national charities whose local branches are relatively autonomous and self-supporting and are therefore effectively community groups.

People and agencies who are not familiar with the concept, or actuality, of community groups as organisations tend to use the term community group in a weaker sense to mean simply a *category* of people: "We deal with various community groups – young people, elderly, women, ethnic minorities."

Groups and networks are the fundamental vehicle for strengthening community life.[2] This is not because they necessarily see themselves in that role, nor are their activities the bulk of what takes place in a community. Compared with everyday conversation and interaction they occupy only a fraction of people's time. But they embody the aspects of community life which are most deliberative, most community-minded and most productive of shared value. Community groups often bring about improvements for their members, and sometimes for other residents who do not even know that the groups exist. And without necessarily setting out to do so, they form a natural interface with the local public agencies and services.

The broad life of a community remains hidden – rightly – from strategy and intervention. It is mostly through the prism of groups that it can be engaged with. You can consult a whole neighbourhood population by means of a survey, or hold a dialogue with part of it by means of a citizens' panel, but to enter into creative collaboration with it you have to engage with the autonomous groups.

Some community-based groups such as Parent–Teacher Associations, Patient Participation groups or Friends of Parks groups will have been set up specifically to interact with a particular public service. The majority of groups, however, will not have had this in mind. Most community groups and networks have a very different culture from that of public agencies. To engage with the community, agencies need to understand this difference and modify their way of doing things in order to meet the community halfway. Equally, community groups need to learn how agencies work if they want to influence and engage with them. Community practice plays a crucial role in facilitating this two-way understanding.

The density or sparsity of community groups amongst a particular population is key to the level of community activity, as discussed later in this chapter. But the majority of community groups are not necessarily found on official lists, and consequently are often underestimated or overlooked. Soteri-Proctor found 58 different community groups in 11 urban streets that were not on any official lists.[3]

Despite the diversity of their objectives, community groups share a number of common features. Often, they will:

• be small;
• be populated by members of the local neighbourhood;
• rely wholly or almost wholly on voluntary input;
• provide an informal service to their members and those around them;
• rely on small, usually self-generated incomes;
• not necessarily be known much outside their membership, even among other people living nearby.

The disparate, random nature of most community groups has been stressed because this range of relatively spontaneous, uncoordinated activity is what is least understood and most undervalued. But some groups grow to a considerable size and become important institutions in the neighbourhood, alongside public services. 'Above' the wide stratum of small groups, or embedded within it, are a number of relatively formal and structured community organisations with more strategic roles, such as community associations, forums, centres, youth clubs and others. These may run premises, employ a caretaker or secretary, have a contract or service level agreement with a local authority, or in other ways be recognisable as public organisations rather than informal groups. They may act as a vehicle for the collective voice for residents on a particular issue, and provide services and activities for other local residents. If they are serving such functions but are still genuinely led by community members, they are still part of the community sector – indeed, a particularly important part. If they have mutated into professionally run organisations which are in reality more accountable to funders and statutory agencies than to their members and users, they are no longer part of the community sector. The job they are doing as a satellite public service is important but should not be confused with being a voice of the community. The status of social enterprises in this sphere has to be judged case-by-case: some are strongly community-based, others entirely separate from the community they happen to be located in.

The Home Office LOVAS study[4] defined community groups as 'voluntary organisations or associations in which the beneficiaries include the volunteers, eg self-help groups … and groups organising communal activities'; as distinct from 'voluntary service organisations', which are 'dedicated to philanthropic provision on behalf of others'.

Productivity of the community sector

Community groups have been focussed on here in some detail because, curiously, although they are so fundamental, they do not occupy a central place in most community development and practice theory. The literature tends to take the importance of community groups for granted, and it also tends to equate them with 'the community'. This masks the fact that there is not much analysis about two crucial aspects of the community group phenomenon: (i) the difference between individual groups and the aggregate of groups across a locality (the community sector); and (ii) the relationship between groups and the substantial part of the local population that is not involved in these groups.

Looked at as a sector across a locality, community groups often cover a wide range of activities. They may include sports groups, tenants' and residents' associations, local campaign groups, older people's lunch clubs, youth activities groups, supplementary education sessions, language groups, mother and toddler groups, social groups connected with churches, synagogues, temples and mosques, arts groups, community associations, choirs, drama groups, arts clubs and more. However, in some areas there is a dearth of groups, and these kinds of activity will be thin on the ground. This will not be obvious to a casual observer. Such a dearth is in itself an important measure of local disadvantage, though hardly ever examined as such in research on poverty and disadvantage.

Even small groups, however, are likely to have several functions, without necessarily setting them up as distinct objectives. Most such functions fall into one or more of the six types of action in Figure 4.1.

These six functions tend to expand into each other as a group grows. Almost all groups have a spontaneous friendship/social capital function (A), though their primary reason for existing is likely to be some form of activity for their members (B). They may specifically seek influence on authorities (C) or develop towards that over time. If they are providing activities or some other benefit beyond their membership, they are also providing a public service (D). This may remain voluntary or, again over time, become a formal arrangement, merging perhaps into collaboration with authorities (E). In addition they may contribute to local economic development (F), either informally, through their activities and services, or by pursuing a particular path such as running a local facility or becoming a social enterprise. Even policies favourable to the strengthening of community life often overlook the richness of these types of productivity. As soon as economic hardship looms, there is pressure to ignore all types of outcome except local economic development, forgetting that this is mostly a consequence of the other functions. New Labour's switch from Neighbourhood Renewal to 'Working Neighbourhoods' in 2008, replacing a wide-ranging programme with a job-creation scheme, was an example of this. Big society's pressure on community groups to become community enterprises is another.

But each of the six functions in Figure 4.1 has its own form of productivity, and all should be boosted in their own right. All of them also have some economic value. Community practice methods should not pressurise any group to go down any particular route, but should provide all possible assistance when it spontaneously shows signs of wanting to do so.

Circumstances often provide a natural prompt. A sports group may focus only on enabling its members to play that sport (function B), and this alone is a big contribution to local health and wellbeing (function A). Then the sports field which the local council has been letting to the group for a low rent is threatened. This leads the group to lobby for the field to be saved. So it develops function C,

Figure 4.1: Functions of community groups

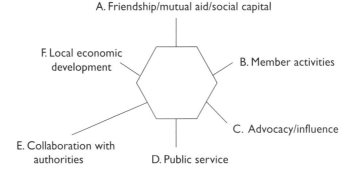

campaigning. The local authority eventually agrees to save the sports field and upgrade it on condition that the sports club looks after the grounds to a specified standard and makes it available to other sports clubs as well. So the group now adds functions D and E, service provision and co-production. Then in order to look after the field and hire it out to other clubs, and financed by that, the group finds it necessary to create paid posts for a groundsman and secretary, thus adding function F, economic development.

But all through these processes it is crucial to retain and increase community participation and members' control (function A, social capital). If the club becomes wholly professionally led, members are liable to feel that it might just as well be a council service, and volunteers may fade away. It might be a good service but it is no longer strengthening the community. If the members remain in control, however, they acquire new skills and roles as the group develops its new functions.

It is possible to start at another point in our six-fold menu, but function A – friendship, mutual aid, member control – is still the fundamental one, and that is where most groups start. Many stay there, and that is fine. A neighbourhood needs a basic floor of many groups at point A in order to sustain a number that will progress to the other functions. The main question for development is not just whether a particular group is climbing up a notional ladder of involvement, but whether the aggregate of groups is expanding 'horizontally' – whether there are enough groups to give all residents a variety of options for involvement, whether groups are increasing their memberships and users, whether groups are strengthening each other by networking, and whether an increasing number of residents are having a personal transformative experience. With this energy bubbling away behind them, a number of groups will spontaneously develop the more complex functions.

Whilst groups often carry out advocacy and exert influence, and this is a key way in which participative democracy functions, it is important not to confuse this with representative democracy. Unless it is their specific intention to try and speak for the whole community and all its concerns, which is not common, groups should not be encouraged to see themselves as representing anyone except their own members, and then only on the issues that the group is about. Groups should be internally democratic and should be open to all residents, but the internal democracy of the group only applies to those people who actually become members. It does not make the group representative of the community. Even for their members, it only makes them representative of what their members agree to do on that issue, not on all issues, which is the role of elected councillors. Representation should be ascribed to councillors rather than groups. Groups should be encouraged to make use of councillors, and councillors should be helped to respond to groups. If the local representative democracy is not vigorous enough, that has to be addressed in its own terms.

Essential conditions for community groups

What conditions are required to enable community groups to flourish? Between 2002 and 2004 the Home Office carried out a review of support for community capacity building, including a wide consultation. The resulting report, *Firm Foundations*,[5] laid down some clear principles: 'The focus for community capacity building is firstly to strengthen the community sector: that is the whole range of existing community groups and organisations through which people take part in collective activity' (p 7).

The consultation set out to determine what conditions and forms of support were most essential to a flourishing local community sector. Five key components were highlighted:

1. Meeting space – available, welcoming and accessible to all.
2. Seedcorn funding, most often small grant funds or community chests.
3. Help from workers with community development skills. This could come from a number of different occupations: 'The critical element is that they have the scope to start from the goals and needs that communities and groups define for themselves.'
4. A forum or network that is inclusive, open and participatory, owned by and accountable to the community: 'This could be for example a network of community groups, a broad-based community association, a tenant management organisation or a neighbourhood partnership. It will ensure that individual actions and initiatives are drawn together in mutual support, rather than left to fragment and divide communities.'
5. Learning opportunities to equip people for active citizenship and engagement: 'These will range from formal courses, through mentoring to informal sharing of ideas and experience.' (p 11)

These conditions are as fundamental now as they were then. Free or cheap meeting space is an irreducible precondition for community groups to flourish. Community centres and other usable buildings need to be placed where different sections of the community can easily access them, and need to be run in a way which is welcoming and helpful to all groups. This is not necessarily best done by transferring the premises as a 'community asset' to the control of single group.

The study by Soteri-Proctor[6] throws light on why small community groups appear to exist on almost no resources, yet are in fact affected by whether a neighbourhood as a whole has resources to support community activity:

> Several of the groups in this study operate with small overheads and need little, if any, finance to sustain their activities. In this sense then, money is not (directly, at least) central for them to sustain themselves. Nevertheless, whether or not aware of this – many of these groups were supported in a variety of ways (directly and indirectly) by paid and

unpaid staff working in the buildings that they use … some received assistance with holding meetings, and there were several examples in which staff helped groups put together applications for small pots of money. More fundamentally, there were staff who worked behind the scenes to ensure that the shared-space was a financially viable resource to the community by bringing in money to sustain their own organisation and, thereby, the building in which these groups meet.

Firm Foundations' recommendation on 'seedcorn funding' also needs to be understood in historical context: the *Firm Foundations* report was compiled in a period when it was assumed that other sources of follow-on funding would be available if community groups reached a more complex stage of development. This may no longer be the case. The point is not to be taken as meaning that groups need seedcorn funding only. Funding for community groups does not increase dependency – it increases volume of activity, which in turn increases volunteering and connectivity. The value of the freely given effort of the activists and volunteers is always the main part of the economy of community groups.

At its core, a community group is defined not only by its purpose but by the nature and quality of the relationships between its members. The effectiveness of a group flows from a combination of formal elements such as aims and tasks and the way it functions as an association: how members participate, communicate, respond and act together; their sense of shared purpose; how they deal with conflict; and how decision making takes place.

Networks

The concept of networks can be even more elusive than that of community groups to those who have no conscious experience of them. 'There are often no clear affiliation mechanisms, and membership itself is a fuzzy category with constantly shifting boundaries and allegiances … The most important and useful aspect of a network is its pattern of connections, which often reflects an underlying value base, a shared interest or simply the geography of overlapping lives.'[7] As Gilchrist shows, networks are just as fundamental to community life as organised groups. Without them, community groups would possibly not exist at all, and the relatively formal life of identifiable groups is often surrounded by a penumbra of face-to-face social networking which touches many more community members precisely because it does not require explicit membership, attendance at meetings or declared commitments. By the same token, however, networks are not formally democratic or accountable and can sometimes be swayed by a few strong personalities.

To work well, neighbourhood partnerships between different agencies and community interests need to function at a networking as well as organisational level. Purposeful networking, indeed, is an essential tool of the trade of community practice. Practitioners need to use networking skills to help community groups make connections – a function which Gilchrist calls meta-networking.[8] In working towards a comprehensive neighbourhood strategy three types of network must be cultivated: (i) the natural personal networks between residents; (ii) networks of cooperation between different public and voluntary agencies, including amongst their front-line staff; and (iii) networks of community practitioners themselves, to build mutual support, cross-referral and a stronger voice vis-à-vis local policy and strategy.

Some community groups are isolated and self-contained, do not see themselves as part of a sector and are content with the level of activity and membership that they have reached. Others are embedded in a web of relationships with other groups and with public services.[9] Local umbrella groups or community projects may play a key role in fostering networks between groups, which may in turn help the member groups in numerous ways. The Wrexham project summarised in Box 4.3 above revealed that individuals who became active through a group that the project had helped to establish often 'graduated' to further community activity if they left the group or it came to an end.[10]

How people interact in groups

Of course, not all is plain sailing in community groups any more than in any other sort of human encounter. There can be stresses in relationships between individuals or between groups, and these can reverberate elsewhere in the neighbourhood.

Group members are usually aware that informal communication is as important as the formal system ('all the best work gets done in the pub after the meetings'), but it is important that both elements are balanced if a healthy and open group culture is to be maintained.

The way an individual behaves within a group will reflect their personality and talents as well as the requirements of the group. Belbin[11] suggests that what matters most in making a group of any kind function well is having a spread of personality types which fulfil different group functions, notably (in summary):

The Chair – the person who presides over the team and coordinates its efforts. A good listener and talker, and works through others. Disciplined and focussed rather than brilliant and creative.

The Shaper – a task leader who likes to get things done. Outgoing and dominant, but can be impatient, irritable and oversensitive.

The Plant – often a source of original ideas and proposals. May be imaginative and intelligent. May be introverted but also intellectually dominant. May also be careless of details and may resent criticism.

The Monitor–Evaluator – carefully dissects ideas and is able to see flaws in an argument. Whilst intelligent and analytic, may seem less involved than the others and can be tactless.

The Resource Investigator – the person who brings in new contacts and ideas, extrovert and sociable.

The Company Worker – the practical organiser who turns ideas into manageable plans and tasks. Methodical, trustworthy and efficient.

The Team Worker – holds the team together by being supportive of others, listening, encouraging, and understanding. Likeable, popular, uncompetitive.

The Finisher – checks the details, worries about timetables, chivvies the others. Can be relentless, but not always popular.

How many community groups are there? How many should there be?

The density or sparsity of community groups is itself a major factor in the character and conditions of a neighbourhood or comparable area. Yet the number of groups in an area is neglected in almost all sociological literature. Even more alarmingly, it is often overlooked even in community development and practice literature. There is a longstanding tendency to concentrate on the individual practitioner and group in isolation.

There has been debate from time to time on the density of community and voluntary groups, and whether the sheer number of such groups in a locality is a meaningful measure. European research in the early 1990s which showed an average of three community or voluntary organisations per thousand people[12] was seen by some commentators as 'over-optimistic'. It was followed, however, by several studies which claimed that it was too conservative – at least for the UK. The Home Office's seminal 'LOVAS' study in the mid-1990s[13] found between 4.5 and 19 community and voluntary organisations per thousand population from one area to another in England.

At first sight the sheer number of community groups that can be found in a given neighbourhood may not seem to tell you much. The number of people who participate is more important. For example, there are villages where there are very few community groups but almost everyone in the village takes part in them. There are other places where there are numerous groups but more than half the population do not take part in even one.

Nevertheless, in a highly diverse and pluralist society the number of groups is significant, for four reasons. First, most groups are small. The smallness is part of what makes them easy and unthreatening to be in. They are able to operate fairly informally, encouraging friendship and sociability, and enabling individuals to play a satisfying personal role. Consequently you need quite a large number of groups in a neighbourhood if you want most residents to be able to access them. Secondly, people join groups in which they feel comfortable, so a larger number of groups makes it more likely that most people could find one that suits them.

Thirdly, a larger number of groups covers a wider range of social issues, so that it is more likely that most important issues will be addressed by at least some fraction of local residents. In a neighbourhood with a strong community sector culture, new groups will form, or old ones will adapt, as new issues come up. This links to the fourth reason, which is crucial to the potential for neighbourhood-wide strategy: a reasonably substantial volume of groups means a better chance of forming a balanced neighbourhood partnership, with some expression from, and access to, most sections of the community. A given density of groups is not a precondition for a neighbourhood partnership, but if a partnership is launched on a sparse base of groups, it should itself foster the proliferation of new independent groups.

Is it possible, then, to lay down an approximate number of groups that a neighbourhood of a given size would need in order to be a strong community? It should be possible to say whether a neighbourhood is well populated by groups or suffering a dearth of groups, and there is enough evidence in previous studies to establish such a benchmark.[14]

How is a comprehensive picture of local groups to be built up? The natural starting point, and a key partner for such an overview, would be the nearest local umbrella group for the community and voluntary sector. This might be a Council of Voluntary Service in a mainly urban area or a Rural Community Council in a rural area. These tend to be fairly small organisations themselves, committed to supporting as best they can all parts of the sector across a large territory, often a whole principal local authority area. Some areas may have their own more local support or fund-raising organisation, such as a Community Development Trust. For strategies on community practice it will be necessary to focus down on the neighbourhood level (usually around 5,000 to 15,000 people). Umbrella groups will not always map their membership by neighbourhood. Where they do, it will often be seen that disadvantaged areas have fewer groups.

In 1998 the government conducted the first comprehensive national survey of third sector organisations across England, sampling the sector in all 149 principal local authorities.[15] The survey sampled all third sector organisations in the locality based on the total number of such organisations found there through formal listings. It was acknowledged that these lists would miss a large number of the smaller and more informal groups. Even so, a substantial number of community groups were included, as well as the more easily located professionally run charities and social enterprises. The numbers for each local authority area can be found on the survey website.

Total numbers of listed third sector organisations in these large local authority areas (community groups plus professionally led and others) ranged from around 200 to 3,000. Examples of the range are shown in Table 4.1.

These figures cannot be directly compared, because they apply to different sizes of population. Nevertheless there are clearly some immense differences in the sheer size of the registered sector in different places. The London Borough of Camden has about 30 per cent more people than the London Borough of

Table 4.1: Total number of listed third sector organisations in selected local authority areas

Barking and Dagenham	394	Liverpool	1,466
Barnsley	465	Oxfordshire	3,213
Bath and North East Somerset	780	Reading	491
Birmingham	2,877	Solihull	538
Bracknell	253	Torbay	361
Brighton	1,001	Wandsworth	860
Camden	2,478	Windsor and Maidenhead	550
Cornwall	2,194		

Barking and Dagenham but eight times as many listed groups. Seaside town Brighton has about 16 per cent more people than seaside area Torbay but three times as many listed groups.

Despite conducting sophisticated analysis of other factors, no analysis was attempted in the survey report of reasons for the large variations in numbers of organisations found per head of population, or the difference that it might make to a locality to be either densely or sparsely populated with community groups or voluntary organisations. Two obvious hypotheses of causal factors would be (i) general level of prosperity and (ii) the local history of community development and practice. Disadvantage both impedes the formation of groups and is exacerbated by their sparsity. This is a key reason why community practice is needed.

Nor did the survey calculate numbers of community groups as distinct from social enterprises and professionally led charities. However, by using the more detailed information it is possible to make a good estimate. For example, if you count as community groups all respondent organisations with no more than two employees, this amounts to 70 per cent of respondents. Looking at funding, 49 per cent of organisations had less than £25,000 income p.a. Given that the survey was based only on groups and organisations contained in official lists, and that social enterprises and professionally led charities were far more likely to appear in those lists than small community groups, it is clear that the majority of groups in localities are community groups: some captured in the survey, many more not.

How much volunteering?

Rather than measuring number of organisations, the Home Office LOVAS study 10 years earlier[16] focused on total number of hours of (formal) volunteering[17] taking place in a locality per head of adult population. But in the course of documenting this figure, LOVAS also counted the number of organisations of different kinds. About two thirds of all formal volunteering took place through community and voluntary organisations and one third through other organisations such as hospitals, schools and the justice system. The figures on total hours of volunteering per thousand adults suggest that there is a rough correlation between amount of volunteering and number of community and voluntary organisations functioning in a locality.

This is another unsurprising but little-remarked aspect of community activity. Governments tend to try and encourage volunteering by reminding people what a good and satisfying thing it is. Most volunteering, however, is generated by people who are already involved in an activity roping in their friends. The most effective thing you could do if you wanted to increase volunteering would be to help people to set up or extend community groups.

As an example of the LOVAS findings, Accrington had the lowest volunteering rate of the 14 areas studied, half the average. This amounted to a total of 22,408 voluntary hours per year per thousand adults resident in the area, ie about 22 hours' voluntary work a year per adult (over 18) resident. In total, 350 independent voluntary/community groups were found, representing 4.5 groups per thousand population. Annual income of the voluntary and community organisations was equivalent to £40 per head of population.

At the other end of the scale, Cresswell, Whitwell and Clowne had 50,188 hours' voluntary work in the year per thousand adults, ie 50 hours' voluntary work per adult resident, and had 194 groups, representing just over 19 groups per thousand population. The annual income of voluntary organisations was equivalent to £225 per head.

Another 'high scoring' example was Billericay, with 50,424 voluntary hours a year per thousand adults, ie again an average of 50 hours of voluntary work per adult resident, from 538 groups, representing 15 groups per thousand population. The annual income of the voluntary organisations was equivalent to £65 per head.

In Huddersfield, as an example of the middle range, the total of voluntary work was 43,396 hours, representing 43 hours' work a year per adult resident, from 1,167 groups, representing 9.7 groups per thousand population, and the annual income of the voluntary organisations was equivalent to £300 per head.

Overall it seems that the sheer number of organisations is a meaningful, but partial, criterion of level of community activity. It is virtually inconceivable, in the UK culture, that a locality could have varied and vigorous community activity without this expressing itself partly through the creation of a rich crop of community groups.

If a local survey cannot find more than three community and voluntary organisations per thousand people, it can be concluded that community activity is distinctly low. This is likely to mean that the community is playing little part in determining and enhancing its own social conditions. It is also likely to mean that councillors and other spokespeople for the community on local partnerships and committees may have few networks to help them reach back into their own communities.

Reaching the uninvolved

If the effects of community practice are to make an impact on the neighbourhood – and show up in social statistics – they must affect the majority of the neighbourhood population, not just the minority who are active.

Different segments of the community can be depicted in a simplified way, as in Figure 4.2.

If a neighbourhood of 5,000 people has our 'standard minimum' of three voluntary or community groups per thousand, that amounts to 15 groups. Typically there will be a handful of active residents at the centre of a group, supported by some scores or possibly in total a few hundred who come to occasional meetings or undertake some volunteering. If it is assumed (generously) that there is no overlap between people involved in each group, and that on average each group is run by a dozen key decision makers, with 25 other regular helpers (volunteers) and another 50 people benefitting or contributing at various levels of commitment, this could still leave two thirds or more of local people uninvolved in any community group.

What are the implications for strategy? Depending on the profile of local groups, a low involvement figure might suggest that more groups would be beneficial or that existing groups might be supported to grow and involve more people. Suppose we raised involvement from 25 per cent of the adult population to 35 per cent, or from 33 per cent to 45 per cent, what effect would this have? It would be likely to mean more people accessing groups' services, a larger minority getting drawn to the active centre, and some of these undergoing a transformative personal experience or gaining some major new understanding of local affairs. It might also mean more useful feedback to public agencies, and more community influence on public service commissioning and delivery, and thus a better fit between services and needs.

Community practice literature sometimes speaks of 'ripples' from the centre of action to the periphery but there are very few studies or evaluations which specifically examine this 'scaling up' process. A 'Social Return on Investment' (SROI) study commissioned by the Community Development Foundation[18] is

Figure 4.2: Levels of involvement in a community

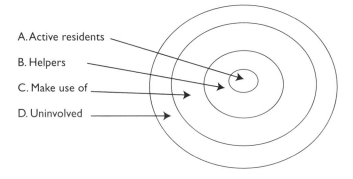

unusual in distinguishing involved and uninvolved residents, and concludes from its calculations that whilst the benefits of community development are most intensive for the active, the total value of benefit for the neighbourhood through the indirect effect on the uninvolved is much greater, as there are so many more of them. 'The wider community benefits from the fact that a significant number of CD activities achieve an improvement in the delivery of various public services, as community needs are better articulated and reflected.' (p 25)

From the experience of participation, the active minority (circle A in Figure 4.2) gain skills and information, widen their social networks, gain recognition by authorities and increase their employability. These are intrinsic participation outcomes for a small proportion of the community (they could be called Level 1 outcomes).

As a result of groups' and networks' activities there are improvements to conditions in the locality. For example the health agencies respond to groups' campaigning by relocating a surgery or dental practice; the housing department or housing associations respond with quicker repairs or more efficient heating; the police respond by removing abandoned cars; the parks department responds by renovating a piece of derelict land. These reach potentially the whole population (Level 2 outcomes).

As activities gain momentum, new volunteers are recruited, and some people who were previously occasional helpers may move towards the inner circle and share their additional benefits. Many residents may know nothing about the developments that have been taking place until they see a park being opened, a dental clinic appearing, repairs to houses being carried out. As a result they start using the new amenities and may ask their neighbours what is happening, attend a meeting or see a newsletter, and some thus become part of the aware or involved community (Level 3 outcomes).

For some people, of course, non-involvement is a conscious choice. Their personal networks or communities of interest (not necessarily bounded by the neighbourhood) may matter more to them than activities in the neighbourhood. Or they may be concerned with the neighbourhood but just not want to play an active role. Research by IpsosMORI re-analysing data from the New Deal for Communities national evaluation,[19] shows that many people can *feel* influential in local affairs without personally taking part. At the same time some who do take part may not feel influential – perhaps because, having made more effort, they feel frustrated at slow progress.

A vision of an ultimately 'developed' community would not necessarily show everyone being active and influential. It might well show a majority of residents aware and approving of the efforts of an active minority and feeling that the results of the activity are beneficial. The problem with what we could call inert neighbourhoods is not that a majority of people are not active in a centralised initiative but that there is not a sufficient, capable, credible minority taking that role and endorsed either actively or passively by the neighbourhood population as a whole.

—

Inertia is unlikely to be because there are no people in the neighbourhood capable of taking the active role. The potential may be hidden because personal relationships and networks in the neighbourhood are poor, and residents have retreated from the social space into personal survival mode:

> The material and psychological disadvantages of living in a neighbourhood with a poor reputation include discrimination in the labour market and in accessing finance; people's self-esteem can be damaged by living in a notorious area. As a means of dealing with these negative effects, residents ... may engage in distancing strategies ...[20]

The ongoing national citizenship survey in England[21] provides information which throws useful light on levels of involvement:

- Proportion of people feeling satisfied with their local area as a place to live: 83%.
- Asked whether they felt their area had got better or worse or stayed the same in the last two years: 65% stayed the same.
- 76% felt they belonged strongly to their neighbourhood and their local area, whilst 87% felt a strong sense of belonging to Britain.

Analysis identified that the lower the socio-economic group, the more likely the strong sense of belonging to the neighbourhood. People in the most deprived areas were more likely to feel that they belonged to their areas than those living in least deprived areas. Sixty-seven per cent of people agreed that people in their neighbourhood pulled together to improve the area. This contributed to their sense of belonging to the neighbourhood. Fifty per cent of people thought that many of the people in their neighbourhood could be trusted. Seventy-four per cent felt safe walking in their neighbourhood after dark, but 38 per cent said they were worried about becoming a victim of crime. Eighty-five per cent agreed that their area was somewhere that people from different backgrounds got on well with together and that people from different ethnic backgrounds were respected, but people's social networks tended to be fairly homogeneous.

Sidelights from organisational theory

The vast majority of books about organisational theory are concerned with the private sector. A small number focus on the public or voluntary sectors but even in these there is rarely anything about community groups.[22] Can these theories help to throw light on the very different world of community groups and networks? Most of the organisational theory which has emerged over the past 20 years has been about much larger and more structured organisations. Some of this theory, nevertheless, is also helpful in understanding community groups and organisations, particularly those which develop into a more structured role. Three of the more relevant areas of theory are touched on in the following.

Psychological contract

Why do people get involved in community organisations? Involvement in a group can eat up a lot of time and energy. Whilst it can be exhilarating and fun, it may also be stressful and challenging. Most people do not set out consciously to join a group but are asked to help out by friends or neighbours. They do not necessarily feel they have joined and are a member of the group, just that they went along to a meeting or two and stayed. Many smaller groups do not keep written membership lists and circulate minutes. But at some point groups begin to think of themselves as organisations, and the people in them begin to think of themselves as members. As groups grow, the methods for keeping track of membership and decisions inevitably become more formal.

The experience of joining an established group is different from helping to start a group. Those who are in at the beginning naturally feel equally involved. When someone joins an established group, they do so as an individual but encounter the group as a collective. They encounter an already coalescing culture, atmosphere, unwritten rules and norms, 'the way we do things here'. The norms may only slowly emerge. New members may only find out about one of these unwritten rules if they inadvertently transgress it.

People have a variety of reasons for becoming involved in a group. They may want to meet people or develop more self-confidence – these can be described as intrinsic motivations. Or they may want to make a difference to an issue in the locality, or to make a new activity available to their children, older people or other residents. These can be called extrinsic motivations. People are often motivated by a mixture of extrinsic and intrinsic reasons.

These motivations are also expectations – the hope that involvement with the group will further that person's desires. By the same token there will be an expectation from the group that the individual will contribute to its running in some way. There is an implicit 'psychological contract' between the individual and the group. This psychological contract is generally unstated, but underpins the 'process of giving and receiving by the individual and the organisation ... the contract works when these two elements are in balance'.[23]

Involvement in any organisation can be either coercive (you are there because you have no choice, such as in prison); remunerative (you are paid to be there); or cooperative (you are there because you agree with the goals of the organisation or you are friendly with the people who are members of the group).[24] In a community organisation the cooperative element is definitive. Members cannot be told what to do, they can only be asked. Those who disagree may refuse their consent or even leave.

In a community group the overall goals are developed through bringing together the extrinsic and intrinsic goals, beliefs and feelings of the members through debate, negotiation, compromise and learning. Difficulties will emerge when the formal goals, and the interpretation of the goals, diverge or become less compatible with some members' own goals and motivations, or when there

—

is a sense within the group that the individual is disruptive or an obstacle to the aims. Sometimes a group feels it has no choice but to expel someone, but this will generally only take place after a long time or when relationships within the group reach a crisis point.

Organisational culture

Charles Handy asserts that 'anyone who has spent time with any variety of organizations… will have been struck by the differing atmospheres, the differing way of doing things, the differing levels of energy, of individual freedom, of kinds of personality'.[25] Small though they are, community groups exhibit the same variety of features. Handy identifies four types of organisational culture:

- *The club or power culture:* structured like a spider's web with a strong personality at the centre, often the founder.
- *The role culture:* structured as a bureaucracy, with separate functions or specialities controlled by procedures.
- *The task or cooperative culture:* job or project oriented and structured like a grid or net. Flat structure, little formal hierarchy.
- *The person culture:* where the structure serves individuals as sources of particular skills, eg as in GP practices or barristers' chambers.

It is easy to see how an individual working in one particular kind of organisational culture might find it difficult or frustrating to be working in another. For example a local shopkeeper or someone running a small business will be used to running things within a power culture, whilst a service provider will be used to working in a role culture model. Both might find working in a task or cooperative culture challenging and either may, consciously or unconsciously, try and shape the group into one they recognise and are comfortable with. Hence complaints such as "It's nothing but a talking shop, I want some action" or "The group has no proper procedures and I'm worried about accountability".

Power and development in groups

Tuckman's ideas[26] about how groups and organisations develop are well known. He argues that to function well, all groups should go through four developmental stages: Forming, Storming, Norming and Performing. This provides a useful structure when you ask yourself 'What's going on at this point in this group's development?' Figure 4.3 illustrates how this might apply to a community group.

   This could be compared with Richard L Daft's description[27] of an organisational life cycle in four stages, each of which leads to its own type of crisis, which drives development onwards:

Figure 4.3: Four stages in community groups

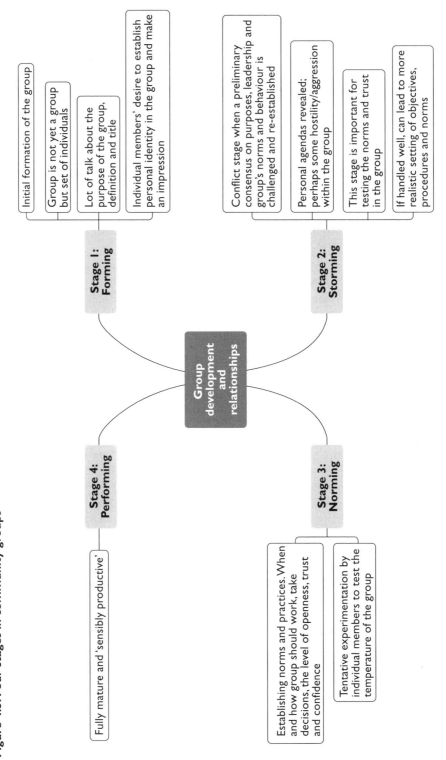

1. Entrepreneurial stage → Crisis: Need for leadership
2. Collectivity stage → Crisis: Need for delegation
3. Formalisation stage → Crisis: Too much red tape
4. Elaboration stage → Crisis: Need for revitalisation.

Even in a small and wholly voluntary organisation much of the culture is determined by the way in which formal and informal power is distributed. Although there may be no financial or coercive power, there are many other sources of power, both positive and negative, for example:

- *Position Power* – from a person's role in the organisation, for example as an officer or a member of a core group. The role allows the holder to make decisions, ask for things and decide things, give permission or stop things.
- *Expert Power* – from being an acknowledged expert in something important to the group, wiser, more knowledgeable or having a greater level of experience.
- *Personal Power* – unique characteristics in a person, be it charm, force of personality, doggedness or determination.
- *Gatekeeper Power* – the gatekeeper is someone who controls access to resources, decision-making systems, information or access to other members of an organisation or a neighbourhood. Gatekeepers can be a source of positive power, enabling and encouraging access to the resources, or they can use their power negatively.

People with either formal or informal gatekeeping powers pervade society. They can help make life easier or more difficult. It is striking how one deeply negative person can have a degree of power within a group that is out of all proportion. A school caretaker may have power in deciding whether to open up the school hall outside school hours. A faith group leader may want to control access of outsiders, to protect their community. It is important to remember that the community practitioner is also a gatekeeper.

An unhealthy level of gatekeeping power can inadvertently become inbuilt into neighbourhood development. A system of area management committees was introduced in a major city in the 1990s, aimed at bringing together residents, council officers and elected members to address local issues. A later study[28] revealed that the system had unintentionally encouraged the emergence of strong neighbourhood gatekeepers who were able to control the access of other residents to the consultative and decision-making system. These were some of the key factors that allowed this to happen:

- The community representatives were co-opted onto the committee for several years, and there was no mechanism for deselecting them even if they moved out of the area.
- There was no system of accountability established between the local communities and the community spokespeople.

- The community representatives received no support.
- Meetings were held in the city centre, during the day for the convenience of the council officers.
- Participants reported that the usefulness of the meetings was not in the formal business, but access to information and informal contacts with officers.
- Prior to the meetings all matters of contention had been thrashed out in advance between officers, or debated by the dominant party grouping privately.
- Decisions at the meeting were often based on simply accepting or rejecting a single option.

Reality check: picturing interaction

These rationalisations of how local groups develop and practice takes place give a tidier picture that would be encountered in reality. This chapter concludes with a depiction (Figure 4.4) of how an initiative to start a group will often find itself situated in a confusing nexus of groups and services. Even a community practitioner supporting a single community initiative may need to work at many different levels within the neighbourhood and public services at the same time; how much more so a team implementing a wide strategy.

In our example, two local parents, Sangeeta and Kathy, want to develop activities for children and young people. Jen, a community worker for Anytown Community Project, has judged that she should support their initiative as she has established that there is a lack of activities for children and young people in the area and new provision will benefit a large number of other families.

The situation depicted in the figure includes several people who are important to the development of Sangeeta and Kathy's initiative. Some of the characters are residents, others are employed by agencies such as the local authority. To get the new group set up with a good prospect of success needs the backing of the school, the community centre and the council.

As the community practitioner concerned with this development, Jen will at some stage become aware of the wider conflicts and issues within the local community (for example potentially competing needs for play, childcare, activities for the under fives, 5 to 12-year-olds, younger teens and post-16-year-olds). She will also become aware that whilst some public sector practitioners and managers of services share the desire to 'do something for the kids' they also face a wide range of constraints, such as personal and organisational priorities, legal requirements and lack of money.

The process of helping develop a single small group drives Jen to function at these different levels:

- *With residents at a personal level* – working with Sangeeta, Kathy and other parents as individuals to help them clarify their vision and understand the implications, develop the skills and self belief that they can play a core role in setting up and running a group.

Figure 4.4: Picturing interaction

- *At a community group level* – working with the members to help shape their ideas and desires for 'something for the kids' into a programme of action that will provide the activity or service; and to help them develop into a cohesive group and later, possibly, a formal organisation. This work may also spread to the community centre management committee as a consequence of exploring with them the possibility of them hosting the children's activity group.
- *At a neighbourhood level* – working across the neighbourhood with the different community and public service organisations to help the children's activity group achieve its aims. One consequence might be bringing the different agencies and groups with an interest in children and young people together to explore the possibility of a neighbourhood-wide strategy.
- *At an agency and department level* – working with public service organisations and staff (practitioners, managers and politicians) to get support for the children's activity group (for example funding and training). If individuals or policies are blocking the development of the group, seeking changes in policies and priorities.
- *At a local authority level* – working with key elements within the local authority to encourage it to become more receptive to community priorities. Change is only likely to come about if the role of community organisations is understood and the interdependent nature of community groups and public services is recognised and supported.

Ultimately the development of a cross-sector neighbourhood partnership is likely to be necessary if these kinds of collaborative arrangements are to multiply and lead towards a transformational tipping point.

Notes

[1] Blyth Valley was a district council till 2009, when it became part of Northumberland County Council. As part of a two-tier system, its budget was relatively small.

[2] Scott (2009); Gilchrist (2009).

[3] Soteri-Proctor (2011).

[4] Marshall et al (1997).

[5] Home Office (2004).

[6] Op cit.

[7] Gilchrist, op cit, p 49.

[8] Gilchrist, op cit, p 105.

[9] Gilchrist, op cit; Rowson et al (2010).

[10] Bell, op cit.

[11] Belbin (2011).

—

[12] Chanan (1992).

[13] Marshall, op cit. The areas studied were: Accrington, Lancashire; Alcester and Bidford, Stratford-on-Avon; Alnwick, Northumberland; Billericay, Essex; Cresswell, Whitwell and Clowne, Bolsover, Derbyshire; Gosport, Hampshire; Great Missenden, Buckinghamshire; Hammersmith & Fulham, London; Huddersfield, Yorkshire; Northwich, Vale Royal, Cheshire; Norwich, Norfolk; Richmond upon Thames, London; Cliff, Nottinghamshire; Torrington, Devon.

[14] This discussion draws on Chanan (2004).

[15] www.nscsesurvey.com. In Chapter Eight we look at other aspects of this survey which are important for evaluation.

[16] Marshall, op cit.

[17] Formal volunteering is through organisations, however small. Informal volunteering is personal help given to neighbours or others outside the family.

[18] New Economics Foundation (2010).

[19] Duffy, Vince and Page (2008).

[20] New Economics Foundation (2010), p 25.

[21] CLG (2011c).

[22] For example Handy (1988); Hudson (2002).

[23] Mullins (1989).

[24] Hudson, op cit.

[25] Handy (1988).

[26] Tuckman (1965).

[27] Daft (2007).

[28] Jeffrey (1997).

FIVE

Towards neighbourhood strategy

Preceding chapters have commented on the piecemeal nature of many community involvement initiatives. If community involvement is to have a more decisive role in the future, it needs a more systematic strategy. This chapter discusses what such a strategy should consist of and how it should be driven. It looks at the spatial basis; at a holistic view of the elements needed for sustainable improvement; and at the interaction of communities of interest with geographically-based communities. Can action in a disadvantaged neighbourhood make any difference to its economic plight? Have government regeneration schemes which tried to improve neighbourhoods in the past made a significant difference? What are the essential factors that make for a sustainable community? How should partnerships operate? Does the big society policy help or hinder neighbourhood partnership working? A number of precedents and models for whole neighbourhood working are reviewed, and the problem of reconciling the 'inside-out' view of residents with the 'outside-in' view of public agencies is highlighted. The discussion draws on whole systems and complexity theory with some reservations, and notes that current models of 'total place' are belied by the absence of any real concept of active communities. The chapter concludes by identifying some of the key skills and concepts that are needed to apply community practice on a whole neighbourhood basis.

Overcoming fragmentation

From 1998 to 2008, as discussed in Chapter Two, there was a period of expansion in community practice in the UK, through programmes on social inclusion, local authority reform, neighbourhood renewal and community engagement. Between 2008 and 2012 there was a contraction in England (though not in Scotland, Wales or Northern Ireland), notwithstanding the 'big society' experiment. Fortunately many previous forms of community practice are still active despite cuts in staffing. This is partly because of the momentum of previous policies and partly because of the age-old process whereby workers and managers at the front line of public services create their own ways of interacting with local groups.

However, most of these practices, whether deliberate or improvised, are scattered and do not see themselves as part of a linked movement or combined local strategy. Without a clear focal point of strategy, coordinated by some form of neighbourhood partnership, community practice may be spasmodic and never achieve cumulative effect. Or it may dwindle unnoticed.

A new community practice strategy needs to be located in a clear coordinating point in each neighbourhood, supporting a network of community practitioners from all services, and supported in turn by policy at higher spatial levels – local authority, region, nation. Agencies need to be persuaded that this is a good use of their workers' time and will have benefits for each separate agency and its objectives. The local authority is the most obvious body to lead coordination but there are a number of other options and different ways in which this can be done.

The neighbourhood, or equivalent space in rural areas, should be used as the main focus for community practice because:

- it is a place which will be recognised by residents;
- it is more or less administratively coherent;
- it is where people have face-to-face encounters and share amenities and settings, so there is a basis for joint activity;
- statistics show significant differences in social conditions at this level.

It would not do to use the notion of community as the main reference point because the meaning of this term is imprecise. It is better to have spatial precision and to examine the state of community action as a feature of that space. This allows us to frame a strategy not for strengthening 'communities' but for *strengthening community activity across a given population,* which can be demonstrated and measured.

A vision of sustainability

The way we envision the future of the neighbourhood will have a long-range effect on what we think we can do to improve it and how we judge success. Some far-sighted holistic thinking on localities was carried out in the 2000s. At the request of then Deputy Prime Minister John Prescott in 2004, industrialist Sir John Egan produced a set of criteria for sustainable communities, defined like this:

> Sustainable communities meet the diverse needs of existing and future residents, their children and other users, contribute to a high quality of life and provide opportunity and choice. They achieve this in ways that make effective use of natural resources, enhance the environment, promote social cohesion and inclusion and strengthen economic prosperity.[1]

From an ecological point of view there is still great waste and unexploited value in most localities. In one of its last reports before being closed down by the Coalition Government,[2] the Sustainable Development Commission (SDC) set out a vision for 'retrofitting' all neighbourhoods through a range of measures such as making homes and buildings more energy-efficient. 'Retrofitting' means both refitting and retrospectively making the places fit for ecologically sound living.

> A well-designed, well-built place could help residents achieve a 75% reduction in their total carbon emissions and a 78% reduction in their

ecological footprint. The most significant contribution can be made from existing buildings. The UK's 21 million homes are responsible for 27% of our carbon emissions. The 1.8 million non-domestic buildings are responsible for a further 18%.

The SDC report shows that the substantial cost of carrying this out would be much less if organised collectively through neighbourhood partnerships. Egan's view was that creating sustainable communities needed a range of specialist skills combined with a range of generic skills which all the contributing specialists should also possess so that they could work together on the unifying objective. This was summed up in a central image which became known as the 'Egan wheel',[3] depicting all the main material and social factors that would add up to a good place to live (Figure 5.1).

Figure 5.1: The Egan Wheel

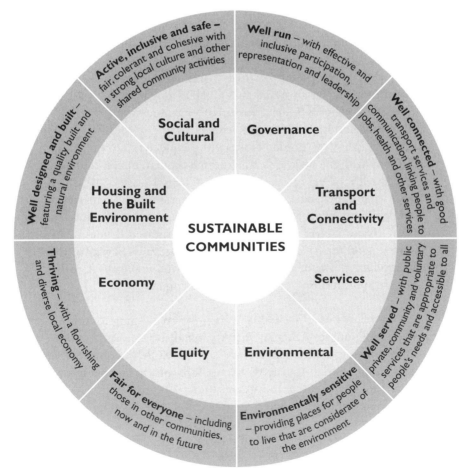

Egan's approach was a major step towards the idea that partnership between all public services and other contributors should become the norm for the way that localities were managed. There had already been wide experience of partnership working in regeneration schemes in disadvantaged areas. The prospect now was to make partnership the universal model for local governance.

Egan's 'transport and connectivity' criterion picks up the issue of the neighbourhood's relation to the wider economy and society and by implication to adjacent neighbourhoods. A characteristic of affluent areas is mobility – not only that the area is seen as desirable but that it is easy for residents to get in and out of it at will, whether for commuting, for leisure or when wishing to move house. Residents may choose to have their community and friendship networks close by or at a distance. What characterises poor neighbourhoods, by contrast, is less mobility, fewer options about leaving, and inescapable reliance on the neighbourhood and its services and amenities. The Egan vision aims to give people in disadvantaged areas more of the options available to those who are better off.

With reference to Belfast and a number of other 'divided cities' across the world, Gaffikin and Morrissey discuss the risks as well as value of neighbourhood development if it does not include connectivity:

> In such cities 'community' can be an exclusive spatial unit. Community planning may encourage each segregated area to attempt to advance its position at the expense of the 'other' community, thereby deepening separatism and sectarian rivalry. ... Local planning in these conflictive circumstances needs special forms of engagement that candidly acknowledge and preclude these tendencies. Participation ... needs to be facilitated by 'border crossers' – people whose contact and credibility with the various factions permit them to operate as honest brokers, without being over-directive or prescriptive ... (CD can bring) local knowledge and credibility, experience and expertise in local development; creative and cultural assets, alongside reliance and resourcefulness ... yet CD can also exhibit significant deficits ... can privilege short term tactics over long term strategy ... elevate process over product ... assume intrinsic virtue resting more on anecdote than evidence and stress outputs rather than outcomes.[4] (p 265)

The Egan report was used in 2006 as a basis for establishing a think tank, the Sustainable Communities Academy (SCA), linked to regional centres to drive forward this unifying vision. Three years later the SCA was absorbed into the Homes and Communities Agency with a remit to inform its then vast portfolio of regeneration schemes. SCA lost its outward-facing role and, with the huge contraction of regeneration activity after 2008, the Egan vision virtually disappeared from view. Like many of the other sources cited in this book, it is well worth considering again as part of rethinking social policy.

Communities of interest and identity

The focus on neighbourhood does not mean ignoring other types of community – communities of interest, identity and culture, or online communities. These forms of association and activity may go beyond or between neighbourhoods. But identifying them through the spatial grid of the neighbourhood ensures that they are also part of the strategic picture. Many community groups are in effect parts of neighbourhood communities *and* communities of interest.

Boxes 5.1, 5.2 and 5.3 illustrate community needs that could not be met simply through a neighbourhood framework: they needed links across a city, through a larger scheme or through focusing on a particular section of the population.

Box 5.1: Negotiating together instead of getting lost in the system

"I work with about 30 refugee community organisations in Leeds ... Most of the groups are very new and rely on people giving their free time. They don't have staff or office space. It's quite hard for the groups to survive ... Refugees are often traumatised when they come here. They also have to learn about what's expected from community groups in this country ... I support the groups with making sure the process of setting up is transparent and the constitution is ok. I also work with them to ensure they understand issues like women's rights and children's rights, because that situation might be very different in their home country. Maybe it's easier to hear that sort of thing from someone like me rather than someone from the council. I came here as a refugee myself so I understand some of the issues they face. One of the things I've done is help set up a Refugee Forum ... In the past the organisations were working alone. But now the forum is acting like a magnet – it's bringing ideas and resources together to help solve problems and improve services ... We have strategic bodies at one level and communities and grassroots activity at another level. Community development work is somewhere in the middle. If you take that out, the structures will collapse, the issues which need to be addressed by the policy makers just won't reach them."

Thapa (2006)

Box 5.2: Organisational development in the community sector

The Neighbourhood Support Fund (NSF) was a programme funded by the Department for Education and Skill (DfES), which helped young people not in education, training or employment. It ran between 2000 and 2006 and was designed on the principle of building greater long-term capacity of community organisations as well as providing immediate benefits to the 50,000 young people who passed through the programme. Largely designed and managed by the Community Development Foundation, NSF showed that medium-sized community-based organisations, not necessarily with a specific remit for youth work, could become effective stepping stones to get young people at risk back on a positive path by involving them in purposeful activity close to where they lived. At the same time it built the capacity of the community organisations to expand their interface with young people. A total of 520 projects were funded for three years. In addition to helping the young people, many of the organisations mobilised many new volunteers and created new community activities. Some also brought young people into the planning and management of the organisation itself.

Based on Bailey (2006)

Box 5.3: Travellers' access to public services

Health authorities in Northern Ireland were concerned about a group of 200 Traveller families which included many children whose access to public services was very low. By working with them as a community the Southern Area Action with Travellers Partnership achieved these changes between 2001 and 2010:

- GP registration increased from 46% to 100%.
- School attendance increased from 45% to 70%.
- Immunisation rates increased from 45% to 100%.
- Preschool attendance increased from no children to 70%.
- After-school attendance increased from 25% to 45%.
- Marked increase in youth club attendance.

Northern Ireland Health and Social Care Board and Public Health Agency (2011)

Communities of interest and identity are clearly a vital component of, and complement to, communities of geography, linking them to different and often broader types of network.

Economic context

The main reasons for the economic contrasts between neighbourhoods are not mysterious. Poor people gravitate to poorer areas, or are placed there by housing authorities. The majority of neighbourhoods are neither starkly poor nor glaringly rich, but at the extremes the contrasts can be dramatic. Differences in life expectancy of up to 10 years can be found between different neighbourhoods in the same city. Regeneration projects are sensibly targeted on the most disadvantaged areas but the same needs and issues also need to be addressed, if less intensively, on a much wider front.

Can disadvantages in neighbourhoods be overcome by economic activity within them? The growth of local social enterprises shows that there is always some scope for independent economic activity, whilst innovative environmental projects point the way to a greater degree of local self-sufficiency in food and certain other products.[5] It is notable, however, that the kinds of business which social enterprises in disadvantaged areas can get are often commissioned by local authorities or other public services. So although the delivery organisation is technically in the private sector, in terms of the overall analysis of the local economy these earnings are not necessarily additional resources for the locality. Reviewing extensive sources on the relation between social and economic factors, Murtagh[6] concludes that there are 'two geographies':

> Only a small proportion of economic activity is organised at the neighbourhood scale. Job markets and major investment decisions operate at higher spatial scales … (but) neighbourhood activities play an important role in terms of quality of life and everyday coping strategies.

Sanderson's review of worklessness in deprived neighbourhoods in the mid 2000s[7] found 'little evidence to support the case for targeting job creation specifically at deprived neighbourhoods … New employment is addressed most effectively at the subregional level in the context of broader economic development strategies' (p 5). Viable solutions – but subject of course to the effects of the global and national economic climate as a whole – seem to lie in a combination of social factors within the neighbourhood and economic factors outside it. Key factors which a neighbourhood partnership can influence include educational qualifications, childminding, transport, employers' recruitment practices and informal information about jobs.

It is extremely unlikely that the larger economic problems of disadvantaged neighbourhoods can be solved from within. The main engines of growth are centred outside them, and it is their relationship to those economic magnets which determines most of their economic opportunities. This means that community practice, even in the ways advocated in this book, can only be part of an overall social policy.

A project or partnership which wanted to increase employment would be well advised to concentrate not on a job creation scheme as such but on exerting leverage on the internal and external factors which link the neighbourhood to the wider local and regional economy: transport; childcare; educational qualifications; active links with jobcentres; lobbying of employers about their recruitment practices; and general social capital factors, such as generating better relationships within the community, improving health behaviours and mental health, spreading information about job opportunities, and in general creating a climate of mutual aid, motivation and optimism.

Regeneration

What evidence is there that larger-scale strategies can improve conditions in disadvantaged neighbourhoods? Government-backed regeneration schemes are a way of channelling and seeking to attract investment into disadvantaged neighbourhoods from outside. Evaluations of regeneration schemes show that they can make a significant but not dramatic impact on economic conditions in disadvantaged areas. Between 2001 and 2007 Neighbourhood Renewal in England reduced unemployment in disadvantaged areas by between 3 and 4 per cent. In total this amounted to 70,000 jobs.[8]

However, the evaluation also shows that those who gain employment often move to better-off areas: 'Population dynamics both reinforce area deprivation and disguise some of the impacts of regeneration activities.' This means that, from a national and individual point of view, regeneration activities are *more* successful than they would appear to be solely by measuring outcomes within the specified neighbourhoods. A number of people will have improved their situation and moved out. But this does not improve things for those within. Indeed, it may deprive the neighbourhood of some of its more enterprising residents, who could have played a positive leadership role.

Disadvantaged areas inevitably make high demands on public services and therefore on public finance. The GDP of areas with weak local economies can consist of up to 60 or 70 per cent public finance, partly through benefits and partly through high dependence on public services. They are also therefore more vulnerable to across-the-board cuts in public services.

The economy of disadvantaged areas consists largely of public sector money so the element of public sector decisions over spending is inevitably large. It is important to get the maximum value out of this spending in terms of alleviating poverty, stimulating personal initiative and spreading mutual aid. Community practice here is not just about helping individual services to work better but needs to faciliate an overall culture of cooperative management of the locality.

It should be remembered that GDP registers only monetary transactions. It does not capture the way people look after themselves and each other, their environment, amenities and morale. In a larger sense, these too are a real part of the local society and economy. The 'asset based' community development movement[9] stresses the importance of recognising the positive features of any locality, and not basing community practice solely on the 'deficit' picture that emerges from statistical profiling of poverty and disadvantage.

The kind of objective judgement which is possible, balancing material and social criteria, is shown by the best evaluations of government regeneration programmes. But these are little known, as they generally appear late in the life of the programmes they describe. The record of policy initiatives and their achievements passes out of currency with indecent haste once those initiatives have been superseded. The Single Regeneration Budget (1994–7) and Neighbourhood Renewal (1999–2008) in particular were major investments, but the picture of what programmes like this achieve is very difficult to discern at the time, and often only becomes clear with objective evaluation some years after the beginning or even the end of the programme. By that time the focus of policy has usually moved on to some new scheme or situation, and much valuable learning is neglected. The definitive evaluation of the Single Regeneration Budget did not appear till after the programme had been closed down (though there were contributory studies along the way). Yet it still has important lessons for partnerships now:

Key outcomes identified in the SRB case study areas were:

- Household incomes improved; there was a statistically significant increase in those employed full-time; the proportion of those unemployed fell in all the SRB areas at a slightly sharper rate than the national rate and the employment rate increased at a rate slightly above the national average.
- Satisfaction with accommodation and the quality of the area increased significantly bringing it close to the national average. Corresponding levels of dissatisfaction fell. There was increased satisfaction with the area against a pattern of national decline and most area-based problems considered 'serious' went down in severity, which compared favourably with national change.
- There was a statistically significant increase in parents believing the local area was a good place to bring up children. The trend was up compared to England, and perceptions of the area as a bad place for bringing up children were also reduced significantly.
- There was a significant rise in those agreeing they could rely on friends/relatives locally for advice or support.
- There was an encouraging increase in the number of people feeling very or fairly safe walking alone at night in their local areas – in contrast the national trend showed a slight decrease.[10]

There was, however, a worrying counter-trend in the area of health:

There was a reduction in those considering themselves to be in good health and an increase in people in bad health, suggesting a considerable widening in the gap compared with the British average. Very few SRB case study schemes had prioritised expenditure on health related activities.

Success was closely associated with the partnership mode of working:[11]

A central feature of the SRB approach to regeneration has been the emphasis on partnership working whereby interested parties come together at the local level to produce a regeneration scheme. The objective has been to tackle multiple deprivation in targeted areas of need and thus to work across traditional mainstream delivery programmes. It was a feature from the outset that the number and range of partners represented in the partnership could vary considerably and that the lead partner could be from the public, private, community or voluntary sector … Good or bad practice is not associated with any specific structural characteristic like lead partner, objective or size. Rather, it is more to do with how it organises and manages itself and its ability to produce a strategy that enhances the core competences of the area and its residents.

Success was also associated with continuous objective monitoring of outcomes, not just to support final evaluation but to feed back into current action:

Successful SRB partnerships also ensured that they had effective monitoring and review procedures in place, capable of informing partners on a regular basis of progress against scheme targets. Too many partnerships had monitoring systems that were relatively good at housekeeping matters but weak at providing the information needed to make strategic decisions. Such information has to be able to encompass relevant themes (e.g. drugs, enterprise, employability) and relevant geographies as appropriate (neighbourhoods, district, region).[12]

New Labour's National Strategy for Neighbourhood Renewal, which effectively replaced SRB, showed a similar level of impact on its targeted neighbourhoods. As well as reducing worklessness by 3 to 4 per cent, there were statistically significant improvements in educational attainment, crime reduction, environmental improvement and the position of ethnic minorities, with health results once again being ambivalent.[13] Partnership again was crucial.

Adapting to austerity

In the 1980s regeneration was seen as being about how to narrow the gap between the disadvantaged areas and a more adequate average economic situation. Although there has never been a period when government budgets could meet all needs, allocations for regeneration and public services were, in the 2000s, relatively plentiful compared to what has been seen in the 2010s. The issue which confronts us now is to discover how far the methods and lessons learnt from the past generation will apply in a period when many more neighbourhoods are at risk of decline, but the national framework of support, and the resources of local public services, have dramatically shrunk.

Underlying this change is a widespread sense that this is not just a gap from which we will return to 'normal' but is part of shifts in the social and economic landscape in ways which we may not yet fully understand. The centre of gravity of globalisation seems to be moving eastwards, and we are only at the start of remoulding economic activity to meet environmental imperatives. The role of local development and governance, whether in rich or poor areas, seems likely to grow in importance in any new pattern of social organisation. But resources for local development may be constrained. To what extent can neighbourhoods improve, let alone be transformed, in these conditions?

National and local frameworks will always remain important even if the resources to implement them are limited. Most staff working at the front line in neighbourhoods are accountable to structures at a higher geographical level, so their ability to contribute to community practice at the neighbourhood level will depend on the scope provided for them by planning at a higher level in their agency. It must always be kept in mind that in much of Britain there is a big difference in perspective between the geographical level of the neighbourhood, at around 5,000 to 15,000 people, and that of the principal local authority, at 200,000-plus. The better that senior and middle managers understand how communities work at neighbourhood level, and how the issues of their respective agencies interact to affect local quality of life, the better the ability of front-line workers to make their particular contributions.

Local authorities and their partners continually reshape their services to try to reconcile resources and needs. Some have seen clearly that this demands an increasing ethos of co-production with their communities. In 2008 Bradford adopted a system of neighbourhood partnerships linked to area and strategic plans across the city of 500,000 people. Five areas of about 100,000 people each contain about six wards of 15,000–20,000 people, which in turn contain on average two or three wards of 5,000–10,000 people. Multi-agency working is coordinated at ward level. Community and voluntary organisations play a key role in neighbourhood working and are involved in an action-learning network. The council also supports them through grants, commissioned pieces of work and joint strategic planning. Liz Richardson's study of the system in action, for the Joseph Rowntree Foundation, contains many insights about the kinds of approach which enable such a system to work effectively.[14]

Belfast, a city of around 350,000 people, produced a community development strategy in late 2011 in order to establish community-strengthening objectives as part of the whole ethos of the city's development, shared between the specialist community development staff and those in other departments:

> The fundamental means by which we foster and sustain good community relationships (includes) … support for capacity building and community involvement … community centres and facilities … and direct advice and assistance to citizens taking action to help particular sections of their communities such as young people, travellers and those living in poverty. (But) community development activity in the council is also wider … We engage with citizens and communities through all of our departments in a wide variety of ways. We work with local groups on a huge number of issues including parks and

—

open spaces, good relations, safety, health and cleansing … We can only deliver effectively on these commitments if we have a shared understanding and commitment to community development.[15]

The strategy is then structured on four 'bases' starting with 'core' community development, which focuses on ensuring that residents have the ability to come together to articulate their needs and priorities; and progresses through engagement with services, then participation in partnerships of communities and service providers, and finally to communities being co-deliverers of services. But it is made clear that whilst the latter stages are built on the earlier, not all community groups would wish or need to progress to the third and fourth stage. Clearly, what Belfast City calls community development across the Council could be described in the terms used in this book as a strategic approach to community practice.

Precedents and models

Major past programmes with a strong neighbourhood component include the Single Regeneration Budget (SRB) in the 1990s and Neighbourhood Renewal (NR) in the 2000s (see Chapter Two). Here we draw some lessons from five types of scheme. The first two are from within NR, the next two from voluntary organisations and the last from the European Union.

Neighbourhood Management

A particular source of experience for bringing service providers and communities together is Neighbourhood Management (NM). NM began in 2001 as a government 'Pathfinder' scheme[16] and was later voluntarily adopted by many local authorities. However, these schemes have now reduced again under the impact of service cuts. A National Association of Neighbourhood Management[17] helped to forge a linked identity and spread good practice.

NM usually entails the appointment by the local authority of a manager for each of the neighbourhoods in question, with support and cooperation from other local services. The manager may have a small team of officers or secondees from other services and will work with local residents and groups. The primary aim is to improve local services and thereby the conditions for residents. The main government-sponsored guide to NM,[18] produced at the height of the Pathfinder programme, is full of useful advice. However, it omits to identify the overall condition of the local community sector as a criterion of success.

The Neighbourhood Element[19]

Introduced in 2005 for 100 particularly deprived neighbourhoods, this was a variation on NM:

—

People living in disadvantaged neighbourhoods experience worse living conditions and poorer public services than those living in other areas. They are more likely to die young, be victims of crime, and live in poor quality housing with unsafe, run down and neglected streets, parks and other public spaces and amenities ... The Strategy ... is premised on the centrality of the neighbourhood as the place for increasing community engagement and improving the effectiveness and responsiveness of services. While recognising that deprived neighbourhoods may not always have received their fair share of resources, the management and coordination of resources and services is often the more serious challenge.

A distinctive feature of this scheme is a suggestion of the sort of team that should be assembled to achieve these aims: neighbourhood manager; policy, research and monitoring officer; community wardens; community development worker; resident outreach workers; administrative staff; plus leverage funding and a small grants community chest. Whilst a dedicated team of this kind would require substantial resources, the spread of team roles suggests some of the kinds of community function which a variety of existing front-line workers might carry out as an extension of their responsibilities. The narrative implies that the team will drive improvement in the quality of public services, with some accompanying mobilisation of residents. The principles emphasise improving public services but again overlook increasing the productivity of the community itself: 'Central to the government's proposals ... is the desire to develop responsive and customer-focused public services, with opportunities for communities to influence and improve (their) delivery ...' However, the model borders on recognising that by making the mobilisation of residents the main mechanism, the residents themselves will drive improvements in the quality of public services.

Community Led Planning (CLP)

This is a participative local development system that was developed in rural areas by Action for Communities in Rural England (ACRE) with the National Association of Local Councils (NALC, ie towns and parishes) and other partners. It follows a staged process over a year and more, using a partnership mechanism to achieve all-round development of a small locality. ('Planning' here includes all social issues, not just spatial planning.) CLP has been applied in thousands of parishes, and there are well-documented case studies.[20]

The parish basis of CLP makes it easy to specify the population boundary and therefore to get evidence of majority consent to a plan for many-sided local development. The Parish Council may be, or become, a basis for partnership between residents and public agencies, though it could be another grouping that takes the lead.

CLP has been spreading more slowly into urban neighbourhoods. It may be that many rural neighbourhoods still have more geographical and social cohesion and self-reliance than many urban neighbourhoods, and are therefore generally more amenable to this approach. Certainly many disadvantaged urban neighbourhoods have a much greater ethnic mix, less obvious boundaries and higher population turnover. The Coalition government has shown signs of trying to bridge these urban-rural differences by giving new powers to parish councils where they exist and, where they do not, setting out a process whereby a neighbourhood community group can become accredited to take on the same powers.

Environmentally based schemes

Local projects by environmental organisations such as Groundwork are found in many parts of the country. The wide spread of their network has also enabled them to collect large-scale data showing that involvement makes people feel safer, more motivated to take part in local groups or organisations, that their neighbourhood is getting better and that there is a greater sense of community between people of different backgrounds.[21] A wide variety of other environmentally based projects are described in one of the final reports of the Sustainable Development Commission before it was abolished in the Coalition Government's 'bonfire of the quangos'.[22]

The aim of the Eco-Towns initiative[23] sponsored by the New Labour government was 'to provide a showcase for sustainable living and allow Government, business and communities to work together to develop greener, low-carbon living' in settlements of around 5,000 homes. The scheme ran into a number of obstacles but the concept is noteworthy for conveying, in addition to its ecological vision, a deeper understanding of the role of community involvement than many initiatives. Planners had to show:

> how developers will support the initial formation and growth of communities, through investment in community development and third sector support, which enhance wellbeing and provide social structures through which issues can be addressed … accompanied by long term governance structures to ensure that … there is continued community involvement and engagement, to develop social capital …

European programmes

European programmes have made an important contribution to the landscape of local projects in designated regions over the years. The EU system of 'Structural Funds' works on a seven-year cycle, and the cycle beginning in 2014 includes an element called community-led local development, based on a long-running rural programme known as LEADER.[24] The aim of the local model is to:

Encourage local communities to develop integrated bottom-up approaches ... to respond to territorial and local challenges

Build community capacity and stimulate innovation, entrepreneurship and capacity for change by encouraging the development and discovery of untapped potential from within communities and territories

Promote community ownership by increasing participation within communities and build a sense of involvement and ownership ...

Assist multi-level governance by providing a route for local communities to fully take part in shaping the implementation of EU objectives.[25]

Key instruments are seen as being local action groups and local development strategies. The action groups are to be made up of 'representatives of local public and private socio-economic interests, such as entrepreneurs and their associations, local authorities, neighbourhood or rural associations, groups of citizens ... community and voluntary organisations'. The strategies should 'define the area and population ... analyse development needs and potential ... and describe the objectives, including targets for outputs or results'.

Projects of the kinds described above are vital sources of experience and may be platforms for neighbourhood-wide community practice.

Inside out and outside in the neighbourhood

How can public service staff and active residents work together in a partnership, seeing that they are in such different positions?

Authorities and communities naturally have different ways of viewing the locality, but the quality of life and conditions depend on both. Communities look at the neighbourhood 'from the inside out' whilst public authorities look at it 'from the outside in'. This is inevitable, considering that the authorities – the local authority itself, or police, health or any other – are responsible for delivering services to the whole population of their designated area. For a principal local authority in England this would be likely to be between 200,000 and 300,000 people.

Decision making at this level is a long way from the neighbourhood. The local authority area could consist, for example, of 25 neighbourhoods of 10,000 people each, or 50 neighbourhoods of 5,000. The divisions are never as neat as this, but whatever the pattern, to plan from the outside-in means in particular to look at statistics of employment, health, education, housing and crime. It is this statistical overview which shows that disadvantages are clustered much more strongly in some neighbourhoods than others, although individual disadvantage can be found anywhere. The most disadvantaged neighbourhoods will also be found to be making the heaviest demands on most public services. So tackling those more effectively is also an economy measure. Public services have to take this into account in allocating resources to meet need; and, more proactively, in seeking to reduce disadvantage.

At the same time, everyone, disadvantaged or not, is entitled to make use of public services, and many more people *would* be disadvantaged if they were not receiving their share of benefits from public services. Whilst community practice makes a particular priority of overcoming disadvantage, it is also very much concerned with boosting involvement by people who are in an average position – the majority of the population.

Service delivery on different issues will come down to each community from several different directions, with different professional cultures and different commissioning and delivery arrangements. It is a common weakness of local public authorities to look at the local community *en bloc*, as if it was an institution like the authorities themselves rather than a fluid mixture of individuals, groups and organisations.

The closer you get to the ground, the more intertwined the social issues are. And the further from the ground, the easier it is to treat an issue like education, health, safety, employment or environment as if it was a system unto itself. Community practice is often ignored at the top because high-level policy has great difficulty formulating cross-cutting approaches to social reality. Community practice gets reinvented at lower levels of policy, because local managers can see that it is easier to achieve their objectives if there is cooperation between services and user participation.

Community initiatives, by contrast, start with what it feels like to live in the place. They begin by people talking to each other, finding common cause and starting an activity or group. The groups are driven by their life situation. Their energy and mutual aid comes from face-to-face relationships. A group might be set up to try to get a better service of some kind or just to do something amongst its members. Often a group will do both: a group of friends who are carers, for example, might start by helping each other out with shopping and giving each other a break, and as they get to feel a bit stronger, realise they have important things to say to the authorities about the way support is or is not provided for them. Then in order to get more credibility for what they want they may contact other carers and organise a more formal group. In doing so they will begin to look and think a little more like a public agency; but at heart they will still see things from the community viewpoint.

A powerful strategy to improve life in the neighbourhood cannot be created solely from one side of the equation. It needs to reconcile the inside-out view of the residents with the outside-in perspective of the public services. Community practice moves across the dividing lines, explaining each to the other and creating an active interface of collaboration, without expecting either side to lose its primary viewpoint.[26]

Joining up the community perspective

To parallel the outside-in view, community practice needs to develop a more joined-up view from the community side. This has often been lacking. Whilst there are copious local case studies of community practice and development, the great majority are depicted in terms of one-off projects, without being clearly situated in a whole-neighbourhood context. We don't know whether the community which they strengthened was at the same time being weakened by other events. We don't know whether the ripples from the action benefitted few or many other residents or what proportion of other residents were aware of them. We don't know, across a specific place, whether community practice and development steadily advanced, was running to stand still or slipped back.

In short, what is generally neglected, even by community projects, ironically, is the overall profile and condition of the local community and voluntary sector itself, as discussed in Chapter Four: how many groups are there in the neighbourhood and adjacent areas? What issues do they cover? Do the local people know about them? Are they easy to access? Are they achieving the objectives they have set themselves? Are they well supported by the local statutory organisations?

Neglecting to profile the whole sector in the neighbourhood is a natural consequence of a community development approach which focuses on the individual worker and the two or three groups with which that worker works. Reports tend to describe the single project as 'the community', implying that if the project succeeds then the neighbourhood as a whole is better off – but without contextual information this cannot be judged.

Joining up the front line

Front-line staff have numerous opportunities to bend their roles towards community practice – if their managers will allow them to do so. This should not be merely a matter of tolerance: it should be built in as a positive remit. This could be done first experimentally, monitored and analysed for cost benefit and if successful instituted as a norm. Our hypothesis would be that 10 per cent of the time of most front-line workers diverted from standard responsibilities to community practice would more than repay its cost through generating better community conditions, better co-operation between providers and users, more volunteering, less pressure on emergency services, better flow of information from communities to agencies and better collaboration between services.

Working more closely with the community leads to working more cooperatively with other local services. Michael Bichard puts it like this:

> Each sector of public spending has its own vertical mechanisms, which translate national policies and priorities into local delivery. However, the people who benefit from these services … use a mix of public services in their daily lives. For example in seeking employment an

individual's experience may be influenced by employment advice, skills training, transport and health services. An excessive reliance on vertical delivery channels will fail to take account of the interconnected nature of the challenges facing local citizens. To collectively meet the needs of citizens, local services therefore also need to be horizontally integrated, with an understanding of customer needs …[26]

However initiatives such as 'total place', 'empowering the front line' and 'place based budgets'[28] capture only the outside-in part of the picture. They would be more likely to succeed if they incorporated a real community practice strategy. The intentions are admirable but lack a concept of the local population itself as a productive force. The public services are expected to effect transition through negotiation with each other. But the relationship of each of them with the community is the necessary medium for the service inter-relationships they are seeking. It is through meeting on the community ground that they actually see how the impact of their particular service interacts with the impacts of the other services. The community's experience of weaving together all the service impacts is the crucible for a more integrated view. Active participation in local problem solving both with residents and staff of other services provides the close encounter that staff need in order to develop an integrated perspective.

Our concern is not mainly with budgeting arrangements, though these are important, but with the remit to front-line staff. Staff time is the main resource deployed by policy: the easiest, least bureaucratic way to bend resources towards community practice is simply to ensure that front-line staff have scope and stimulus to cooperate more flexibly with the communities they serve. This can equally serve to 'empower the front-line' in the sense expressed by Michael Bichard, which requires management hierarchies to be more responsive to what those on the frontline want to tell them about how their services interact with the community.

A holistic view with some holes in it

Joining up the inside-out and outside-in views could be described as taking a holistic or system-based view to the locality or neighbourhood. However, that is not to say that there is any 'system' or 'whole' which is actually comprehensive, all-embracing and self-contained. Every locality whatever its size is affected by things outside it, and every type of analysis highlights some features at the expense of others. In this book a qualified 'whole system' approach is adopted in the sense of looking at neighbourhoods so far as possible as a whole, being aware of their interacting parts, and questioning how they contribute to the goal of strengthening community life. A holistic approach should be one which moves nimbly from the big picture to the details and back again as necessary to solve problems and improve conditions. It does not assume that the neighbourhood is self-contained and can wholly control its own destiny and conditions. What it does assume is that local people will achieve greater influence if they increase their internal relationships and cooperation and thereby exert greater leverage on surrounding factors.

By the time one gets to the local implementation level there is very little wiggle room left in policies, organisational strategies and budgets unless understanding of the role of community practice has been absorbed higher up in the hierarchy. Without this, community practice often has to be squeezed in at the end of the chain, with insufficient funding and clout. The space and conditions for an appropriate level of local autonomy – just as for individual human rights – have to be guaranteed at national level, built into policies at regional, subregional or large local level, and implemented at very local level. Chapter Nine describes this policy cascade in more detail.

A holistic approach is not, therefore a 'total' approach. It does not (or should not) claim to explain the whole of its chosen system from within its boundaries. It is, rather, a corrective to over-generalisations or to approaches which focus only on single causes for single effects.

Community and complexity

The clash between the two types of culture – the culture of the community and the culture of public authorities – can be illuminated by Complexity theory. Geyer and Rihani[29] describe the use of Complexity in social analysis (moving on from its origins in physical science) as an antidote to the rigidity of social and political systems based entirely on trying to maximise order. The 'British Westminster model', they say, is a prime example of an over-orderly model, which is replicated in British local authorities. In their judgement this culture denies and tries to suppress all disorder, and therefore fails to achieve its objectives, because life is not like that. The implication of this is that social policy which makes space for the unpredictable or even for a degree of disorder will be more successful or at least less damaging. This is an important principle which should encourage local public agencies to give their managers and front-line workers sufficient flexibility to participate actively in neighbourhood partnerships.

However, it would be a mistake to caricature the formal agencies as being completely rigid and orderly. The 'Westminster model' is in reality not as fixed as Geyer and Rihani describe it. The formal aspects are the surface rules of the game. But as in any game, the skill consists in weaving between the rules as well as observing them. Politics is 'the art of the possible'. Skilled players know perfectly well that there are unpredictable factors. Central government is well aware that it does not wholly 'command and control' local government, public services and even its own departments (hence the popularity, even with politicians, of the 'Yes, Minister' satire on the illusions of decision making), let alone the public, press and unions. All of these influence the course of events, and government has to use a mixture of directives and negotiation to keep on top of a constantly evolving situation. Sophisticated local authorities know that the same is true in their sphere.

Conversely, in the sphere of community practice, in contrast with many top-down policies, there can be a surfeit of *dis*order. There is a danger of muddling along with unclear definitions, avoiding focusing on outcomes, and limiting evaluation to the perceptions of the providers or participants themselves.

Eileen Conn provides a way of visualising the interface between the two cultures, postulating a 'space of possibility' between them.[30] She judges that many unsuccessful attempts at community involvement stem from failure on the part of public services to understand that communities have a radically different culture from themselves. The problem, she claims, is not merely lack of understanding but that public institutions seek to deal with communities as if they were also institutions and expect them to behave as such. The service agencies have a prevalent concept of a simple relationship between two blocks, in which the aim of community engagement is simply to draw local residents into the concerns and processes of the services.

The reality however is that virtuous interactions between services and communities take place by building a third space between the two cultures, in which each modifies its nature to some extent (Figure 5.2).[31]

Community development, says Conn, is the only occupation which has consistently argued for and supported independent community groups for their own intrinsic value in supporting people's life strategies directly, whilst public

Figure 5.2: Building the creative space between communities and public agencies

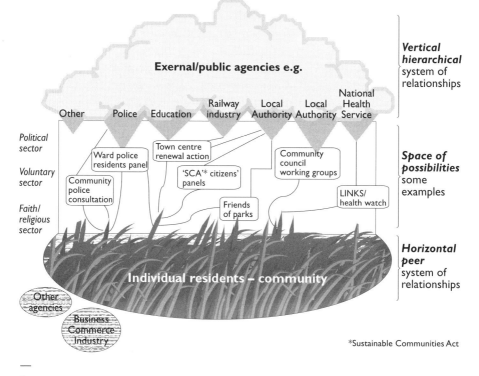

*Sustainable Communities Act

services have an inherent tendency to see them, if at all, as voluntary mini service-providing agencies (p 13ff).

Snakes and ladders

The much-quoted ladder of participation[32] is therefore not the best guide to what should be happening here. It tends to suggest that the ultimate desirable form of community participation is complete community control. The main idea is that at the bottom of the ladder is a community which is controlled, passive and manipulated, and progress is represented by the community firstly becoming better informed, then more participative and influential and eventually achieving complete control itself. To be fair to the originator, Sherry Arnstein, the original article put this forward as a model for experiment and debate, but it has been seized on and expanded as if it was a complete theory.

The general direction of travel is no doubt desirable. The problem is that the ultimate goal of complete control implies that localities are to be run *either* by government *or* by communities. 'Influence' is halfway up towards complete takeover of control. This ignores the fact that government and public services exist because they are empowered by the population – that is, by the aggregate of all communities – to carry out functions which are best carried out collectively or through specialised agencies accountable to the whole population.

In the co-production model the top of the ladder for a community would not be complete control, because that is either unrealistic or suggests an isolated community. The community of communities already has overall control through the national and local democratic process. The top of the ladder for a local community is to have a high degree of influence, and to be able to collaborate confidently with the public services.

To put it another way: the ultimately desirable position is indeed that the population has complete control of its society, but through a number of different mechanisms and levels, of which the local community is only one. The citizenry splits its control into a number of arms. On one arm it delegates to government decision making over matters that concern the whole of society, and it should vigilantly hold government to account for the decisions it makes. On another arm it exercises strong influence over local issues and over the way that national decisions are carried out locally. If services are not being well enough delivered, citizens need to exercise their control at *both* levels in appropriately different ways. To pitch the local community *against* the local services, to place it in competition with them, is to pitch one arm of citizen control against another, to pitch it against itself.

Notes

[1] Egan (2004).

[2] Sustainable Development Commission (2010).

[3] Egan, op cit.

[4] Gaffikin and Morrissey (2011), p 265.

[5] See for example www.incredible-edible-todmorden.co.uk.

[6] Murtagh (2010).

[7] Sanderson (2006).

[8] Amion Consulting (2010), Chapter 5.

[9] Foot and Hopkins (2010).

[10] Tyler and Rhodes (2007).

[11] Rhodes, Tyler and Brennan (2007), Chapter 17.

[12] Rhodes, Tyler and Brennan, op cit.

[13] Amion Consulting, op cit.

[14] Richardson (2012).

[15] Belfast City Council (2011).

[16] SQW (2008).

[17] www.neighbourhoodmanagement.net.

[18] Dwelly (2005).

[19] ODPM (2005b).

[20] www.acre.org.uk/our-work/community-led-planning.

[21] Groundwork (2009).

[22] Sustainable Development Commission (2010).

[23] CLG (2009).

[24] 'Liaison Entre Actions pour le Developpement de l'Economie Rurale'.

[25] European Funding Network (2012).

[26] FCDL/National Empowerment Partnership (2008).

[27] Bichard (2009), p 72.

[28] Immediately after the 2010 general election the Local Government Association made a case for 'Place Based Budgets' (Local Government Association, (2010). However, by 'places' they indicated the subregional level (cities, counties or similar) not neighbourhoods.

[29] Geyer and Rihani (2010).

[30] Conn (2011).

[31] Ibid.

[32] Arnstein (1969).

SIX

Building partnership

Transformative neighbourhoods?

In the 1960s and 70s, regeneration was often thought of as enabling disadvantaged areas to 'catch up' with an overall increasing national prosperity. EU funds were allocated to what were called 'lagging' regions. It will always be necessary to measure material improvement in terms of reducing gaps in income, work, education, safety and health, but it is surely no longer appropriate, if it ever was, to think in terms of one part of society being the norm and another part trying to catch up. Society as a whole is seeking for some sort of transformation to a more equitable, cohesive and sustainable way of life. A transformative neighbourhood would be one that is part of a society in a process of transformation, playing its part in that change: from widening inequality to narrowing; from public services as top-down provision to co-production with communities; from accelerating consumption and global warming to a new equilibrium.

It is not possible to see what a transformative neighbourhood might look like only by reviewing the average performance of the big regeneration schemes as we have done in previous chapters. We can see more exciting possibilities by looking at exceptional neighbourhoods. In 2004 Dick Atkinson, a leader of resident-led regeneration in Balsall Heath, Birmingham, from the 1990s, reckoned that there were 20 neighbourhoods in England which had achieved an exceptional degree of change and could guide others in how to do the same.[1] These were some of their common features as he saw them:

the process of resident-led recovery has been under way for some years

the level of participation within local associations (community groups) has risen markedly

many people now feel confident and able to shape the quality of their lives

there are a growing number of resident-led activities and voluntary associations

the associations have come together in some form of umbrella association this association holds regular and annual meetings and employs people to do a variety of tasks

these staff and their employers have a neighbourhood development plan, parts of which they will deliver, other parts which will be delivered by statutory partners

there may be a neighbourhood manager and an interagency team of professionals working with the manager and the association of residents

progress has been made towards improving ... the economy, education, safety, health, the environment, housing and the image of the area

there is determined local leadership and vision

the local authority and/or other statutory agencies are linked in productive partnership with the residents' forum and other local voluntary organisations.

Some of the neighbourhoods in Atkinson's 'top twenty' at that time were described like this:

Castle Vale, once Birmingham's sick council estate, now transformed. People are living longer, are better educated and more people are in work. It is pioneering neighbourhood management practices.

The Eldonians (in Liverpool) redeveloped their own estate and provide a range of homegrown services.

Royds (in Bradford) took ownership of an SRB programme and acquired land and property. Today they employ over thirty staff, run a variety of local projects and are fiercely proud of their achievements.

Balsall Health was Birmingham's blighted red light district. Today that is a thing of the past as residents support each other through 22 self-help associations. House prices have risen and people no longer wish to leave the area. Statutory partners help residents to implement and review a neighbourhood development plan.

Bromley by Bow (in London) started its transformation in a run-down church which now houses a nursery and craft activities. A park and healthy living centre are amongst its achievements.

Interlocking systems

A neighbourhood is a complex set of interlocking systems – a meeting point of families, organisations, buildings and public spaces, and private, public and voluntary organisations. It is also a 'crossroads' for influences and connections from adjacent neighbourhoods and further afield. Figure 6.1 is a simplified representation of some of the kinds of interaction which exist in neighbourhoods. Quality of life is affected by how these elements mesh together. The neighbourhood is also affected by external elements, such as local government, other public services, national government and the global economy. A partnership would seek to optimise all these assets and influences, but 'making partnerships work effectively is one of the toughest challenges facing public sector managers'.[2]

Partnerships and networks are vital to developing a comprehensive approach to improving neighbourhoods.[3] For many organisations the need for networks and partnerships is becoming increasingly important:

> Very little is accomplished by the single organisation acting alone ... It cannot embrace the connections and relationships needed for the way in which products and services are now designed, developed, produced and delivered. This is especially so when tackling intractable problems, the 'wicked issues', and moving to more preventive and sustainable outcomes.[4]

Figure 6.1: Neighbourhood as interlocking systems

Engage, a voluntary sector forum that was set up to promote participation in the East Midlands, sees six key benefits in effective neighbourhood partnerships: better decision-making; more effective service delivery; greater community support; community development; renewal of local democracy; and increased resources.[5]

Like any organisation, a partnership requires a sense of purpose and direction of travel, more than simply being a place where information is shared. It should have its own strong sense of identity, a positive organisational culture and a commitment to learning and reflection.

Neighbourhood partnerships: who drives?

Some neighbourhoods will already have a partnership with potential for locating different pockets of community practice, assisting them to network with each other and coordinating them to produce greater synergy. Others may need to create one.

Who is to 'own' and drive forward such a partnership? As holder of overall democratic responsibility for the area, the local authority is in the best position to initiate the development. But another major agency might be better placed to take a lead at a particular time. The new local health bodies set up in England by the Health Act 2012 have to show, amongst other things, 'meaningful engagement with patients, carers and their communities'.[6] Although there has been a long, and not very successful, history of 'patient and public involvement' in previous health policy, this new framework puts local health agencies in a more proactive position to take initiatives on community practice, especially in conjunction with local authorities through collaboration on the new local Health and Wellbeing Boards.

The principles of neighbourhood policing, introduced by David Blunkett as Home Secretary in the early New Labour period, have proved durable despite other changes, putting local police teams in a favourable position to contribute to neighbourhood partnerships. The Coalition government's introductory Green Paper on policing maintained the idea of partnership between people and police by 'enabling and encouraging people to get involved and mobilising neighbourhood activists ... increasing community involvement ... and empowering individuals and communities ... Solutions to local problems are often best found within communities'.[7]

The Paper implies that this was overturning previous practice, but the preceding government's directives on community policing were equally eloquent, with the added dimension of joint working with other local public services:

> Core principles include:
> * strong local leadership at strategic level to drive integration
> * clearly defined and agreed neighbourhoods
> * shared and publicly negotiated local community safety priorities ...
> * teams consisting of police, local authority and other relevant organisations

- coordinated working to tackle problems effectively …
- a neighbourhood lead, eg neighbourhood manager or coordinator
- strong joined-up community engagement …[8]

Having the police as an active local partner has the added value of bringing access to another form of evidence of local outcomes, and one which can sometimes respond quickly to community practice. Community policing is credited, for example, with reducing crime in an industrial estate in Bangor in Wales by 45 per cent, and in Rubery, West Midlands, by 60 per cent.[9]

Equally, housing agencies, fire and rescue services, social services, youth services and others have their own histories and experiences of community involvement, any of which could be a jumping-off point to reach agreement with the other services on creating a new, dynamic neighbourhood partnership between all of them and residents. Favourable national and local policies are vital but initiative and creativity can come from anywhere within the system.

Whatever the partnership structure, as the Young Foundation emphasises, 'connections are key':

> The best local partnerships between civil society and the public sector manage to connect the time, energy and creativity of users, volunteers and community groups with the capacity and strategic networks of the public sector. When they do so they connect unmet social needs with underused resources and assets, transforming unproductive … or conflicting relationships into dynamic ones that achieve results.[10]

Part of designing the partnership is ensuring a balance between inward-facing and outward-facing perspectives, by distinguishing features such as in Table 6.1.

A model for the crucial early steps in developing a neighbourhood partnership is 'C2', developed by Hazel Stuteley and colleagues[11] and subsequently adopted by the Health Empowerment Leverage Project.[12] It is based on a seven-step process (Table 6.2).

The C2 model builds partnership on a careful balance whereby residents are in the driving seat but front-line staff of local services have a clear complementary role. Although the C2 partnership building process is carefully designed, the mobilising of new energy that goes with it is largely intuitive and organic. The aim is to create the right conditions for development, not to direct it from the top down. New possibilities come on to the horizon, as the reality of initial wins sink in and the atmosphere of the neighbourhood changes to one of hope and purpose. Hazel Stuteley and Susanne Hughes, who run C2 and facilitated the Townstal project (Box 4.5 in Chapter Four), write:

> We prefer to speak of capacity release rather than capacity building, which … can tacitly assume that communities are 'empty vessels' waiting to be filled. It would not be possible to build capacity if it was

Table 6.1: Internal and external perspectives of a neighbourhood partnership

	In the neighbourhood	In the partnership
Vision	– Vision for the community in the future	– What is the partnership for? – What will the partnership be like in three years' time? – How do we want the partnership to function as a group?
Links with community and services	– How will the partnership relate to and communicate with the wider community and partner services? – How should partner organisations relate to the partnership?	– What should the values and culture of the partnership be? – How committed are partner organisations to the partnership?
Setting objectives	– The work programme should reflect the wider community's concerns	– Improve the skills of partnership members – Develop ways of reviewing effectiveness
Action	– By the community amongst itself – By the services individually – By the services jointly – By the services and community jointly	– Choose and support officers – Develop meeting and action processes – Agree who is responsible for doing what – Ensure that people and agencies do what they say
Evaluating progress	– Annual neighbourhood consultation and feedback event. Impact on the quality of life and the way services are delivered. Are residents better off and do they feel they have more power over what happens in their community? (See Chapter Eight.)	– Is the partnership functioning in the way the members want it to function? What needs to be done to improve or develop it?

not already there. Capacity may be latent and become overlaid with mistrust, lack of confidence and the stress of coping with multiple disadvantages. What is needed to bring it out is respect, empathy and relationship building. People will then get involved at the level that suits them. Many will eventually help out as activities grow, following the lead of a minority who by nature have the ability to be change agents ...

What we are looking for is the potential for multiple effects, many simultaneous leverage points which will reinforce each other so as to gradually influence the whole social climate of the neighbourhood. But precisely because we can see that every issue is ultimately connected to the larger picture, we know that any issue, however minor it may seem at first, can lead into wider development. Effective development conveys the message 'I want to connect with *whatever* motivates you'. By doing so we are actually boosting not one but three capabilities: (i) the hopeful, positive, productive side of the individual's personality; (ii) their willingness to see the public services as creative and helpful rather than rigid and off-putting; and (iii) their ability to relate to

Table 6.2: The C2 seven step model

STEP 7. Partnership firmly established and on forward trajectory of improvement. Two or three key residents employed and funded to co-ordinate activities. Measurable outcomes from community action plan and evidence of visible transformational change, e.g. new play spaces, improved residents' gardens, reduction in ASB, all leading to measurable health improvement and parallel gains for other public services

⬆

STEP 6. Evidence of community strengthening and self organization characterized by setting up of new groups and activities increasing social capital, catering for wide spectrum of age groups and targeting health priorities. Accelerated responses in service delivery from partnership agencies, leading to increased community trust, co-operation and reciprocal uptake.

⬆

STEP 5. Monthly partnership meetings, providing continuous positive feedback loop to residents. Celebration of visible 'wins' e.g. successful application to funding streams which support community priorities, and promote positive media coverage, leading to improved community confidence, more volunteering and increasing momentum towards change.

⬆

STEP 4. Constitute partnership which operates out of easily accessed hub within community setting, opening clear communication channels to wider community e.g. regular newsletter, estate 'walkabouts', links with other community groups and interface with strategic organisations.

⬆

STEP 3. Steering group hosts 'listening event' and produces report on identified issues, fed back to residents within 10 days. Commitment established for resident led, multi-agency partnership to tackle issues. Exchange visits undertaken to meet communities who successfully self-manage.

⬆

STEP 2. Hold workshop to consolidate connections within steering group and embed skills and mindset needed to support residents to lead change and become self- managing. Jointly plan 'listening to community' event to identify and prioritise neighbourhood health and well-being issues.

⬆

STEP 1. Identify and nurture key residents. Establish partnership steering group of front line local service providers, key residents and other stakeholders who share common interest in bringing about change and improvement within a targeted neighbourhood to jointly undertake the 7 step process towards a resident-led partnership.

---

other people and bring out *their* positive side. The need to find the 'trigger' issues overrides, at first, the prescribed issues of the public services – but you can be sure it will lead to them.[13]

Teamwork and leadership

Most community development and practice literature contains very little description of how teams and partnerships work. It is strange that a field whose ethos continually invokes solidarity and equality should mostly depict its own practice in individualistic terms. It is essential to develop a team consciousness in order to address the full profile of issues across the population of a neighbourhood.

During the period of expansion of community practice in the 2000s, a number of local authorities evolved a three-fold approach:[14]

- Working at neighbourhood level, supporting existing groups, helping residents develop new groups and encouraging groups to network with others in the neighbourhood.
- Working at an area or local authority wide level to encourage the development of partnerships and fora and ensure that they included the voice of the community sector (as a distinct stratum within the third sector).
- Working at a strategic level (organisational, departmental, local authority or even regional) to develop policies and strategies aimed at providing adequate resources, such as access to small grants, training and specialist staff, to provide support for the community sector.

However, being drawn into management and social planning created a degree of unease amongst some practitioners who felt their authenticity lay in being 'on the side of the community'. But such workers will have gained managerial and cross-departmental experience which would be valuable in organising new, wider networks of practitioners.

The challenge for new community practice is, despite having fewer specialist workers, to address the whole of the community sector in the neighbourhood.

A wider pool of groups will allow exceptional groups to come forward. Others may reach a plateau and stay there, or eventually dwindle. This does not matter as long as the overall momentum is increasing and the community sector profile is widening. Instead of thinking of community practice as a rare resource that has to make a painful choice of whom to support intensively, it should be thought of as primarily a lighter touch form of support that should reach all groups and potential groups. This depends critically on all available practitioners being well networked across the neighbourhood and having a fluid culture of cooperation and cross-referral through the neighbourhood partnership.

Structure and coordination

Although the neighbourhood partnership should have a generally cooperative ethos, it is likely to need coordination and direction to ensure that decision making is effective and accountable. The chances of success will be greatly increased by the neighbourhood partnership employing the services of skilled person who is neutral with regard to local interests, whether in the community or the services – a community practice coordinator or manager with the right outlook and skills. Twelvetrees argues that an independent facilitator is virtually essential to moderate the varied interests and capacities of the local members:

> There are effective and ineffective partnership players ... Developing a partnership well cannot easily be done by somebody with a strong allegiance to any one organisation ... If there is potential conflict within a partnership, a great deal of work needs to be undertaken outside formal settings ... While it is illusory to expect all stakeholders to want the same thing, it *is* realistic to ensure that they all understand what each other wants ... (but) some individuals and organisations may not be entirely sure what they want or may be reluctant to reveal it ...[15]

As the coordinator would not have line management control over most of the contributing workers, this requires a special set of skills combining management, persuasion, negotiation and vision. Table 6.3 suggests what some of the key skills would be.

Table 6.3: Skills for community practice coordination

1. Understanding the mix of formal and informal structures that go to make up the life of a neighbourhood or community.

2. Looking at the locality and neighbourhood as a system and as an ecology.

3. Ability to identify the range of existing and potential community practitioners across the neighbourhood and situate yourself as an actor within the network.

4. Ability to take the long view of the development of the neighbourhood but focus on timed milestones.

5. Ability to understand social statistics and use them to illuminate policy and practice.

6. Ability to form action plans out of disparate factors. Ability to design community projects.

7. Ability to relate to people under the stress of multiple disadvantage and gradually get people and groups on to a positive development track.

8. Ability to relate to people working within a service specialism and gradually get them to take a broader problem-solving approach.

9. Ability to create and sustain networks of practitioners across different occupations.

10. Ability to understand the development of community groups, support them appropriately at different stages and guide others in how to support them.

11. Ability to manage community practitioners both directly and through guidance to other managers.

12. Ability to explain community processes to senior decision-makers, coordinate evidence and negotiate long term support.

Supporting community groups

For concentrated practitioners, ie dedicated community development workers, the kinds of role to be carried out were described succinctly in *The Community Development Challenge*[16] in the form of a cascade from getting individuals together, through supporting individual community groups, to fostering the relationship of such groups with public authorities:

1. Help people see that they have common concerns about local or other public issues that they could benefit from working on together under their own control
2. Help people to work together on those issues, often by forming or developing an independent community group, supporting them to plan and take actions, and encouraging evaluation and reflection as a way of improving effectiveness
3. Support and develop independent groups across the community sector non-directively but within an ethical framework, and increase networking between groups
4. Promote values of equity, inclusiveness, participation and co-operation throughout this work
5. Empower people and their organisations to influence and transform public policies and services and all factors affecting the conditions of their lives
6. Advise and inform public authorities on community perspectives and assist them to strengthen communities and work in genuine partnership with them.

For the less intensive practitioners the input might take the form of time spent on:

- supporting an independent community group or network;
- meeting with community group members or other residents to get feedback on services they are using;
- taking part in meetings with community groups and other public services to discuss issues and jointly solve problems in the locality.

Supporting groups can be one of the most rewarding but also challenging aspects of community practice. The worker will often develop close bonds with those involved in the group and to some extent share their highs, lows, frustrations and triumphs. Practitioners need to be aware of the power dynamics within a group and between groups. Problems may occur around issues of power, relationships, group culture and stresses in the psychological contract between the members and the group.

When a group reaches a formal stage of development it may need to know about issues such as charitable status and personal liability of trustees. Members may need to be talked through the process of developing a constitution or terms of reference. This is often seen as something of a chore, and there is the temptation to simply adopt an existing template. However the development of a constitution, particularly the aims and objectives, can be used to create a collective vision and to explore in depth what the group is there to achieve.

Information and advice on these issues may be available both locally, through specialist third sector support groups such as Councils for Voluntary Service

(CVSs), nationally through the Charity Commission (online and via guidance and advice documents[17]) and through helpful guides.[18]

Well-established community development literature, such as *Skills in Neighbourhood Work* by Paul Henderson and David Thomas[19] and *Community Work* by Alan Twelvetrees[20] also provide invaluable step-by-step guides to many of the practical aspects of supporting and developing community groups, whilst Alison Gilchrist's study of networks and connectivity[21] explores the relationships and links that underlie the way communities work. The National Communities Resource Centre at Trafford Hall[22] in Chester provides training on practical skills at extremely reasonable rates for community groups.

In working with community groups it is useful to think of the role of the community practitioner as providing technical assistance or a kind of management consultancy. Traditional community development was often selective about which community groups it would prioritise. This was partly because of limited resources and partly because of a desire to give intensive help to groups that the practitioners judged to have most potential for lobbying service providers on behalf of the community. This can lead to tensions. A new pattern of community practice will have to continue to deal with these tensions but may be able to alleviate them in part by adopting a more comprehensive and possibly less intensive approach to supporting groups. This has to be achieved through better practitioner networking and cross-referral, even though full time practitioners may be much rarer. The model should be that every community group, however small, has access to at least a part-time community practitioner, and each practitioner has at least one group to nurture.

Power in partnerships

As Charles Handy and others point out, organisational cultures can play as significant a role in the way an organisation functions, as do the organisation's aims and objectives, constitution, terms of reference and decision making structures. This applies equally to partnerships.[23] What really matters is what goes on in the meetings, how issues and solutions are identified, and how the partnership oversees actions and assesses impact. Also important is the way the partnership functions as a social group: the way in which it ensures a pleasant atmosphere, enjoyable activities and friendly relationships; how it learns and develops; and how it celebrates success.

The membership of a neighbourhood partnership is likely to be very mixed, including residents (as individuals or as representatives of community organisations), services providers (often including a mix of practitioners, and operational and strategic managers), and local councillors (who may also have a senior responsibility within the local authority). The power dynamics can be complex, not only between the professionals and residents but also between individuals from different services.

The professionals representing services and the local council will generally have more power than the residents. But this does not mean that the residents are powerless. They may have formal power within the partnership (as officers of it); they may have formal or informal gate-keeping powers in relation to particular organisations in the area; they may have persuasive powers within their own community and within the partnership; above all they may be able to mobilise opinion and action across the community.

The power of the service providers and politicians is also constrained by other factors. Most public service representatives will be part of a complex organisation that functions through a hierarchical management structure. Practitioners and operational managers tend to have limited scope to make decisions and to act independently, and they also have to abide by relevant legislation.[24]

As individuals, partnership members will have competing demands on their time and energy, so the pleasure and rewards of taking part need to be high. For service staff the competing pressures may include: organisational demands and workload; reorganisation in their agency; job insecurity; cuts in resources; and changing local and national government policies and priorities. For residents other factors may loom large: time for volunteering, family, work, health, relationships, confidence and competence in meetings.

A partnership aims to bring everyone together to see and understand the whole, breaking down the organisational barriers that exist within a neighbourhood. Pratt et al summarise types of activity which can be used to build a common understanding, such as:

- *System Mapping:* examining a situation from a wide range of perspectives, sharing and learning together to develop a deeper understanding of the system.
- *Future Search:* a tightly organised process where participants spend two days creating their shared future together, grounded in reality of past and present.
- *Appreciative Enquiry:* replacing the traditional problem solving focus with a 'possibility finding cycle'. Participants share stories of accomplishments, the 'core life giving factors of their organisations' and deliberate on the aspects of their organisation's history that they most value and want to bring to the future.[25]

Whatever the resources and skills available, the development of the plan should be guided by the same set of principles:

- involving as many residents as possible along with service providers;
- making sure the process genuinely encourages open discussion, focusing on issues and problem solving; and
- ensuring that participants are challenged to go beyond the easy wish list.

Pitfalls

Neighbourhood partnerships also present a number of challenges in terms of power dynamics, sustainability and accountability. Experience is not always positive – these structures may not live up to initial hopes and expectations. Partnerships can fail through neglect, indifference or even hostility from some key stakeholders. Sometimes they fail because relationships within the group have broken down or because a key leader or champion of the group leaves. Attendance begins to drop off, members are less committed and may complain that the group is nothing more than a talking shop.

On the other hand some neighbourhood partnerships continue to flourish after many years. They are well thought of by their members, the wider community and local services, and achieve significant changes and improvements to their areas.

By bringing the relationship between systems together in a structured and transparent way, partnerships can provide opportunity for residents, service providers and others to form a powerful problem-solving mechanism. By this means, local people will also have a greater degree of say over what goes on.

Gawlinski and Graessle illustrate pitfalls that can prevent a team or partnership from succeeding. They contrast effectiveness with other forms of thinking that often deflect purpose, such as:

'Committee Thinking': the capacity of some teams to take decisions with which no one is happy, simply in an effort to arrive at a consensus

'Expansion Thinking': equating growth with progress. A tendency to do anything for which money is available or to make unrealistic plans and promises

'Charismatic Thinking': allowing the enthusiasm of one person to blind everyone else to the realities of what's being proposed

'Personality Thinking': the trap of thinking that all problems in the team are to do with personality issues

'Tree Thinking': where a team is too busy to know what it is doing, e.g. 'we can't see the wood for the trees'.[26]

Does the big society theme help?

Is the big society theme and the policy on localism introduced by the Coalition government helpful to neighbourhood partnerships and the spread of community practice? The original idea of big society as expounded by David Cameron before the general election of 2010[27] gave the impression that it would mean a boost to community strengths and the voluntary and community sector (VCS) and locally based social enterprises. In the event, voluntary and community organisations suffered from cuts both directly and indirectly through cuts to local authorities and other services which traditionally supported them.

Support to the VCS has never been more than a very small fraction of public sector expenditure, yet it is a vital lifeline to local VCS organisations. The introduction of 'big society' did not include any specific protection for the VCS despite the predictable fact that this sector was particularly vulnerable to cuts. A year after beginning the cuts process, Communities and Local Government Secretary Eric Pickles circulated to local authorities a request to protect the VCS where possible.

In contrast with the Coalition government's reorganisation of the health service, there was evidently no pre-prepared plan for big society. Indeed, planning was said to be inimical to its development. It will remain difficult to assess the success or failure of the idea because there was no baseline for it; also because a proportion of VCS organisations rapidly rebranded themselves with the big society slogan to protect themselves in the new policy climate. The signs are, however, that the VCS is likely to be found to have shrunk in this period.

Cuts to community development were more direct, including the three English national community development organisations,[28] suggesting that the government saw no connection between community development and big society, or even saw community development as an obstacle to the new concept. By contrast the devolved administrations in Scotland, Wales and Northern Ireland did not take up the big society theme, but ramped up their support for CD, as being even more vital in a period of austerity.[29]

Positive measures under the big society banner include the training of 1,000 community organisers a year (5,000 over the Parliamentary term) to assist local people and groups to take more action in their neighbourhoods. In all, 500 people are to be paid as 'senior community organisers' with 4,500 part-time and voluntary workers. The contract to organise this scheme was awarded to Locality,[30] a body newly formed from two organisations with long experience of local development, i.e. BASSAC and the Development Trusts Association. Locality rapidly developed a vigorous programme of local recruitment and projects, hopefully providing real practical help to a number of communities. But in the larger picture this scheme cannot avoid looking like a poorly-resourced substitute for the community development capacity and experience that had been disbanded. Drawn from the local communities themselves, the organisers are expected to be highly motivated and enthusiastic for change, but they have little leverage in relation to the major public bodies which administer their areas.

As the Coalition government bedded in, big society was embodied or invoked in a number of pieces of legislation. The provisions of the Localism Bill and the Open Services White Paper[31] focus mainly on physical planning, but they could also be a stimulating framework for addressing wider social issues. The Bill sought to:

- make it easier for local people to take over the amenities they love and keep them part of local life
- ensure that local social enterprises, volunteers and community groups with a bright idea for improving local services get a chance to change how things are done
- give people a new way to voice their opinions on any local issue close to their heart
- enable local residents to call local authorities to account for the careful management of taxpayers' money.[32]

The language is brave but the thrust and mechanisms of the Bill are still mainly directed towards public services or amenities being taken over by communities.

An analysis looking at London in particular, but with general implications, judged that big society would be unlikely to make an impact unless it was crystallised in specific local mechanisms such as 'Community Improvement Districts' (echoing Business Improvement Districts). These would need to be:

> community led, capable of raising resources and, so as to avoid creating permanent additional structures, time limited … have sufficient formality to be business-like … and demonstrate that they enjoyed local support and could deliver real improvements to all local people.[33]

Big society could have heralded a genuine rethinking of the relationship between society, government and public services, and it is still early days (at the time of writing) to make a final judgement. An underlying weakness in the idea is its failure to examine how community activity and public services interact or 'co-produce', and how they could do so more productively, 'delivering public services in an equal and reciprocal relationship between professionals, people using services, their families and their neighbours'.[34]

Flattery of the idea of community control, which began under the preceding government,[35] has contributed to the misguided principle that the ultimate in community strength is for community groups to take over public services. Misconception about the nature of communities is redoubled by encouraging them to borrow money from the 'Big Society Bank', launched in mid-2012. This policy exerts pressure on community organisations to turn themselves into competitive businesses.

It is appropriate for some community organisations to go down this route, as social enterprises, and it is natural for many community centres and similar bodies which have the use of their own premises to recoup some of their costs by hiring them out cheaply to smaller local groups. But to seek to reshape the whole community sector on a business model is to undermine its fundamental reciprocal nature, the value of which is precisely that it lies outside the cash nexus. It is also dubious whether communities should have to purchase amenities or services which already belong to them as citizens; or whether such assets should be sold to individual community groups, whose members are only a fraction of the local population, and which are not accountable to the whole community.

One part of big society policy which approached the neighbourhood more holistically is the Community Budgets programme. Based at the Department for Communities and Local Government, this is a version of the 'total place' idea, seeking ways to rationalise budgets from different programmes and services by looking at needs from the perspective of users. Originally focussed on coordinating services needed by 'the most troubled families', the programme expanded its scope in 2011 to experimentation in a small number of neighbourhoods and localities.[36] The driving aim is to reduce costs but the programme provides opportunity for innovation and community input.

Notable amongst other forward-looking initiatives outside government is the National Lottery's 'Big Local' scheme, which endows up to 150 neighbourhoods, which have acute needs but have been overlooked in previous government funding, with £1m to invest over 10 years against a plan for local improvement drawn up by the local community.[37]

Principles to take forward

In summary, the kind of arrangement needed as the core vehicle for this strategy would have these features:

- The neighbourhood needs a solid partnership between residents and service providers. Leadership should be a balance between residents and service providers, but with residents in the driving seat, by occupying the key officer posts.
- The partnership should adopt a problem-solving, aspirational improvement ethos – the community doing things for itself which are in its own power, advocating and influencing services about things which are not in their power, and collaborating with services on things which need joint power.
- The local authority councillors for that neighbourhood, and parish councillors if any, might play a pivotal role, both as residents and as a link with the governance of local services.
- All key services should be invited to nominate participants in the partnership. However, these would not be *representatives* of their service, to avoid any difficulties about conflicts of interest.
- Supportive policies should be embedded high up in each agency – managers should see the neighbourhood initiative as an essential part of their operating environment. Agencies should license their front-line workers to work with the neighbourhood partnerships, and should be open to ideas and recommendations which those workers bring back.
- The service nominees should be, or become, community practitioners to some extent – ie they should be doing something with one or more community groups or networks as well as being on the partnership committee.

- Other front-line workers should also be guided to do community practice as part of their job.
- The partnership should facilitate a network of all front-line workers who are doing some community practice.
- The partnership should seek to draw on community development expertise and experience on how to support and develop community groups.
- Baselines and objectives should include the condition of the community sector: how many groups are there, how many people are active in them, how easy is it to access them, how well they cooperate, what range of issues they cover, and how far they are achieving their objectives.

Notes

[1] Atkinson (2004), pp 72–3.

[2] Audit Commission (1998).

[3] Gilchrist (1995).

[4] Attwood et al (2003).

[5] Clark (2001).

[6] NHS Commissioning Board (2012).

[7] Home Office (2010), paras 5.4–5.6.

[8] Home Office (2008), para 1.30.

[9] Ibid, para 1.43.

[10] Savage et al (2009).

[11] Connecting Communities (2012) – with thanks for granting us permission to reproduce the seven-step model in Table 6.2.

[12] www.healthempowermentgroup.org.uk.

[13] Stuteley and Hughes (2011).

[14] Miller (2008).

[15] Twelvetrees (2008), pp 58–60.

[16] Community Development Challenge Group (2006). See also Chapter Eight, Table 8.1.

[17] www.charity-commission.gov.uk/Charity_requirements_guidance.

[18] Such as Hayes and Reason (2009).

[19] Henderson and Thomas (2012).

[20] Twelvetrees (2008).

[21] Gilchrist (2009).

[22] www.traffordhall.com.

[23] Handy (1993).

[24] Mintzberg (1983) refers to this type of organisation as a machine bureaucracy.

[25] Pratt et al (1999).

[26] Gawlinski and Graessle (1988).

[27] Cameron (2009).

[28] The Community Development Foundation, Community Development Exchange and Federation of Community Development Learning.

[29] See for example Christie (2011); also www.scdc.org.uk and www.community developmentalliancescotland.org.

[30] http://locality.org.uk.

[31] HMG (2011).

[32] CLG (2011a) and CPRE (2012).

[33] Travers (2011).

[34] Boyle and Harris (2009).

[35] In the rhetoric of the 2008 White Paper, *Communities in Control* (CLG), although the substance of the policy was about co-production.

[36] CLG (2011b).

[37] www.biglotteryfund.org.uk/prog_biglocaltrust.

SEVEN

Different perspectives

New directions can emerge from anywhere within a system, not just from its formal leadership. This chapter illustrates – fictionally but based on real sources – ways in which strategic thinking can emerge from different places and viewpoints in the local landscape. The first story shows the thinking of a local political leader, mobilising various players from his central position in the hierarchy. The second story is told from the viewpoint of a community practitioner who is building up a neighbourhood health project, starting with a group of residents and gradually finding the need to facilitate collaboration with a range of service providers. Concluding comments find some common elements in the different approaches, not least that there is no single ideal platform for change but that there is always the possibility of assembling favourable components from different directions.

Multiple pathways

The impetus to work towards transformative neighbourhoods can come from many places in the system, for example as part of council policy, the growing demands of a group of local residents, the work of a neighbourhood practitioner or the ideas of an operational manger with an interest in exploring new ways of delivering a service. But wherever they fit within the system, those working to pursue an empowering strategy will face a number of similar challenges, such as:

- formulating the strategy and translating it into a plan of action;
- getting buy-in from others who will play an important role in taking things forward;
- identifying necessary resources – people, time, money, local assets;
- creating an atmosphere in which players strive to move forward rather than stay in fixed positions.

Story one: A political initiative

The background

Jim Harrison is the local leader of a political party in a large town in the Midlands. The town still has some of the character of its market town origins. It also has a history of light manufacture, now declined, and is a university town (a 'redbrick' established in the 1960s). There is an increasingly large student population. The university has also played an important role in encouraging the development of a rapidly expanding base in new media and software development.

The town has several areas of relative poverty. Mostly these are outlying postwar social housing estates but they include some areas in the centre where there is a complex mix of housing association properties and small 'first time buyer' terraces. Increasingly, private landlords are buying up these houses for student lets.

Jim's party recently (and rather to its own surprise) took control of the council with a slim majority. The party's local election manifesto had a strong commitment to increasing community empowerment by developing a network of local partnerships.

Jim's background is as an estate agent – he set up one of the most successful independent businesses in the area, which now has 10 branches. It also has a strong record of community involvement, including playing an important role in the local 'Business in the Community' group and in encouraging staff to get involved in community activities. Jim retired from the business a couple of years ago, and subsequently became more involved with local politics. This is his story about an initiative he launched and the first year of its implementation:

Jim's story

I grew up in one of the local estates and still have a lot of relatives and old school friends who live there. So maybe I am 'the local boy who made good', but I have not forgotten my roots. I'm dismayed to see what's happened to my old area and the other estates. Don't get me wrong, they were always pretty tough places. There always was a problem around low educational achievement and they had a poor reputation. But there was also neighbourliness, and there was a good chance of getting some sort of job even if you didn't have many qualifications. With generations of families growing up there, there was a strong tradition of extended families, who looked out for each other – and also indulged in a fair bit of tribal warfare, to be honest.

This has changed. The local kids still tend to achieve little at school, but they also stand little chance of accessing even minimum waged jobs. This is because the students from the university are soaking them up. Best-educated bar staff and waiting staff in the country! Also, low cost housing is disappearing as private landlords buy the place up for student lets.

My involvement in politics is a way of trying to put something back into the community and town where I grew up. We have a lot of great things happening, including the expansion of the university and the development of the new industries and businesses. My own business has benefited. But the town has also paid a price, particularly in terms of people's jobs, starting a family and so on. I sometimes feel that the new people, the well-heeled, self-confident, well-educated ones, are basically elbowing out the working class families who have been here for generations. Added to this has been the arrival of a large number of Eastern Europeans, which has been resented by some. These changes have changed the town, in many ways for the better, but it is a different place from when I was a lad.

When we started preparing our local election manifesto our party wanted to promote a sense that whilst we have deep roots and a strong commitment to the town, we also want to try and do things differently. A central plank of our campaign was a strong focus on our 'Flourishing Communities' strategy. The idea was to focus on developing local communities 'from the bottom up', and to achieve this would require community engagement. Our means of achieving this would be through the development of a network of neighbourhood partnerships.

When we set this out in the manifesto it seemed a relatively simple idea. We had heard about the success of community empowerment initiatives in other parts of the world, such as participatory budgeting in Brazil,[1] and the Seattle initiatives that sought to bring government closer to neighbourhoods.[2] We were also aware of the relative strengths and weaknesses of initiatives much closer to home, such as the last Labour government's sensible but brief experiment with Neighbourhood Management. These are examples of how you can get services and communities working together. But experience of these kinds of initiatives in this town is pretty limited. Neighbourhood management never got off the ground here because the last administration was opposed to it. They didn't like it because they thought that it would provide a new power base for the opposition.

My own experience of community involvement is limited. Some years ago, before I became a councillor, I was involved in a local residents' group. The group got quite a lot of support from one of the then council community development workers. The worker helped get the group going and then supported lots of other initiatives in the area. But I always thought her approach had rather limited ambitions. There was lots of talk about community empowerment, but this seemed to begin and end in the development of a few local groups. I think the assumption was that these groups would then develop the self-confidence and skills to influence the council in some major way for the better. I guess the community development worker felt she had to be cautious, as she was employed by the Council, and may have felt she could not be seen to be encouraging groups to become stroppy with it.

We got ourselves elected with this big idea of working with local communities and giving them more power, but if I'm honest we had little real idea of how we would achieve this. One of the first things I did was try to set up a working party of key people, including colleagues from the Cabinet, departmental directors and a number of people from the voluntary sector. The aim was to start developing ideas about how our strategy should be developed. But things did not get off to a very good start. While most of the people in the group were chosen because they seemed to be committed to the aims of the Flourishing Neighbourhoods idea, and would play a key role in taking the programme forward, at the meeting it became apparent that there were a lot of different views on what we should be doing. We couldn't reach a consensus, and I felt that some people (including some council directors) had difficulty separating their own interests from the need to develop the strategy. There was a lot of jockeying for position, claiming of expertise and grandstanding.

I found the whole thing rather dispiriting, so after the meeting I got in contact with an old friend who has been involved in a lot of community engagement projects around the country. I wanted some advice on how we might proceed. My friend asked a series of questions. Initially these seemed quite straightforward, but they were pretty hard to answer:

- Why do you want to increase community involvement or community empowerment – what do you think this will achieve?
- What will community empowerment or engagement look like when it has been achieved?
- What is your longer-term vision – how do you envisage things in, say, four years' time? What do you hope to be able to say to the electorate about what has been achieved?
- What do you mean by 'bottom up'?
- What do you mean by community engagement and community empowerment?
- Are community engagement and community empowerment the same thing? If not, how are they to relate to each other?

My friend thought that one of the reasons the first meeting was not a success was because it was organised too soon in the process. We had tried to leap into something without sorting some basics out first; in particular we were unable to answer these basic questions. And if we could not answer them why should we expect the others to do so? In effect the roots of failure had been written into the project from the beginning, as no one had bothered explaining what was meant by the phrases that defined what the project was seeking to achieve.

So we needed to start again. We agreed that this was a long-term project and we needed to avoid the usual short-termism that is endemic in local government. Usually what happens with these kinds of strategies is that they are set up as time limited projects, but little or no thought goes into how these initiatives will be linked with the longer-term decision-making structures of the Council or the other public services, or how local councillors fit into the scheme of things. And no thought is given to how local people should be supported and involved.

We finally agreed that, because of the complexity and ambition of the project, we would involve as many people as possible. However, this could only be done within available time and resources. We also agreed it was essential that the cabinet and party leadership develop their own idea of what was wanted, why we wanted it, and how we'd know we had achieved what we wanted. We were the people responsible for the policy and for taking it forward. It was our responsibility to communicate our vision to the others, the people who would actually be pulling the details of the policy together and implementing it.

Another priority was to be clear with the Council's senior managers, operational staff and the front line staff about what our vision was, what we wanted to achieve in the long term and why it was important to us and to them.

We also needed to develop a joint communications strategy with our partner organisations. The attitude and understanding of senior managers, other services such as police and NHS was as important as council staff, managers and councillors. The attitude of the other organisations would affect the way in which their staff would be involved in the local partnerships.

The key throughout the life of the project was to get buy-in and a sense of ownership from as wide a range of stakeholders as possible. So there was a need to set out the longer term vision, anticipating what results would be visible by the end of our first term, and the steps that we would take to get there. We'd start small, in just a couple of areas, and learn from them, involving all those engaged in the action. We would come together on a regular basis to discuss how things were going, the blockages, successes and what we had learned.

To develop the strategy we organised a series of away days:

- Firstly, with the Cabinet and the group of people from my party I had worked with on our manifesto, who had dreamed up the idea in the first place.
- Secondly with the Council's senior management team.
- Thirdly, over the following 12 months, with virtually everyone in the council.
- Lastly we organised a series of confidential briefings with senior colleagues in the other public services, particularly health, the police and the fire service.

The party meeting was confidential. My colleagues needed to feel they could share their greatest concerns and that they could disagree, on the understanding that in the end we would develop a joint concept of what we wanted to achieve. It was an exhausting but amazing day. I'm not sure we have had such a searching conversation for a long time.

We started the day by asking participants the six questions posed by my friend. The response was pretty varied but included the following comments. The strategy should:

- act as a vehicle, at a local level, for taking forward some of our key party priorities and policies;
- form an important local powerbase for the party, particularly in the marginal wards;
- improve services by making them more accountable to local people and their needs;
- link up with government policies, so we would be able to access more resources and government grants;
- give people more of a say in their area.

I also outlined my views on what I believed to be the core aims of the strategy: first of all, our party had a commitment to extending democracy and human rights. Flourishing Neighbourhoods could play a key role in this because it offered an opportunity to develop a system of 'participative governance' at a local level.

I said that we needed to wake up to the fact that the number of people voting in local and national elections was falling, and it was getting harder to recruit good, committed candidates to stand for local elections. Membership of all the main political parties was falling and people were cynical about politicians. At the same time people felt they had no power and were excluded from the decision-making process. So the strategy had to be, first and foremost, about extending local democracy and citizen engagement. We needed to develop an opportunity for local people to work with public, voluntary and private sector organisations, as equals, in order to tackle the issues and problems in their neighbourhood that most concerned them.

Some of my colleagues responded by saying they were worried that we were biting off more than we could chew. The Flourishing Neighbourhoods strategy was only one of a number of important policies. The media and the opposition could portray the strategy as a huge but trivial project at a time when we faced substantial cuts in the Council's budget. This was a fair point, but it was important to recognise that we were starting something which would save money in the long run. The development of the network of community partnerships would take several years and we would need to build them up step-by-step, learning as we went along. By the end of the meeting we agreed to proceed with the development of the strategy and that its core aim was to develop a structure for local 'participative governance' over the lifetime of this council.

The awayday with senior management was quite tough. It was clear that some of them were quite enthusiastic, some were, at best, lukewarm, but most sat on the fence. Most of the senior officers seemed only to understand issues that were directly related to managing local services, irrespective of residents' sense of ownership and involvement. Several pointed out that there could well be a clash between what the communities wanted and the Council's ability to deliver, particularly during a time of cuts.

This reminded me of some management theory I had read years ago. According to Henry Mintzberg, a council is an example of a 'machine bureaucracy': the core aim is delivering services and implementing policy through a hierarchical command and control structure. There are strict rules on how the work is undertaken. When the budget shrinks, this inevitably strengthens the tendency to rigidity, as it imposes tighter levels of supervision over who gets the service and how it is delivered.[3]

Perhaps this kind of culture reinforced the resistance I encountered from some of the officers. A couple of the senior people pointed out that what we were proposing was not the way most Council managers and staff were used to working. Others feared that opening up the Council to varied community influence might bring it into conflict with legal obligations and statutory guidance on, for example, planning and education. This could be a real problem, but it might also be that some staff found the concept of 'Flourishing Neighbourhoods' a huge challenge to their own role.

Other senior officers, including, I'm pleased to say, the Chief Executive, were supportive of what were aiming to do, and understood our point about the need to develop better forms of community governance. He also understood that the strategy provided an opportunity for getting council and other services to work better and more creatively together. Council staff would need encouragement, support and training. Their operational managers would need to have a flexible approach and also be willing to roll up their sleeves and get involved in the partnerships. There was also the question of our colleagues from other organisations. Clearly we had no control over how they were managed and trained, and we could not compel other services to get involved in the partnerships. But we could tell them what we were doing and urge them to join in. One person said she had learned that most of the people who worked for the Council and other services were not mindless bureaucrats. Many already worked in neighbourhoods, and came into regular contact with residents. Many were already deeply committed to the idea of engaging more effectively with local residents and working in partnership with other services, and this was a good place to start.

The first 12 months

The process during the first 12 months of the strategy followed more or less the cyclical sequence: *vision and policy – strategy – implementation – learning – adapting.* The Flourishing Neighbourhoods management group tried hard to embed a process of learning within the work. Because of our sequence of awaydays and 'whole systems' days we were able to predict some of the issues that would confront us. But, as always, there was nothing like the doing of something to reveal the problems.

Vision and policy

We were able to set out a reasonably clear vision: that we aimed to develop, over the next three years, a network of community partnerships consisting of local people and service providers that would take on increasing responsibility for longer-term planning, decision making and managing resources. The purpose of the partnerships was to develop a local response to local issues and priorities, to support the community to develop its own independent organisations and services, to develop new and innovative projects to address local issues and needs, and to encourage services to work more effectively and efficiently with each other.

Strategy

The strategy aimed at developing at least eight neighbourhood partnerships in a cross-section of wards across the town. Support for the development of the partnerships was to be provided by a new Council team (of existing, seconded staff) and a senior management group.

Implementation

Implementation initially focussed on two neighbourhoods. One had quite a strong record of community action, with a lot of community of groups and organisations. The other was 'quieter', with fewer community groups. Some said that the second area was apathetic, but others argued that the lack of activity was a result of the area having been neglected by the Council.

Learning and adapting

We learned a lot about how partnerships work. Effective partnerships require a lot of goodwill and trust, but it is also important to be aware of the power dynamic that plays out in these groups. We started to get complaints from local residents that they felt the partnership meetings were tokenistic and that the services remained in control – the relationship was not an equal one. However the residents also thought that at least some of the service providers seemed to be trying very hard to be inclusive.

We realised that more thought was required on the membership of the partnerships. We also realised that an area where there was a variety of community groups and a network between them was different from an area with just one or two groups. This raised the question of the status of the community representatives in the partnership. In the area with a strong network of groups, community representatives could be put forward by the network, but in the area with only a few groups, they could only really represent themselves.

We also learned that neighbourhoods require support to enable them to participate. We needed to support the development of community groups, the individual residents who were active in the groups, and those who represented the community in the partnership. We needed to focus on helping the local groups be as open, democratic and accountable as possible in order to properly represent local residents.

Staff who were involved in the partnerships required a hands-off approach from their line management. The local partnerships needed active participation from the staff side, not participation which required taking back all decisions to be made at HQ, where they could get bogged down in the bureaucratic line management systems of the service providers.

At one stage we faced some discontent from the local ward councillors. They complained that they felt alienated, sidelined from the process. So we spent a lot of time, through the councillors' support team, on helping them define their role in the context of the partnerships. It was important to remind everyone that the councillors were constitutionally elected representatives of the area, whilst the community reps were really representatives of the community groups, not of the residents at large, or were essentially a self-selected group of local people. It might be best to call them something other than representatives, so that they didn't seem to be conflicting with the councillors' role. We needed to work on the fundamental question of where participative governance ends and representative democracy begins, and how they should interface.

The other services naturally had their own organisational and professional cultures, management systems and decision-making processes. These sometimes helped and sometimes hindered the partnership process. But the success of the other services' involvement in the partnerships was mostly dependent on the attitude of the practitioners who were involved and their immediate line managers. In short, everyone involved in the development of the partnerships, not just the residents, needed 'capacity building', space and time to participate, along with the appropriate level of skills, knowledge and attitude.

Progress

Towards the end of a year results began to show through. The pilot partnerships began to raise issues that we and our partners had overlooked or not tackled well enough. Could an alley which had become a no-go route into town since someone had been mugged there have better lighting and a periodic police presence? Could empty shops in the neighbourhood centres be turned into community enterprise nurseries? Could a bus route be reinstated as its closure had made it difficult for some residents to take up wider work opportunities? Could community group leaders be trained in how to recruit and retain more volunteers? Could the area with few groups have visits from groups in the other area to stimulate new groups being set up? Many of the issues were not new, but because they were now raised as part of partnership business they were taken seriously, and the partners began there and then to discuss solutions.

A landmark at the end of the year was a 'whole system review day' where we brought everyone together – residents, partnership members, senior managers from the council, cabinet members, ward councillors and colleagues from other services. Reflecting on what we had learned, I said I was glad we had gone ahead with the pilots, with a strong commitment to learning and adapting as things developed. A comparatively small development like setting up the local partnerships was clearly going to reap rewards both for residents, the Council and the other agencies, and yield useful learning about how to work with residents, how to manage staff in that relationship, how services relate to local people and how council-wide strategy now must pay careful attention to what is emerging from the partnerships. The exciting thing was that the issues that had come up were not just extra demands on resources – they were wealth-creating in themselves. Rolling out the other partnerships was clearly justified.

Story two: A community health project

Jenny's story: the background

The Smallbury Down Community Health Project is a one-year-old neighbourhood project based in a large, mixed housing estate on the outskirts of the town. The estate has a mixed population, about 60 per cent White British, 20 per cent Sudanese and others including Asian and Chinese. The project is funded for three years by the Public Health unit in the Council, and reports to a steering group of residents and services. It employs a full-time community development worker and a part-time Sudanese health link worker. A project manager is seconded from the Council's public health team.

Jenny, the project manager, has been a vocal advocate for the need for health services to work more closely with local communities. She has some experience of community practice, and it was largely through her efforts that funding for the project was secured. The community development worker has considerable practical experience. The Sudanese health link worker is herself from Sudan and has a background in research.

The steering committee is chaired by the local Anglican vicar, and has four resident representatives, including a local Sudanese shopkeeper, a local councillor, the manager of the local Children's Centre and a police sergeant. This is Jenny's story, firstly just after the project was set up and then a year later:

The initial steps

It's all very new here, a new team, people have only been in post a couple of weeks. The steering group has been around for a while as I was set up to oversee the initial development of the project. At the moment it's all excitement, energy and confusion. We don't know each other very well and we are all on a bit of a learning curve.

I have fairly good experience as a manager, as I managed a community health education team for a few years. Several colleagues have said to me that they think I have been shoved sideways into a non job. I don't feel this way. The project is very important to me. I really believe in what we are trying to do in the area. However I'll be the first to admit that my experience of community practice is limited. I'm also a bit nervous about our work with the Sudanese, and it's important that we get this right. I have already heard mutterings from some people saying why should the Sudanese get special treatment, that it would have been better to spend the money reopening the old youth club.

Over the years I have become increasingly sceptical of some of the traditional approaches to improving health in communities. I think the evidence shows that health education initiatives, and special groups such as to stop smoking or reduce obesity, have had only limited success. There has been quite a lot of work in healthy eating groups, advice to families about dental hygiene and so on but there remains a 10-year difference in life expectancy here in comparison with the richer areas of the town. The health issues faced by local people are profound. More people die from heart disease. There is a higher incidence of cancers, and higher levels of teenage pregnancy than anywhere else in the town. The initiatives may have made some difference – the gaps could have been even worse – but they clearly haven't cracked the problems.

Our overall aim is to improve the health and wellbeing of the residents of Smallbury Down. We have four key objectives:

- developing a minimum of four health or wellbeing groups per year, at least one within the Sudanese community;
- working closely with other local public and voluntary services and community groups in the area;
- reducing 'silo working' by encouraging and supporting closer working between services;
- exploring new ways of delivering health services by supporting joint community and public service initiatives.

My strategy is to approach things at two levels: externally, with the community and other service providers, and internally, establishing an effective team and developing the steering group. This is important because what we have at the moment is just a disparate bunch of people with a lot of goodwill, enthusiasm and commitment. We are still in the initiating phase but we have a basic structure, a general sense of what the project goals are, and a rough outline of how we will achieve them. But I'm not sure we have a very clear vision of how to achieve our overall project aim. The original service specification was pretty sparse, simply stating that, over three years, the project would employ community development methods and develop a number of community based activities aimed at improving the health of local people.

Amongst the new team members and steering group there are a lot of diverging views on what community development is and how much flexibility should be used in defining what kind of community groups might bring health benefits. In the end we agreed that we'd work with local residents in an open-ended way, encouraging and supporting them in developing the groups they wanted. We also agreed that there would be a need to support existing groups. Practically any involvement in a community group would bring mental or physical health benefits to those participating, and also for those using the service provided by a group. We hammered out broad principles for the way we wanted the team to function and learn together, and the role of the steering group.

These discussions helped cement the steering committee and staff group together, because we allowed people to be open and honest about their views, but challenged people when they started using easy jargon such as 'bottom up', 'community engagement' or 'empowerment'. We agreed we needed to:

- establish a strong relationship with the local community and with other services;
- map the existing network of community groups and local service provision and identify any gaps;
- develop a sense of what local people and service providers felt were the key issues and priorities in the area;
- develop a team and individual work programme to carry out these tasks.

The project 12 months on

It's good to be able to look at how things have developed. Some of it has been very good but we have faced some big and frustrating challenges. At first I focussed our effort on supporting and developing community groups that would have a positive impact on residents' health and wellbeing. I then planned to move on to the other objectives about working with the public services. What I had not anticipated was the way the one led into the other, like ripples in a pond. Policy decisions and priorities were sometimes directly affected by our work at a very local level with a relatively small group of residents.

Here is an example: about three months into the start of the project we began work with 20 residents who wanted to set up a local action group. They were concerned about a number of different issues – the social isolation of older people living in the area and the need for some basic environmental issues to be sorted out, including traffic calming and clearing rubbish. They also wanted something done about the 'noisy gangs of young people hanging around the shopping area, making trouble'. We helped them set up the Smallbury Down Action Group. Its aim was to 'improve the quality of life for the people living and working in the area'. The group agreed three core themes:

- Environmental improvement
- A safer neighbourhood
- Action for older people.

This was an ambitious agenda. It quickly became apparent through discussion that improvements on these issues could not be achieved by residents alone, so in order to plan action we borrowed an idea from Cormac Russell on 'asset based community development':[4] we set out action in terms of things the community could do for itself, things the community and authorities could do together, and things the authorities ought to do (Table 7.1).

These were just some of the many ideas that the group came up with, but they served the purpose of focusing the main tasks so that they did not seem so overwhelming. Our role was to support this group of residents to become an effective and self-confident group that could develop a strategy to make these things happen.

Table 7.1: Complementary actions of residents and services

Things the group and other residents could do	Things services could and should do	Things that residents and services could do together
Improving the environment		
Report fly-tipping	Introduce traffic-calming measures	Organise neighbourhood clear ups
A safer neighbourhood		
Organise Saturday football club and other activities for young people	Police to patrol shop area more, establish a better relationship with the young people	Organise meetings with young people to see what they want
Action for older people		
Organise social events and trips	Provision of weekly health clinic in the area	Organise a neighbourhood watch/ good neighbour project

Working with local services

At this stage links between members of the action group and local services were pretty tentative. It was clear that, if the group were to achieve any of their goals, they would need to develop a closer relationship with local service providers.

We organised a series of meetings about each of the objectives with the appropriate service providers. Most of them were happy to meet the action group, although some seemed a little nervous, as this was a first for them. Sometimes these meetings had a rather bumpy beginning, as the residents outlined what they'd like to see happen and then some of the service providers immediately launched into reasons why they could not do anything, or prevaricated. But there were always some people who were keen to cooperate and do something. At times it could be frustrating. When we talked about environmental improvements we were amazed at the number of different agencies and services affected and therefore the complexity of accountability. For example highways and roads were the responsibility of a different council from rubbish collections, and the police and the fire services also had their own way of doing things.

Things got heated at times. The residents would get angry at the apparent intransigence of some agencies who seemed to be keen to find all sorts of excuses as to why they couldn't do something, or why it would take ages for them to get a decision from their managers. On the other hand some of the service providers were clearly getting frustrated with the residents' seeming inability or unwillingness to understand the problems the service providers faced.

We tried a technique to help loosen things up: we got everyone to start filling in a grid that encouraged people to plot the actions they were suggesting in terms of the impact they would have and the ease of undertaking the action (Table 7.2).[5]

We created tables for the residents' activities, the service provider activities and the joint activities and we asked the participants to put a rough timetable on each of these, ie whether an activity could take place in the short, medium or long term.

Table 7.2: Impact and difficulty grid

		Level of Difficulty		
		Easy	Medium	Hard
	High			
Level of Impact	Medium			
	Low			

This worked! There was a change in the atmosphere and attitude between the residents and the service providers, from one of near confrontation and lack of understanding to one where, in order to complete the task, a dialogue between the participants began to take place.

One of the things the residents wanted to do was work with the highways people to identify where some of the most dangerous areas in relation to traffic were. The highways people took some persuading, as they had their own guidelines and models for identifying if and when traffic calming and other measures are required. But in the end they relented and we organised a community survey. We asked residents (including local children) where they thought the roads were the most dangerous. The programme of putting in the traffic-calming measures has now begun.

The action group also had an impact on the decision making processes at a strategic level in some services, such as the NHS and Adult Services. A number of focus group meetings were arranged between older residents and service providers. The information and 'case studies' were fed in to the way the public health department and adult services were reorganising their services.

What we learned

With the benefit of hindsight it's easy to understand how we might have approached things differently if we were to start again. I should have realised from the beginning that practically everything we did in some way affected the service providers. This was particularly true of the action group, which was to play a key role in the subsequent development of things in Smallbury Down.

As we developed the action group, there was a four-fold process of simultaneous change:

- how the group's proposed actions and initiatives were developed and implemented;
- how residents and services providers communicated and worked together both within and outside the group;
- how the group developed in response to the changed relationship;
- how the services adapted their way of working to respond to the changed relationship.

It's clear to me now that we would have achieved even more if we had understood that the action group was going to need to develop into a kind of partnership between the residents and the service providers. We were naïve in assuming that there would be a simple communication process between the residents and the services as the action group presented its agenda to the service providers. The development of a workable agenda required an open dialogue and sharing of information and ideas between the residents and the services. The job of the project was to support the residents in terms of their capacity and self-confidence, whilst at the same time working with the local services to help them develop the confidence and skills to work in an open way with the residents. It was a two way street!

Commentary

Our stories illustrate how two people, occupying different positions within the system but equally committed to strengthening the community, forged a pathway to help bring this about. Each approach has some strengths and some limitations.

As leader of the Council, Jim Harrison would appear to have considerable power to drive the local authority to develop and implement his Flourishing Neighbourhoods strategy. Jim's instinct was to work through a traditional 'cascade' approach, from the top down, starting with his colleagues within the party leadership, then the departmental directors and senior managers, and bringing in the senior people from the other agencies as seemed appropriate. Once all these were on board, the next stage was to inform and involve operational managers and their staff. Jim's approach is what you might expect in a local authority or a large organisation as it starts to develop an important new strategy. Jim recognised that the strategy meant that the Council would need to change the way it operated, and he rightly anticipated some difficulties when expecting Council staff to adopt new and different ways during a time of budget cuts. During the implementation process, which sensibly focussed initially on two neighbourhoods, Jim was pleased to find that most stakeholders of all kinds were willing to learn a lot, particularly on the functioning of the neighbourhood partnerships, the power dynamics within groups, the support needs of both residents and service providers and the role of local councillors. However, in this wide emphasis on participation there was perhaps some loss of focus on other types of outcome, and he was left with a number of questions to be tackled during the future course of implementation: would all this participation necessarily lead to improvements in local conditions and quality of life? Would it absorb a great deal of energy? What would need to take place within the local community to ensure that local people felt more empowered? How would participation need to be linked to the way local services were managed and delivered?

In the second story the focus was naturally on the project in question. Jenny sought a project-based strategy to fulfil the aims and vision that emerged from the community as well as the original project design. She saw involving her team members and the project steering group as paramount. But her previous experience and training had not predicted that what she needed to enable the project to succeed was to create a more collaborative relationship between residents and service providers.

What is the common ground? Any strategy to strengthen communities will need to be both outward facing to the community and inward facing to the initiating body, whether this is a local authority, a neighbourhood partnership or a single project. As suggested in Chapter Five, a strategy should work towards a qualified 'whole systems' approach. There is no absolute whole system, so it is necessary to be clear what one is regarding as 'the whole' or 'the system' in a particular case, and be aware of its externalities. At a very local level the designated 'whole' may be the neighbourhood. Strategy here would seek to involve all the factors operating within the neighbourhood, but also take account of the surrounding factors such as the local authority area. At the larger local level, the local authority area can be regarded as a relatively whole system, and the aim is to seek to work with all the main levers affecting the life of the locality.

Notes

[1] www.unesco.org/most/southa13.htm.

[2] www.seattle.gov/neighborhoods/.

[3] Mintzberg (1983).

[4] www.assetbasedconsulting.co.uk.

[5] With thanks to Development Focus for this and other tools and approaches to co-production and planning: www.developmentfocus.org.uk.

EIGHT

Outcomes and evidence

Inadequate evidence has held community practice and development back. This chapter reviews the way that the focus of social policy gradually moved from provision to outcomes, the hesitant response of community practice, and the establishment of objective indicators of community strengths within New Labour's local government system. The National Survey of Third Sector Organisations which emerged from this system is a particularly rich model for how the local community sector could be profiled. A shift in the community practice evaluation culture to more objective measures is advocated, and the kind of logic framework and indicators which could be used are suggested.

The evidence imperative

Building community strengths[1] is a good phrase for what we are doing *in a neighbourhood* and across neighbourhoods. It is not enough to know that a group or initiative is benefitting its participants, though that is vital. It is also necessary to map the whole sector of community groups against the perceptions and conditions of the population as a whole. If the sense of community, community activities, community cohesion, community capability are to be improved, this must be done against a stable territorial and population background, rather than trying to do so against the unstable notion of 'community' itself.

Community practice, we have seen, is scattered through a variety of occupations. What sort of impact can it make and what sort of evidence can demonstrate it? In the absence of systematic evidence, the value of community practice is often judged intuitively, or it is seen simply as a technique and is not assessed separately. This leaves it half invisible and less effective than it could be.

For the more concentrated form of community practice, community development, there are a number of types of assessment. But the methods are mostly designed for self-evaluation by the practitioners and participants directly involved, and are not widely recognised outside the field. Without more transparent and objective forms of evaluation, it is unlikely that community development, and community practice as a whole, can achieve the fundamental place in policy which it ought to occupy.

Public services have a long history of being provision-centred rather than outcome-centred. The relatively recent focus on better outcomes was partly driven by the realisation that much government policy, and not only in the UK, suffered from 'short-sightedness, fragmentation and orientation to process, not results'.[2] Writing in the mid-1990s, Mark Friedman, an influential US commentator, equated poorly conceived outcomes with waste of public money:

> Government organisation is often a maze of interrelated, overlapping and sometimes duplicative structures. These structures tend to carve up and compartmentalise problems ... Budgeting systems tend to be slavishly devoted to process rather than results ... Outcomes or results are usually considered only in terms of what individual agencies and programs produce ... Citizens outside government do not view success or failure in these terms ... Current budget systems allow and even promote the paradox of programs claiming success while conditions get worse.[3]

Friedman's remedy emphasised:

- the importance of using a shared and common language across partner agencies;
- population accountability, which is about improving outcomes for a particular population within a defined geographical area;
- performance accountability, which is about the performance of a service and improving outcomes for a defined group of service users;
- asking 'How much did we do?', 'How well did we do it?' and most importantly 'Is anyone better off?'.[4]

Evaluation of community practice has traditionally been weak in these dimensions. The potential for a stronger model has emerged over the past generation, alongside successive governments' attempts to make public services more outcome-focused.

Cost and quality: the Conservative approach in the 1980s and 1990s

The Conservative government of the 1980s approached the question of efficiency in public services by analogy with the private sector. It believed that the introduction of private sector methods into public service agencies would automatically improve quality and contain costs. One anxiety about public services was that there was no 'bottom line' – no profit motive from which one could clearly judge success or failure. There was therefore no natural and necessary constraint on ever more expenditure, since there were always more needs to be discovered. Limits had to be put in place by policy, in contrast with the private sector, where failure was said to be self-eradicating in the sense that businesses which failed to make a profit collapsed.

Expressing concern with cost and quality is a convenient platform for those whose underlying motive is to reduce provision. Nevertheless, since we are collectively spending a great deal of our common resources on public services it is in everyone's interest to ensure that these funds are spent to greatest effect.

If little of this argument was directed at community practice, that was because it was seen as a marginal issue. Seeking a more central place for it in public policy and services, the same question must be confronted: why is it worth spending public money on community practice?

The John Major (Conservative) government (1990–97) introduced a structured approach to ascertaining quality in public services. This took the form of the Compulsory Competitive Tendering system (CCT). Public services had to be open to bidding from any competent provider, whether in the public, private or voluntary sector. Public authorities could themselves continue to provide the service if they won the contract, which had to be judged partly on cost.

Regeneration of disadvantaged areas was a vital incubator for community practice. Here the search for effectiveness was interpreted in an ingenious way under Environment Minister Michael Heseltine. Disadvantaged areas, having concentrations of need, absorb more public service expenditure than other areas. Companies are reluctant to invest there, further reducing job opportunities, and increasing the dependence of local residents on public services, so that public expenditure becomes the main basis of the economy of such areas. They therefore take on an unnatural kind of life in which the fundamental connection between work and reward is broken. Young people see few opportunities, and those who can find jobs by moving elsewhere, do so. Thus even though the prosperity of the country as a whole may be rising, the gap in prosperity between these and other areas continues to widen.

The Heseltine innovation of City Challenge (described in Chapter Two) attracted private business, especially property developers, into disadvantaged areas through the prospect of receiving long-term rents on houses, leisure amenities and shopping centres. The local schemes were required to specify outputs in terms of numbers of houses improved, jobs created, and services delivered. The challenge was addressed to local authority bidders, which would compete on the quality of the plan for local improvement, including attracting private investment. The Minister thus contained government expenditure by attracting private investment whilst stimulating effort to improve the quality of plans.

Unfairly, residents were at the mercy of the talent of their local authority bidding teams. But one of the major criteria by which quality was judged was how well the plan included community involvement. Soon the City Challenge model would spread far and wide through the similar but much larger Single Regeneration Budget (SRB) which replaced it from 1993. In the remaining four years of the long Conservative administration, whilst sleaze and scandal seemed to be running out of control in Westminster, a significant expansion in community practice and support to local community groups was taking place through the year by year rounds of the expanding regeneration portfolio.[5]

Continuity and change under early New Labour

On its accession in 1997, New Labour set out to seize the nettle regarding evidence and quality in public services: henceforth policy would not be ideologically driven but 'evidence based'. Methods would be modelled on 'what works'. In abolishing the Conservatives' compulsory competitive tendering system, as putting price above quality, the new government did not abandon the requirement that public services should prove they were being delivered in the most cost-effective way. It instituted instead the 'Best Value' process.[6] In order for Councils and Authorities to be measured against Best Value, 90 performance indicators were introduced. These were known as Best Value Performance Indicators (BVPIs). The Audit Commission (itself later abolished by the Coalition government in 2010) was given the job of overseeing the implementation of the system.

The BVPIs covered four dimensions:

• Strategic objectives – what the service is for.
• Service delivery outcomes.
• Quality of the service, as judged by users.
• Ease of access to the service.

No one likes being inspected, judged and controlled, and over a few years there was increasing criticism and resentment of the 'target culture' and the over-centralised management which at first accompanied it. But standards of public services were shown to improve, and at the same time the government modified the system to reduce micromanagement. Best Value was phased out but outcome indicators were retained and developed. Public service agencies were given 'freedom and flexibility' in their methods so long as they could show they were achieving the agreed outcomes.

How did pressure for proof of results affect community practice? At first there was little effect, since community practice was treated, as before, simply as a method to assist other issues. But gradually community strength, and by implication community practice, came to be recognised as an issue in itself. A stepping stone to recognition was the identification of 'safer and stronger communities' as a priority for local authorities, in conjunction with the police. Even then, at first, there was a tendency to regard community strength merely as an aid to policing. Gradually it was realised that measures of equal status were needed to recognise whether a community was strong in itself. The connection with policing was only one of many connections across public issues. A stronger community would also be healthier, better educated, more employable, more tolerant and more caring of its environment. Much of its importance was, indeed, its effect on other issues, but this was also true of the other issues themselves: each public issue has both an intrinsic importance and a secondary importance for its effect on other issues.

The main vehicle for local collaboration and monitoring was the Local Area Agreement (LAA), introduced in the mid-2000s. The LAA was an agreement between government and each locality about how services were to be improved for three-year periods. The agreement was enacted through the Local Strategic Partnership (LSP) – the arrangement for joint effort between the local authority and its partners, both other services (police, health, fire etc) and the voluntary and community sectors. The best LSPs were not just high-level talking shops but a forum for a wide variety of more local and thematic partnerships, the LSP 'family', all helping to spread participation more widely (Figure 8.1).

The combined effects of all the forms of local action were to be captured in a selection of indicators. These were, in effect, objectives stated in the form of desired outcomes. Together with its partners, each local authority made a selection of action priorities for a three-year period from a menu of 198 outcome indicators (a massive reduction from the 800 indicators that had previously accumulated under previous separate development of all the relevant departments and agencies).

For advocates of community practice, the key question posed by this system was how their discipline should feature within it. Would it once again be seen as merely an adjunct to other objectives? If it was to have equal status with other factors, its aims would need to be couched in terms of measurable outcomes. This was unfamiliar and uneasy territory for community practice advocates.

Figure 8.1: Example of an LSP 'family'

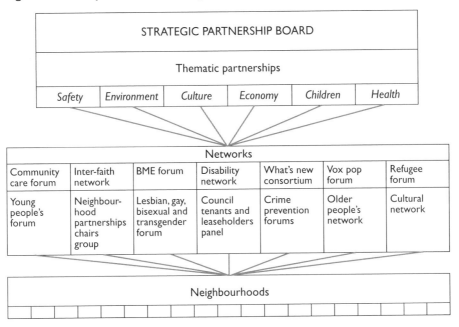

The community practice response

Many champions of community practice were uneasy about reducing the value of community involvement and groups to facts and figures, which they saw as being externally imposed and inimical to the fluid nature of community life:

> For years community development has argued against predetermined targets and performance criteria, asserting that intervention strategies must be non-directive and nurture organic development rather than

deliver an external agenda. This is the difference between the top-down imposition of rigid action plans with pre-set outputs versus a bottom up approach that works *with* the grain of the community, helping them to define and achieve their own solutions using processes that simultaneously empower and educate.[7]

Whilst successive governments looked for outcome indicators for public services, there were some important attempts to reframe community development in terms of modern evaluation, whilst keeping to its non-directive principles. Key examples were the creation of National Occupational Standards for community development across the UK and Ireland (CD-NOS) and the National Standards for Community Engagement in Scotland. The Federation for Community Development Learning led the development of the CD-NOS under the Sector Skills Council for Lifelong Learning. The NOS went through three versions, the last being issued in July 2009.[8] Separately, National Standards for Community Engagement were commissioned from the Scottish Community Development Centre (SCDC) by the Scottish Government in 2005.[9] SCDC was also commissioned by the Northern Ireland Office to produce an evaluation framework which came to be called Achieving Better Community Development (ABCD), and led on to a further version called Learning, Evaluation and Planning (LEAP).[10] Both these and CD-NOS came to be used widely across the UK. Another useful framework created slightly later was Axis of Influence.[11]

Important as these frameworks were, and are, in helping practitioners to plan their work, they do not crack the problem of objectively capturing changes in residents' situations or local conditions resulting from community practice. The CD-NOS are based almost exclusively on the perspective of fieldworkers (despite the NOS system supposedly being driven by employer needs), reflecting what practitioners see themselves as *doing*, with little about outcomes.[12] The ABCD and LEAP models do urge the importance of outcomes, but leave it to the users of the model to determine their own outcomes and indicators. This is consistent with the principle that communities and practitioners should control the purpose of the work, but it has two drawbacks. First, it greatly underestimates how difficult it is for individual projects and practitioners to establish meaningful and measurable indicators. Secondly it means there is no particular consistency between assessment of one community initiative and another.

Establishing measurable indicators is a research activity involving considerable expertise and discipline. This is disguised by the fact that well-known indicators look simple, because they have been painstakingly pared down to single unambiguous statements. Getting them into this form is precisely what is difficult. For most practitioners and project designers this is counter-intuitive. When you are trying to deliver a powerful programme to meet complex and intractable needs the natural impulse is to want to compress as many judgements together as possible, because they all seem important. This results in multiple statements of objectives which are impossible to measure. One Neighbourhood Renewal guide asked partners to use an indicator of whether there had been 'robust, in-depth analysis of local problems, underlying causes and a range of solutions'. It is impossible to collect systematic evidence on such a dense bundle of judgements.

Generic community practice outcomes can be predicted

The determination of community development advocates to keep the definition of objectives within the control of community groups rightly warns against poorly designed projects which seek to impose arbitrary top-down objectives on individual groups. Each community group can only function well – often can only be formed in the first place – by choosing its own objectives and its own pathway of development. Nevertheless all community development and practice, whatever issues it chooses to focus on, implicitly adopts certain generic objectives about strengthening the community. This is particularly clear if one looks at community practice across a whole neighbourhood rather than a single group. The strength of community life in a particular place is recognisable, as illustrated in Chapter Four, by how many community groups there are, what activities they carry out, how many people participate in them, what issues they cover, what services they provide, what condition they are in, and what effects they have on their participants, on non-participants and on public services.

Even on the question of what social issues the groups take up, at neighbourhood-wide level, the range of community concerns, especially in disadvantaged areas, is largely predictable because the main issues are universal. The greater the number of residents and groups that are created, consulted or involved, the more their combined objectives will equate to the full range of issues addressed by the public authorities. There may be tensions between residents and services on all sorts of matters but there is rarely much difference on the overall aims of reducing crime, improving education, increasing employment, improving housing, amenities and environment, taken up in different ways by different groups.

The evidence required for progress on the overall strategy for strengthening communities is therefore different from the kind required to assess the progress of an individual group. The individual group needs to know if it is advancing towards its chosen goals, which might be limited to one issue or another and to a small subsection of the community. A neighbourhood strategy or partnership, on the other hand, needs to know about the aggregate effect of all contributors to community practice across the local population – Friedman's 'particular population within a defined geographical area'.

During the 2000s some community development literature had already started moving towards identifying the generic outcomes long implied in practice. *Firm Foundations* suggested these:

- A higher level of social capital (trust and cooperation) amongst local people

- A wider, stronger, better networked, more varied, accessible and inclusive local community sector
- More effective community groups and organisations, including in the delivery of their own forms of public service
- Greater participation in local activity and in decision making ... by all sections of the community
- Greater capacity amongst community groups and organisations to engage in joint working with public authorities.[13]

Soon after, *The Community Development Challenge* showed that outcomes were implied in the main community practice roles (Table 8.1).

These are the kinds of objective which should be established as an overall framework at partnership level. In a sense these objectives are therefore top-down or outside-in. But they do not interfere with the freedom of groups to

Table 8.1: Six outcomes model from *The Community Development Challenge*

Role	Outcome
1. Help people see that they have common concerns about local or other public issues that they could benefit from working on together under their own control	– Reduction of isolation and alienation – Increase in social capital and co-operation
2. Help people to work together on those issues, often by forming or developing an independent community group, supporting them to plan and take actions, and encouraging evaluation and reflection as a way of improving effectiveness	– Creation or improvement of bona-fide community groups – Increase of opportunities for activity in the community – More effective community activity
3. Support and develop independent groups across the community sector non-directively but within an ethical framework, and increase networking between groups	Increase in: – community sector – volunteering – mutual aid and autonomous services – learning between groups – improvement in local conditions
4. Promote values of equity, inclusiveness, participation and co-operation throughout this work.	Increase in: – participation – social capital – co-operation – community cohesion
5. Empower people and their organisations to influence and transform public policies and services and all factors affecting the conditions of their lives	– Community engagement and influence. – Better dialogue between community and authorities. – More coherence and effectiveness of public policies.
6. Advise and inform public authorities on community perspectives and assist them to strengthen communities and work in genuine partnership with them	– Increased capacity of agencies, authorities and professions to engage with communities – Improvement in delivery of public services – Increased resources for the community sector

Source: Community Development Challenge Group (2006).

choose their own issues, or with practitioners' ability to 'work with the grain of the community, helping them to define and achieve their own solutions'. On the contrary, they rely on these. Whatever issues an individual group chooses will automatically contribute to one or several of the generic outcomes and one or several of the recognised social issues addressed by public authorities. Each group chooses its own direction of development, but an overall neighbourhood plan can still actively look for a specified range of outcomes. Indeed, the overall plan should in turn influence the work of the network of practitioners. It is not contrary to good community practice for practitioners to nudge groups in rewarding directions, or encourage them to fill gaps in the overall map of social issues. Even the most non-directive practitioner is in any case likely to do some nudging to encourage groups to adopt community development values of equality, inclusiveness and participation.

Changing the community practice evaluation culture

To people working on a project on the ground, the intentions of the project often seem clear and obvious. They are tackling poverty, building people's confidence, delivering childcare or pursuing some other worthwhile cause. But these intentions may be far from clear to people a bit more distant from the action, whose support and understanding they need – funders, public authorities or community members who are not part of the inner circle. A clear statement of intended outcomes establishes good communication with stakeholders and enables supporters and co-operators to understand what the project is aiming to do.

By starting with a clear vision of outcomes and then working out what actions would bring those about, there is also less likelihood of adopting arbitrary and ineffective methods, less danger of wasting resources on unproductive action and less likelihood of getting bogged down in a process which has no clear direction. Expending effort can easily be mistaken for achieving progress. To check whether progress is really happening it is necessary to periodically stand back from the process and ask whether the conditions or problems which are being addressed are really changing. That will need evidence beyond the perceptions of those who are closely involved (though including them).

Another pitfall that can be avoided by clear outcomes is the trap of unrealistic expectations. People who create or deliver social projects are often more than a little idealistic and want to improve everything in a short time. Funders and commissioners are often only too keen to believe that more can be delivered for less, and politicians like to promise the earth. Projects often therefore set out very wide-reaching goals with limited resources, and if these are not fully achieved, later on this will make it look as if the project has failed. Setting down outcomes within a realistic plan, and proportionate to the resources available, can help to avoid this, leading to a deserved record of proven success when results come in.

Attempts to codify community practice criteria have been hobbled by four factors found widely in community development literature which need to be rethought:

- Attachment to the provider-centred rather than user-centred perspective: only practitioners themselves are trusted to judge whether their work was effective.
- Focussing only on the minority of residents with whom the community practice is directly carried out, instead of using Friedman's principle of measuring by the effect on the whole population of a defined geographical area; therefore switching to the perspective of a whole neighbourhood and a practitioner network and team, rather than taking the work of the individual practitioner as the basic unit of delivery;
- Lack of detachment: since evaluation is treated as part of the relationship with the community, nothing is allowed to be seen to fail – the imperative of encouragement and boosting of confidence overrides other considerations;
- Scepticism about statistics to the point of avoiding them altogether.

However, professional researchers and evaluators have also had difficulty in bringing together subjective and objective evidence of strengthening communities. Even government-commissioned evaluation models which are of high quality in other respects[14] rarely combine public service records, resident perceptions and profiles of the community sector across a neighbourhood.

Much policy narrative tends to assume that the community and its organisations are simply there to be tapped into. A shallow revolution has taken place whereby most social planners now accept the need to 'involve the community' but do not see that 'the community' can be in a strong or weak state, with sparse or abundant community groups, vigorous or feeble community activity, inclusive or narrow social networks. It is only when this is understood that the role of community practice is grasped.

Measurement of community practice will never be watertight – nothing in the social field ever is. The point is not that this measurement and knowledge should be 100 per cent accurate but that it puts the matter into the public domain, crossing a threshold into public endorsement. How to carry out brain surgery remains a mystery to 99.9 per cent of the population but patient survival rates can be understood by everyone. It is this kind of visible outcome that community practice needs to make in order to establish itself as a matter of permanent public concern.

The primary outcome that should be highlighted is the strengthening of the local community sector itself. Ironically, this is something that community groups themselves often overlook. Asked what they want, they will usually answer in terms of their priority issues – better housing, better care, better environment – rarely in terms of the condition of themselves as groups and networks.

The indicators breakthrough

With help from the Community Development Foundation and the Audit Commission, the Department for Communities and Local Government (CLG) developed a suite of evidence-based indicators of strong communities, as part of its public sector and local authority reforms of the mid-2000s. The group of indicators of community strengths (Table 8.2) occupied the first seven places within the indicators framework. Others covered the main familiar social issues. Evidence for the community indicators was mostly in the form of large-scale statistical collection of resident perceptions through a 'Place Survey' conducted

Table 8.2: Community strength indicators from the England Local Government Performance Framework 2007–10

Number and name of indicator	The question/s asked or definition of evidence
1: % of people who believe people from different backgrounds get on well together in their local area. (Cohesion)	'To what extent do you agree or disagree that your local area is a place where people from different backgrounds get on well together?' (Places Survey Q18)
2: % of people who feel that they belong to their neighbourhood	'How strongly do you feel that you belong to your immediate neighbourhood?' (Places Survey Q5)
3: Civic participation in the local area (Equalities)	Preamble 'In the last 12 months have you been – a local councillor (LA, town or parish) – member of a group making decisions on local health or education services – ... regeneration ... crime ... tenants' committee ... services for young people ... other ...?' (Places survey Q16; targeted especially to equalities groups by gender, ethnicity, disability, age, religion/belief, sex orientation) (not poverty, income or class)
4: % of people who feel they can influence decisions in their locality	'Do you agree or disagree that you can influence decisions affecting your local area?' (Places survey Q13)
5: Overall satisfaction with the local area	'Overall how satisfied are you with your local area as a place to live?' (Places survey Q3)
6. Participation in regular volunteering	Preamble + 'Overall how often over the last 12 months have you given unpaid help to any group(s), club(s) or organisation(s)? Please only include work that is unpaid and not for your family' [at least once a week/at least once a month/ less often/ not through any organisation]
7. Environment for a thriving third sector	'How do the statutory bodies in your local area influence your organisation's success?' (Q23 in separate third sector survey commissioned by the Office of the Third Sector)

throughout the country. (In the second column of Table 8.2 the exact question asked is given, since this is not always obvious from the name of the indicator.)

As an integral part of the Local Area Agreement in each local authority in England, the suite of seven community indicators set in train a national effort to improve these features of society. Programmes, budgets and action plans followed. Strengthening communities was thereby, for the first time, established as a form of productivity in its own right.

What all this meant in common-sense terms was that practitioners could give straightforward answers to straightforward questions which had previously caused bafflement, like 'What effects is your work meant to have?', 'What changes do you expect to find two years from now?', 'What does a strengthened community look like?'.

A strengthened community is a neighbourhood where a high proportion of people:

- from different backgrounds are getting on well together;
- feel that they belong to their neighbourhood;
- who are from 'equalities' categories serve on decision-making groups;
- feel they can influence decisions in the locality;
- are generally satisfied with the area;
- participate in regular volunteering; and
- where the third sector, particularly community groups, is thriving.

Community indicators such as these had been variously developed and used previously for research and information, but integrating them into policy was an entirely new level of significance. They were amongst the highest priorities chosen by local authorities from the Local Area Agreement menu of options.

Community influence and cohesion

Let us look at a few of the indicators in more detail. Two of the largest aspects of community involvement were influence and cohesion: did residents feel that they could influence local decision making? And how well did residents from different ethnic backgrounds, different generations or different cultures or religions get on together in the locality they shared? A single indicator could not of course capture the complexity of each of these major issues but it provided an objective focal point for what had till then been a frustratingly amorphous debate. It also gave action projects something measurable to aim for.

The *influence* indicator (no4 in Table 8.2) became the headline for the Empowerment unit in the Department for Communities and Local Government (CLG). It remained in the form of a single question ('Do you agree or disagree that you can influence decisions affecting your local area?'). The national baseline when the Local Area Agreement system started in 2006 was 39 per cent of people believing they could influence local decisions, 61 per cent believing they could not, or not knowing. This suggested a high degree of civic alienation or indifference, way beyond disadvantaged areas. In order to try to improve it, the Empowerment unit sponsored a wide variety of initiatives to interact with the efforts of local services. Notably it commissioned, through the Community Development Foundation, a network of 'Regional Empowerment Partnerships' to boost training, research and communication. These produced a wealth of documentation within the short time they were to have before the governmental changes of 2010.[15]

The *cohesion* indicator (no 1) was also a single question: 'To what extent do you agree or disagree that your local area is a place where people from different backgrounds get on well together?' Here the national baseline was much higher, at around 85 per cent. Interestingly, cohesion, by this measure, was often higher in *highly* diverse areas such as London boroughs than in areas where there were concentrations of particular ethnic minorities, such as some northern cities, or in areas of low diversity, such as most rural areas. Again there was a CLG unit to foster this issue. But the concept of community cohesion had only been coined in recent years, and there were few direct hooks in field practice. Most of the practical work on the ground on cohesion was in fact improvised by community practitioners as an integral part of their practice, based on values of equality. CLG produced guidance and a small-grants programme for community organisations which fostered better relations between diverse cultures and ethnic groups. A small number of specialist jobs were created. Probably more could have been achieved if there had been a structured relationship with community practitioners, and resources available to them to boost this side of their work.

The relationship between community groups and local public bodies

Indicator 7, which included help for community groups from local public bodies, is particularly important for future development. Most community practice works by helping community groups, and a strong community groups sector is arguably the single most important aspect of community strengths.

The collection of evidence for this indicator was handled by the Office for the Third Sector (OTS, forerunner of the Office for Civil Society) in the Cabinet Office. Rather than relying on a single question, OTS carried out a nationwide survey of local voluntary and community organisations.[16] The central issue for government was the relationship between the local voluntary and community sector (VCS) and local public bodies. This was embedded in a 40-question survey covering the whole condition of these organisations – their size, objectives, amount of volunteering, number of employees, grants and earnings, social issues addressed, support wanted and received, communication, influence on local decision making and confidence in their future. The survey is a major landmark for the prospect of establishing universally recognised objective indicators of community strengths.

First carried out in 2008 and reported in 2009, the survey was designed to be repeated every two years, and was duly repeated in 2010, after the change of government. This was the first ever comprehensive national survey of the voluntary and community sector, with a sample from every local authority in England. With a 47 per cent response rate in 2008 from a sample of over 104,000 groups and organisations, this is undoubtedly the most comprehensive picture of the VCS in England that has ever been compiled.

Table 8.3 shows some of the findings of most importance to community practice.

Table 8.3: Selected findings from the National Survey of Third Sector Organisations

	2008	2010
Total sample of listed 'charities, voluntary groups and social enterprises' in England*	170,552	154,851
	%	%
Response rate to survey	47	41
(a) Organisations with 1–20 volunteers	68	63
(b) Organisations with 21–100 volunteers	18	20
(c) Organisations with no employees	56	53
(d) Further respondents with up to two employees	14	15
(e) Organisations with annual income below £25,000	49	48
(f) Organisations with annual incomes below £5,000	23	24
(g) Organisations who felt local statutory bodies were a positive influence	16	18
(h) Organisations who felt local statutory bodies were a negative influence	14	11
(i) Organisations who had little or no direct dealings with local statutory bodies	69	69
(j) Organisations satisfied with their ability to influence local decision-making	16	16
(k) Organisations dissatisfied with their ability to influence local decision-making	27	24

* The survey acknowledges that, relying on established lists, it overlooks a large number of unlisted bodies, mostly smaller community groups. Even so, community groups were also clearly represented amongst respondents. We discuss the significance of the limitation below.

Sifting the responses

It should be remembered, as mentioned in Chapter Four, that the third sector is in fact a yoking together of two considerably different sectors: on one hand, professionally run charities and non-profit organisations; and on the other hand self-sustaining community groups, the community sector. The functions, viewpoints and interests of the two parts of the sector are not the same, though there are some organisations which straddle both parts.

The survey clearly captured a mixture of, on one hand, local community groups, and on the other national or regional charities which happened to be based in the locality: 69 per cent said the main area they worked in was the neighbourhood or local authority, and 26 per cent said they mainly worked regionally or nationally. The latter would be of less concern in a local community practice strategy.

The overall results of the NSTSO survey are therefore of less concern in the context of this discussion than the results for the community groups sector alone.

By using the cross-tab facility on the website it is possible to distinguish results for smaller organisations from those for larger organisations for each question. But this is a laborious process, and it is to be hoped that The Office for Civil Society will commission the researchers, or ask the Third Sector Research Centre, which it sponsors, to produce a cluster analysis showing the overall differences in results for community groups and professional voluntary organisations.

Even without focussing down on the community sector, the overall results are of interest to community practice since 69 per cent of respondents are functioning locally, and most of these, judging by income and staffing, are community groups. Around 90 per cent of respondents saw themselves as having been very or fairly successful in achieving their objectives in the past year, and around 85 per cent were very or fairly confident of success in the year to come. Around 50 per cent regarded themselves as social enterprises – a surprisingly high figure when one considers that 56 per cent had no employees and a further 14 per cent had no more than two. The given definition of a social enterprise, 'a business with primarily social objectives whose surpluses are principally reinvested for that purpose in the business or community', must have been understood very loosely in many cases – especially as most community groups by definition have no 'surplus'. The odd definition is evidently an import from a different sector and mindset.

An important limitation of the national survey, however, is that, working from existing lists of organisations, it could not hope to capture anything like the full range of smaller local organisations and community groups. So there is an acknowledged bias towards the larger groups and professionally-run charities. Even so, well over half the respondents were small organisations or community groups, and the difference of perspective between larger and smaller groups can be sifted out by comparing their responses. Of the responding organisations, 56 per cent had no employees (point c in Table 8.3). These were certainly community groups. So also were the further 14 per cent who had no more than two employees (point d). It can also be seen that 49 per cent had incomes of less than £25,000 p.a. (point e), but the income of many of these groups was far lower than this: 23 per cent had less than £5,000 p.a. (point f). Community groups could be defined as those with no more than two employees, income of no more than £25,000 a year and who worked in their own locality. Different thresholds of money and employment could be chosen but these seem a reasonable reflection of how community groups actually work.

Low baseline – high potential

Why is this extraordinarily rich source of data so little known and used? There is little guidance to stakeholders on how they could use this information in local strategy and practice. A slim 'user guide' issued by OTS in 2010 related the key success factors to five action areas:

- strengthening partnership working;
- improving communication and influence;
- boosting indirect support from public bodies and umbrella groups;
- supporting the whole sector, especially smaller groups;
- improving the funding relationship and the economic dimension.[17]

Perhaps a major blockage has been that the results are not very flattering to the stakeholders. In 2008, only 16 per cent of organisations felt that they owed some of their success to the support of local statutory bodies (point g in Table 8.3), and 14 per cent felt that local statutory bodies had a *negative* effect (point h). Proportions improved, slightly but significantly, over the next two years. The great majority of organisations, however, still had either no contact or very little contact with local statutory bodies (point i), and the number dissatisfied with their ability to influence local decision-making was significantly greater than the number of those who were satisfied (points j and k). The minority of organisations which felt that local statutory bodies were helpful were largely those which both had contact with them and felt able to influence them. Many of the remaining majority regarded the question of their relationship to statutory bodies as not applicable to them, which is perhaps even less encouraging for community involvement than outright dissatisfaction.

However, this rather painful picture is precisely what makes the survey so valuable as a baseline. There is a long way to go before there are broadly dynamic, co-operative, co-productive relationships between statutory bodies and the bulk of the local community sector. But by the same token, new initiative stands to reap major rewards. Cross-tabulation analysis shows that the top requirements which third sector organisations express are not, as public authorities might fear, money, grant aid or contracts, but communication, contact, encouragement, recognition, valuing of their experience and opinions.

Other points that could be considered for local strategy include:

- ensuring that all staff who interface with the community sector understand the multiple value of cultivating a positive relationship with it;
- ensuring that front-line staff have sufficient flexibility and time to build this collaborative relationship;
- encouraging elected members to be fully involved with community organisations in their ward;
- mapping the issues and beneficiaries of existing community organisations against need, and offering stimulus and support to new or existing organisations which would fill gaps;
- stimulating and supporting networking, intercommunication and collaboration between community groups;
- providing help and guidance to groups on how to obtain funding where needed and develop trading where appropriate.

Building local evidence

For our purpose it is not only the results of the national survey that are important, but the questionnaire, which is a source of tried and tested questions that can be adapted to carry out a locally-owned survey. Although the survey was conducted in every principal local authority area, the findings are anonymised in such a way that it is not possible to obtain a full local profile of the VCS from them or break them down into neighbourhoods. But it is a full profile of existing groups which would be most useful for local strategy. And the national survey's failure to capture the full range of small community groups can be remedied in locally-conducted profiling, through the knowledge of local agencies and front-line workers. Improvement of the national survey itself is an equally important but separate issue.

The fact that numbers at neighbourhood level are likely to be too small to be statistically significant does not matter: it is the actual profile of groups and organisations that is needed for local strategy. As discussed in Chapter Four, the known size of the VCS per head of population varies substantially between one local authority area and another. Contrasts are likely to be redoubled between one neighbourhood and another, concealed by the local authority average. There is every likelihood that the numbers of community groups in disadvantaged areas will be fewer, sometimes far fewer, than in average and well-off areas. A dearth of community groups is itself a form of poverty.

The national community indicators established in the mid-2000s are not the last word in objective evidence. They should be capable of improvement over some years.[18] Their importance is that they show that objective measurement of generic community practice outcomes is possible. It remains to show what inputs make this happen. Indicators are vital but they alone will not achieve the sea change in community practice which is needed. Strategy must be driven by the development of a more explicit logical story for what community practice is trying to do.

The logic of community practice depends on a hypothesis which is rarely articulated but could be put like this:

1. Contributory factors to poverty, exclusion and disadvantage include low social capital, dearth of community activity, ineffective community activity, social exclusion, conflict between communities and lack of productive dialogue and collaboration between communities and public services.
2. Conversely, high social capital, vigorous community sector, harmonious community relations, effective community activity and productive dialogue and collaboration between communities and public services contribute to overcoming poverty and disadvantage, and lead to a more fulfilling life for residents.
3. Multiple disadvantages also result in disproportionate pressure and costs in public services and benefits.

4. Community activity, social capital, community groups and collaboration between communities and public services can be increased in both volume and effectiveness through community practice.

5. These increases will have two kinds of value: (a) *intrinsic*, meaning improvement in relationships, cooperation and mutual aid inside the community; (b) *extrinsic*, in terms of beneficial influence on local conditions, amenities and the way public services are shaped and delivered.

6. Both the intrinsic and extrinsic improvements will also, other things being equal, reduce excessive costs of public services and benefits in that place, by reducing crime, increasing employability and improving health, education and other factors.

This implies the need for six types of evidence:

A. The level and effectiveness of community activity, assessed through people (eg by residents' survey).

B. The level and effectiveness of community activity, assessed through community groups and organisations (eg by survey of groups and organisations).

C. Conditions and support for community activity (excluding community practice), eg buildings, grants and responsiveness of public services to community views and initiatives.

D. Community practice input, including its costs.

E. Views of key informants from both communities and agencies about causal relationships between input, outputs and outcomes.

F. Public service statistics (subsets from different agencies) and, where possible, estimate of the cost benefits of the outcomes, eg savings in public service costs resulting from reduced crime or improved health, attributable to increased community activity and influence.

No new information should be collected till there has been a thorough investigation of what relevant evidence already exists or is being collected by local agencies. The effort required to assemble the necessary evidence may consist more in locating it in agencies or departments, getting access to it and putting it into an easily understandable form than in collecting new primary evidence.

New community practice would aim to:

• add new input, especially in the form of a coordinator to link the work of the different practitioners, including front-line staff of different agencies with a community engagement remit;

• boost existing input through stimulus, training, networking and a team approach;

• make better use of resources such as community buildings and other assets;

• actualise latent community practice, for example where front-line workers have a community engagement remit but this is treated in a tokenistic way;

- guide community groups in influencing public services and maximising community benefit obtained from them;
- guide all practitioners to focus on intrinsic and extrinsic outcomes for the community, for example:
  - *intrinsic:* higher social capital, new friends, energy, confidence, skills, information, new or extended community groups
  - *extrinsic:* improved relationships between the community and service providers, beneficial community influence on services, new amenities.

Table 8.4 shows some examples of the various components of community practice strategy and what sort of evidence would count for them.

Table 8.4: Components of evaluation and performance management

	Component	Example	Eg of source of evidence
1	Social conditions	– Baselines: Poor housing, low employment, high crime etc – Outputs and outcomes: improvements attributed to 3 and 4 below	Index of multiple deprivation; Joint Strategic Needs Assessment; records of individual agencies; level of demand on services; costs of provision
2	Audit of support for community activity (excluding community practice)	Amenities, community meeting places, grants for community groups, training for volunteers	Review of supportive conditions; intelligence from residents, practitioners and agencies
3	Level of community activity	– Baseline: Not many community groups, low % of population involved. – Output: Five new community groups formed; five existing groups increase level of activity. – Outcome: increase in usage of groups' services and activities; number of residents regularly involved in community activity increased from 5% to 10%	Survey of community groups; intelligence from residents, practitioners and agencies
4	Effectiveness of community activity	Groups' satisfaction with effectiveness; level of activity and usage; interaction with public services	Survey of community groups; intelligence from residents, practitioners and agencies
5	Input: Existing community practice establishment	Two community workers in Housing department; one in Leisure; one in VCS Umbrella Group; 12 other frontline workers in different agencies have community engagement in their job description	Information from agencies (including voluntary sector agencies with a community practice remit)

(continued)

Table 8.4: Components of evaluation and performance management (continued)

	Component	Example	Eg of source of evidence
6	Input: new community practice	Community practice coordinator and assistant appointed; seedcorn fund for new groups set up; agreement of agencies that their community work and other front line staff will participate in a new neighbourhood partnership; establishment of network, with news training and team approach to coordinate community workers' and other frontline workers' help to community groups and initiatives and advice to agencies on engaging with the community	Contracts; inter-agency agreements
7	Cost of input	Cost of 2 + 5 + 6 for overall cost. Cost of 6 alone for cost of change in methods	Accounts
8	Intrinsic outcomes	Increase in residents' confidence, information, social capital, employability, informal and formal volunteering (via personal help/via groups and organisations)	Community groups survey Residents survey
9	Extrinsic outcomes	Better relationship between residents and police; improved dental service; increased health visiting; successful lobbying for new street lighting and bus route between the estate and town centre, widening travel-to-work area and access to amenities.	Community groups survey Residents survey Key informants focus groups
Contributions to issue-specific outcomes:			
10	Employment	Increased employment; new social enterprises set up	Economic records
11	Education	Improvement in school leavers' qualifications	School records
12	Police	Reductions in crime Reduction in fear of crime	Police records
13	Fire	Reduction in fires; reduction in rescue emergencies	Fire service records
14	Housing	Improvement in satisfaction with housing; fewer people wanting to leave the area; more people wanting to move into the area	Housing agency records
15	Health	Reductions in hospital admissions; reductions in ambulance call-outs; reductions in teenage pregnancies	Health service records
16	Environment	Derelict open space reclaimed and turned into safe play area	Environment records

Cost benefits

An outcomes-based approach opens the door to the potential for demonstrating the value of community practice in terms of cost–benefits. This cannot be a perfect science but it can be a good deal more concrete than seen up till now. Indeed, even costs alone are rarely included in community practice reports. There is too little experience of outcomes evaluation in this field as yet to provide a firm model and examples of cost benefit analysis, but there have been some promising experiments.

Some outcomes can be imputed a monetary value in terms of reduced pressure on services, especially emergency services. The ability to calculate this, however, depends on the quality of statistics kept by the services in question. Health agencies and the police normally keep detailed statistics and can translate some changes into costs or savings, for example the cost of an ambulance call out or emergency operation, or the cost of a judicial process and custody.

Cost-benefit assessments also have to be placed in context. It will be necessary to assess whether any improvements are greater than would have been expected from other known factors independent of community practice, such as improvements within mainstream services. Conversely, if local conditions have deteriorated due to other factors, such as the closure of a main employer, it will be necessary to assess whether deterioration has been any less than would have been expected from the impact of those factors.

The Health Empowerment Leverage Project (HELP) reports an embryonic model for estimating cost benefits of community practice in health.[19] The model consisted in obtaining figures from a neighbourhood on the incidence of a number of main health conditions and comparing these with the national average. A review of research literature was used to show that increases in community activity led to improvement on those health conditions.[20] They then described the increases in community activity, social capital and influence on service delivery flowing from a new community practice initiative with a known cost; and estimated how much health service cost would have been saved on the assumption that those improvements in community life led to a 5 per cent reduction in the specified health factors in that neighbourhood.[21] This relied on the fact that the health service has a tariff of average costs for treatment of all conditions. The total estimated saving represented a return of 1 : 3.8 for health alone on the community practice expenditure. Adding savings produced by reductions in crime and anti-social behaviour from the same community activities produced a higher return, and with economies from applying the method simultaneously in three nearby neighbourhoods, a return of 1 : 6.4 was estimated.

A rare study focusing on the financial value of community development was carried out by the New Economics Foundation (NEF) in 2010.[22] The 'Social Return on Investment' analysis attributed monetary value to resilience, self-esteem, positive functioning, supportive relationships, trust and belonging, but not in terms of specific savings to service budgets.

The NEF report found a return to the value of £3.45m over eight years from an investment in community development of £233,655 by local authorities in four areas. From the LA point of view this was a return of almost 15:1. Interestingly a much earlier CDF report[23] had also found a value of 15:1 in a town-wide project on the basis of the amount of volunteering generated by the input of paid community workers.

Notes

[1] As in Skinner (1997).

[2] Friedman (1995), pp 4–5.

[3] Ibid.

[4] Chamberlain, Golden and Walker (2010).

[5] DETR (1997).

[6] DETR (1998a).

[7] Gilchrist (2009), p 123.

[8] www.fcdl.org.uk/nos

[9] www.scdc.org.uk/what/national-standards

[10] Barr and Hashagen (2000).

[11] Changes UK (2006).

[12] For a critique and alternative outcome-oriented framework see Practical Standards for Community Development, www.pacesempowerment.co.uk

[13] Home Office (2004), Appendix.

[14] For example Dickinson and Prabhakar (2009).

[15] NEP (2009).

[16] www.ncsesurvey.com

[17] Cabinet Office (2010).

[18] See for example Richardson (2009).

[19] Health Empowerment Leverage Project (2012).

[20] Fisher (2011).

[21] Griffiths (2012).

[22] New Economics Foundation (2010).

[23] Bell (1992).

Conclusion – strategy for community practice

We have sought to show, in the preceding chapters, both the necessity and the potential for a coordinated approach to community practice at neighbourhood level. In this final chapter, we review key points and draw together a framework of the main conditions and factors that would make this possible. We first review the various levels of policy which go to make up the environment for community practice. Reaffirming the centrality of partnerships at neighbourhood level, we then assemble principles for action, including some changes in approach that would be needed if new strategy was to be led by community development. We conclude with 12 pillars of strategy that need to be in place for community practice to achieve decisive and measurable improvements in neighbourhood conditions and people's lives.

The policy chain

We have suggested throughout that the potential for neighbourhoods to improve their conditions is reliant on policy frameworks at local, regional and national level. These policies can be liberating or inhibiting. But the ultimate determining factor is what is done in the neighbourhood itself, by the residents and local public service workers together. This is not something that can be done by residents in isolation. Erosion of mainstream public services would make it increasingly difficult for neighbourhoods to function, let alone transform themselves.

Before drawing together the neighbourhood components, it is useful to look briefly at the other interlocking levels of policy that need to be activated if the most favourable conditions for neighbourhoods are to be provided. The six most fundamental are shown in Figure 9.1.

Neighbourhoods do not contain or determine the whole participative life of citizenship but only the very local part. Issues that are decided at large local, regional, national, continental or global levels demand participation at those levels (though these may also need local vehicles, for example local branches of national political parties or international environmental campaigns). Of these other levels the most important is the national, as this also determines the scope of the local arena below it and the international arena above it. There would be no international without national entities to create it, and there would be no local autonomy without national policy to protect it.

To be a fully participating citizen, you need to exercise multi-level citizenship – contributing to national issues by participating in national vehicles, local issues

Figure 9.1: The policy chain

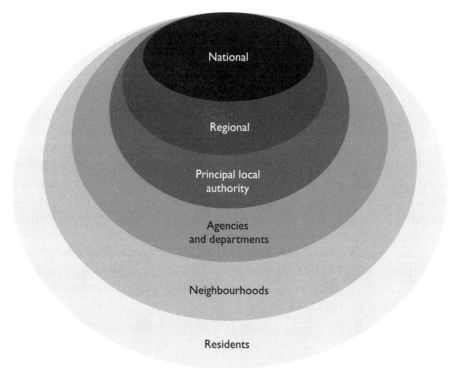

by activity at local level. The slogan 'think global, act local' should be triangulated into 'think global, act local, influence national'. At the same time, communities of interest may interweave with any of these levels. The same could be said of the international element. It does not sit above the national as a controlling structure but impacts at all levels through global trade and communications, the turbulence of the global economy, environmental issues, cooperation and conflict.

Ideally there would be a consistent link between policies affecting local community practice throughout this chain. It is vital that 'higher' spheres act in ways which liberate and resource the 'lower' spheres to act effectively. However in reality there is often a poor fit between the levels. There are optimum policies and practices to be sought at each level, and some of the key ones are sketched in below. But none of this determines exactly how local action should be played out. At the end of the day, neighbourhood strategy is a matter of synthesising inputs from all levels into a unique action plan.[1] The following paragraphs comment on the role of the different levels.

National level/central government

The key roles of national government regarding strengthening communities are: (i) to recognise that this is a vital national issue which needs strategic support but cannot be closely directed from national level; and (ii) to ensure that there are effective resources and frameworks available through the policy delivery chain, and in particular through policy making and resourcing in local authorities, local health agencies, police and other bodies.

This role includes providing, in collaboration with the partners at other levels, frameworks and resources for regeneration of disadvantaged localities and enhancement of average ones. This should include outcome measures in which the strengthening of local community life has a central place, treated with the same objectivity as health, education, employment, safety and the other fundamental social issues.

In present conditions, as the historical review undertaken in this book has shown, national policies affecting community practice are in a state of disarray in England. They are a patchwork of legacy from the New Labour period, which itself built to some extent on preceding governments; a 'big society' policy which is piecemeal and lacking in strategy; community engagement policies at different levels of development in different departmental silos such as police, housing and planning; varied levels of commitment to community involvement by different local authorities and even by different departments in the same local authority; a community development profession that has been depleted; a wide scattering of other community practitioners who are uncoordinated; and the variable histories of different neighbourhoods.

This is by no means a hopeless base to build upon but it offers few firm landmarks. There are many components and assets that could be marshalled at local level by a shrewd and visionary plan, and it is probably by devising such plans that community practice will progress in these conditions. Scotland, Wales and Northern Ireland provide illuminating alternatives. Every avenue should be pursued to develop effective national plans for the future. Government and other interests should consider how a national focal point for advancing community practice in England could be established.

Regional level

The term 'regional' in the UK has had shifting meanings. Across the UK, especially after the devolution of domestic governance, Scotland, Wales, Northern Ireland and England are referred to as four nations but they are also, at least in a geographical sense, regions of the British Isles. The European Union developed a system of regions of approximately equal population size across the member states in order to distribute assistance to the most disadvantaged regions through its structural funds. In this mapping England was divided into nine regions, which the governments of the 1980s and 1990s regarded as equally convenient for a number of other purposes.

English regions have distinct histories, cultures and identities, illustrated for example in enduring different accents, and marked economic differences. Experimentation under successive governments appears to show little popular appetite for developing a distinct layer of regional governance. However, a widening economic gap between south and north in the climate of austerity, and examples of independent social policies in Scotland, Wales and Northern Ireland may in time change that.

The English regional level remains vitally important, in any event, for community practice. This could hardly be otherwise, given the different economic histories, character and conditions of the regions. The existence or absence of a policy structure at this level (about 5m people – similar to the population of Scotland) can be an important factor in determining whether community practice will flourish. Between 2007–10 a network of English 'Regional Empowerment Partnerships', sponsored by the Department for Communities and Local Government (CLG), began to show that this level of networking could make a difference to the spread of community involvement innovation, skills and methods. This was swept away in 2010. A future national strategy should look afresh at this level.

Local authority level and local agencies and departments

Despite cuts, many local agencies have retained or even strengthened the community engagement ethos which they had begun to develop – mostly with all-party support – over the past generation. However, practice is inevitably patchy, and there is often little coordination across neighbourhoods. A system of neighbourhood partnerships is needed to pull the different contributions together and drive a strategy forward.

The principal local authority (LA) level remains critical for neighbourhood action even though, at populations up to 250,000 or more, LA decision-making is a long way from the neighbourhood. This gulf was partly bridged by the Local Strategic Partnership (LSP) system introduced by New Labour and now voluntarily maintained to varying degrees by different LAs. There are usually also a spread of thematic sub-partnerships on crime, health, education and so on, and these considerably widen the channels of participation. However, there are simply too many neighbourhoods – perhaps 50 or more in a principal LA – for them all to be influential on the LSP or have their very local issues considered in detail.

It is clear, however, that if significant numbers of residents are to feel involved in decision making, involvement has to be mainly at neighbourhood level. But what can make such involvement meaningful if all the major decisions are taken at a higher geographical level? This is the classic dilemma of participation. There need to be policies at the higher levels which ensure increased scope for very local decision making. What this 'proactive subsidiarity' might mean in practice is not only encouraging citizen participation but linking it with providing greater scope for frontline workers of public agencies to join with residents actively in flexible local problem solving and feeding back recommendations on service change to their employing agencies.

The mutual adjustment between communities and agencies is therefore not a shift of power from agencies to communities, as it has sometimes been described.

It is rather a gain in power for both systems: the community gains greater power over its conditions and the way the public agencies serve it; the public agencies gain power to achieve more effective outcomes. This requires some change of mindset on both sides. Communities need to understand and be able to engage with the organisational formality of public agencies, and agencies in turn need to loosen the formalities and make space for more flexible problem solving.

Equally this broadening of horizons at the front line needs to feed back into the agencies to help them as learning organisations, using the kinds of approach described, for example, by Peter Senge:[2]

> *Systems thinking*: analysing and managing organisational dynamics in holistic and systematic terms. Seeing the interrelationships and patterns of change rather than snapshots

> *Building shared vision:* powerful learning occurs when people are highly committed to accomplishing things that matter deeply to them in concert with their peers

> *Team learning:* encouraging collaboration and energy flow between people and ideas; teams can be synergistic – ideas spark off ideas

> *Building personal mastery:* individual learning does not guarantee organisational learning but without it no organisational learning can take place. Learning organisations provide their members with continuing opportunities for personal and professional development

> *Mental models:* the influence of taken for granted ways of seeing things and patterns of thought are recognised and are exposed to critical examination.

Neighbourhoods at the centre

Neighbourhoods are the centre of the action, not because they contain self-sufficient communities but because:

- they are the spatial level at which people share amenities, landmarks, some friendships, institutions such as schools, pubs, places of worship, meeting places, and therefore are natural bases for collective action;
- most people have some attachment to and identification with their neighbourhood;[3]
- people are more dependent on their neighbourhood if they have children, are old, are ill, are immobile or out of a job;
- most community groups are based in a neighbourhood even if their network is wider or narrower than the neighbourhood;

- effective action needs a clear territorial and population base, otherwise there is no hope of measuring progress.

By neighbourhood, in this book we mean an area of usually between about 5,000 and 15,000 people. It could be a small rural area, a cluster of villages or any other reasonably distinct grouping of population. It could be much smaller or somewhat larger. It may have a natural and obvious boundary such as a village or estate, or it may sit tightly alongside other neighbourhoods, as in many cities. In those situations the boundaries may not be obvious or natural, and it may be necessary, for purposes of planning and measurement, to specify boundaries using wards, super output areas or some other way of mapping. Action to strengthen community life in a neighbourhood should not exclude people from nearby areas who are drawn in, but measurement of effects should use the specified boundary and population for statistical consistency. Equally, harmony and collaboration with other nearby neighbourhoods is an important goal, and some issues need to be addressed outside the neighbourhood framework, at a larger geographical level or through a section of the population which does not necessarily align with neighbourhoods.

The focus on geographical neighbourhoods includes concern with communities of interest, identity and culture. These may be within the neighbourhood in question or may link with other neighbourhoods or with regional, national or international networks. At some point they intersect with neighbourhoods. Our aim is to be comprehensive on a population basis and therefore to be concerned with all types of community grouping, however large or small, inclusive or selective, that manifest within the population of a specific geographical area.

Neighbourhood partnerships

The best hope of making a significant difference to the wellbeing of a local population is to mobilise the fragments of latent and quasi community practice within the area around a small specialist team which can coordinate and strengthen this aspect of their varied roles. This amounts to some form of neighbourhood partnership. To work well, such a partnership must also mobilise and embody strong leadership from residents.

At neighbourhood level the daily interaction of people, the building of social capital, the face-to-face influence, in short people's influence on each other, is a real operative factor in safety, education, health and all other issues. This is the level at which community action can best make a difference to conditions without major new financial investment, through better coproduction between community organisations and public agencies across the board. Fostering a dynamic community partnership dedicated to local improvement is a highly economical way to enable interaction between public services and the local population.

The local strategy needs to link up all the different forms of community practice input that can be mobilised for that neighbourhood, make them aware of each other, form them into a sustained network and elicit an effective division of labour, mutual support, cross-referral and greater collective effectiveness.

This also means that each parent agency of the community practitioners needs to appreciate and buy in to the fact that by allowing their staff to play an active part in this cross-sector community of practice they, as a specialist agency, stand to gain enormously from the reciprocal value of community practice by other agencies.

Principles for strategy

The process of drawing up a strategy for neighbourhood action could start with these principles:

- The aim is to strengthen community activity, benefits and capabilities throughout the whole population of a given neighbourhood, and in cooperation with other neighbourhoods.
- The strategy should be vested in a neighbourhood partnership owned jointly by residents and service providers.
- The strategy should be outcome based, and the outcomes should be rooted in baselines and monitored by milestones.
- The strategy should address the neighbourhood as a whole, and its entire population and community sector, but linking with larger local, regional and national frameworks, not as a self-contained system.
- There is a need for leadership and expertise. This may come from experienced community development workers/teams/units if they exist in the locality and are in tune with this approach. Otherwise it must be found elsewhere. Traditional community development methods and style may need to be adapted and reinterpreted for the new situation.

The bulk of resources will need to be found largely through redirecting a margin of the time of existing and potential community practitioners across the public services and voluntary sector; plus private sector input if possible and appropriate. A relatively small amount of new funding may be needed to employ a coordinator, provide training and other central functions. Cost should be offset against projected and monitored savings from greater coproduction between services and the community.

All areas may contain a good deal of latent or potential community practice. Several front-line occupations contain, explicitly or implicitly, actual or potential elements of community practice within their remit. Examples may include youth workers, health visitors, health trainers, regeneration workers, tenant participation officers, police officers, police community support officers, teachers, voluntary sector workers as well as community development workers by name. The community practice element in these roles, such as supporting independent community groups, organisations and networks, could be boosted at little or no cost.

There may be useful links to be made with initiatives taking place under the big society heading, but it is not advisable to use big society as the platform, because it embodies the idea that community organisations should try to take over public services rather than coproduce with them.

From community development to community practice

Policy to strengthen community life in England reached a high point under New Labour and has fallen back since. But a result of different forms of support over the past 20 years is that there is potential for development of new local strategies based on linking practice from a variety of sources around the best community practice experience.

We have followed Banks, Henderson, Butcher and their colleagues[4] in using the term community practice for the whole spectrum of support to community life that has emerged over the last generation.

It would be possible to describe the present landscape of community support in a number of other ways. You could say that community development had become wider and more varied but under other names; or on the other hand that 'true' community development, as a practice radically critical of the role of the state, had retreated whilst weaker substitutes advanced.

We think the most realistic formulation is to say that community development first grew and has now somewhat declined in numbers, while community practice has considerably expanded. This is an opportunity as well as a dilemma. Community development tended to focus on the lone intrepid practitioner working intensively with two or three groups. The new community practice needs to be carried out by a linked network of practitioners helping all groups in the area which want such help, with a lighter touch but a more comprehensive strategy.

Some of these quasi-community practitioners may lack strong techniques and focus. The important thing is to organise the wide network of practice and bring it closer to the sustained approach of community development but with certain new emphases such as better evidence and wider links with public services. This should partly be driven by the way community practice is commissioned and partly by continuing development of its own professional ethos.

Community development leadership and change

Insofar as it takes it bearings from a long tradition of community development, community practice stands to inherit a wealth of experience and value, especially a range of techniques and insights on how to involve residents, strengthen community groups, influence authorities and work collaboratively with them to improve conditions for the whole neighbourhood. The main differences between community development and community practice are not just theoretical but also contingent: moving from small numbers of full-time dedicated community development workers who often feel isolated and marginalised, to small fractions of the time of people employed in a much larger number of occupations, who are carrying out aspects of community practice more loosely, often without clear criteria or support.

There is a rich community development literature to draw on, which has strengths and weaknesses. It provides numerous techniques and operating frameworks. But sometimes it tends to reinforce the isolation and adversarialism of community practice by assuming that the practitioner is operating as an individual plunged into an unknown situation to improvise action virtually without management or context. On the other hand, some local authorities have produced wide-ranging and sophisticated community development strategies.

With these cautions, it might be asked whether community practice should necessarily take its bearings from the community development tradition or should perhaps regard itself as a wholly new movement. Our view is that despite its weaknesses, the community development tradition contains a profound occupational identity and values basis for a field that is extremely complex. Without establishing itself in relation to the community development platform, new community practice might have little chance of establishing an identity. The solution therefore, in our view, is an alliance of community development and other forms of community practice under an agenda of rethinking and reform.

We are conscious of a danger of creating a caricature of 'traditional' community development. In reality there are many variants. But at the risk of oversimplification we need to pinpoint some shifts that would need to be made from prevalent community development methods in order to lead a wider community practice network (Table 9.1). These are not diametrical opposites but changes of emphasis.

How much planning?

No neighbourhood intervention can follow a wholly prescribed plan. Sometimes the realities, both opportunities and blockages, are very different from the starting assumptions. But this does not mean there should not be a plan. Numerous projects pursue 'change' without saying from what to what, and at the end of the day do not know whether they have changed anything or not. They may have been running to stand still. They may even have gone backwards. *Plus ça change.*

Evidence of results is patchy because it is often not clear what is to count as a strengthened community. While we, like others, use community as shorthand for a complex phenomenon, we have made clear our view that any viable strategy which is to include measurement of progress needs to be based on a systematic mapping of all the key factors, both within the community and in its material conditions.

Baselines, intervention and evidence of improvement need to be conceived together. Baselines of social conditions indicate which neighbourhoods need most help. The same factors must be used to assess improvement. A 'deficit' mentality should be avoided by appreciating and building on the human and material assets of the neighbourhood, whatever its problems.

Table 9.1: Six points of divergence in community development models

Traditional community development (CD)	New community practice (CP)
1. Main focus on support to individual community groups, with emphasis on exclusive resident control	Support to all existing and potential community groups , overseen by a partnership jointly led by residents and service providers. Main focus is on the shaping up of the community sector as a whole, including the networks between groups
2. Issues only taken up if raised by residents	Potential for take-up of all social issues anticipated by involving wide range of service providers proactively to listen to the community's priorities and link with them
3. Building residents' skills and confidence	Building skills and confidence both of residents and frontline workers
4. Viewpoint of public services and community seen as liable to be in conflict	Viewpoint of public services and community seen as potentially convergent through joint learning and development whilst recognising different starting points and experiences
5. Indefinite timescale. CD seen as bound to take many years	Clear timescales for stages of intervention, e.g. two years to establish a neighbourhood partnership, opening the way to long-term self-renewing development
6. Qualitative self-evaluation by participants, with emphasis on process	Evaluation of impact on all stakeholders including non-participants, with emphasis on outputs and outcomes, and linking them to respective agency objectives

Complexity theory critiques the 'command and control' model of social organisation which it attributes to state agencies. Community practice needs a local strategy. A strategy is a plan. It is therefore an attempt to exert some degree of 'command and control'. But the complexity approach tacitly assumes a degree of order and a stable policy environment to allow things to 'emerge'. The question is what *balance* of order and flexibility to aim for, in order to get the necessary mix of planning and participation. We know from countless examples and from the nature of local life what range of issues will come up from the community. The emphasis in traditional community development on privileging 'the issues that the community choose' is to some extent a product of focusing on the single isolated community development practitioner. One practitioner with one or two groups may be faced with hard choices and have to prioritise a limited number of issues. A network of 10, 15, 20 or more practitioners from different occupations working across all groups in a neighbourhood will come up with the full range of predictable issues as well as perhaps some additional surprises.

If, however, a profiling of all the groups in the neighbourhood shows that there are not many, or perhaps none, dealing with health or housing or one of the other major issues, this is an objective gap which needs to be filled. Practitioners should try to stimulate the formation of such a group. The community has not yet addressed something which is undoubtedly of importance to it. But it might have tried and not been able to, or been blocked. To take a holistic approach is to try to energise all the operating factors, both top down and bottom up, both command and control and participative and emergent.

Twelve pillars of strategy

To encapsulate our main recommendations, the 12 factors shown in Table 9.2 need to form the pillars for neighbourhood strategy. These are discussed briefly below. Because of all the surrounding complexities, this relatively simple central architecture for neighbourhood improvement has often been lacking. Asserting it now as a *framework* does not mean abandoning the essential flexibility of *method*

Table 9.2: Key factors in community practice strategy

Factor	Desired outcome	Action
1. Policy context	Supportive policies and provision from national, regional and local authority levels	Locate relevant existing policies and use to the full; advocate improved policies
2. Community sector profile	Wide variety of community groups taking up the whole range of social issues, to the ultimate benefit of all residents	The central function of community practice – find existing, incipient and struggling groups; match practitioners' help to groups; negotiate better help from local voluntary organisations
3. Neighbourhood partnership	A solid partnership with credibility across all residents and public services	Lead a dynamic strategy for improvement affecting all sections of the neighbourhood population, including communities of interest and identity
4. Community practice leadership	New type of leadership based on the factors listed here	Recruit leader team; train/retrain as necessary; draw on the community development tradition but critically re-evaluating its strengths and weaknesses
5. Network of community practitioners	Active coordinated network	Mobilise wide range of front line workers to share in the community practice scheme
6. Agencies' and departments' community engagement strategies	All social agencies and departments supportive of community practice and providing the conditions for their front-line staff to incorporate it in their roles and collaborate through neighbourhood partnerships	Negotiate with agencies and departments as necessary

(continued)

Table 9.2: Key factors in community practice strategy (continued)

Factor	Desired outcome	Action
7. Spaces for community meetings and activities	Sufficient community buildings/ spaces for community meetings and activities and to help groups grow	Survey existing spaces and seek improvements
8. Income for community groups	Sufficient income for groups to function and grow, through a combination of grants, contracts, trading and donations	Survey existing income levels across the sector locally and seek improvements; support trading activity and community enterprises where appropriate
9. Personal networks of residents	Connectivity between residents; abundant social capital	Basic personal interaction with residents by the network of practitioners, including emphasis on reaching marginalised people
10. Community groups and networks	Strong and abundant sector of community groups. Mutual support and where appropriate strong collective voice vis a vis local policy and decision-making	All members of the network of community practitioners support at least one embryonic and one mature community group; some also support network building
11. Resources for the new community engagement strategy	Sufficient resources to carry out this strategy	Negotiation with major local agencies; drawing on national schemes; micro 'Total Place'-type analysis leading to redirection of investment into community practice
12. Relationship to mainstream issues: health and wellbeing; safety; education; employment and income; housing and environment; culture, leisure and other issues	Improvements attributed by the relevant professionals to community practice	Actions linking with the agendas of each of the relevant agencies.

or the need to be alert to *unintended outcomes* both good and bad. Undoubtedly there are even more aspects than those we list but for manageability we would see these as the most crucial.

First there must be a *clear territorial and population basis*. If this means having somewhat arbitrary boundaries such as those of a ward, estate or designated output area in order to make it easier to use existing statistics, so be it. This need not compromise the flexibility of practice: people from nearby do not have to be excluded in order to achieve a result for the specified population. It may mean that measurement is based on something less or more than 100 per cent of the core population, but the variation is unlikely to be great. It may be sensible to accept a degree of imprecision for the convenience of access to a range of existing statistical information.

Secondly, attention must be given to the *policy context* cascading from higher geographical levels (point 1 in Table 9.2). Are there propitious national and regional policies? Can anything be done to influence them? Are there European policies and programmes which can be accessed for help? Are there apparently helpful policies which should be treated with caution, as we have suggested about 'big society'? A powerful national policy promoting the strengthening of communities would be an immense boon, but the practical effects must be looked at critically. Even more vital are positive policies at local authority level. It is at local authority level that priority neighbourhoods must be chosen, and that negotiations with public service bodies must be carried out to create the space, conditions and resources for dynamic neighbourhood action.

Engagement with the prioritised neighbourhoods must begin with establishing a *profile of the existing community sector* (point 2 in Table 9.2). Again, this is remarkably neglected in many community projects. Existing groups, however small, are the product of people who have cared enough about some aspect or activity in their neighbourhood to dedicate personal effort to it. They should not be fobbed off as 'the usual suspects'. They are sources of crucial experience and should be given every opportunity to play a part in further development. They should not however be automatically given power to decide the scope of such development. Newly active residents must also have space to develop new activities. Local professionally run voluntary organisations also need to be mapped. While they may be primarily service providers rather than part of the community that is being strengthened, they may play a key role in the strategy that is to be developed. Local voluntary and community sector umbrella groups will be particularly relevant and might be able to play a key part.

Mapping the community sector is also needed as a baseline. It would be impossible to map all networks – many are too fluid and informal – but any group that has a name and a contact address should be included. It is important to know firstly how many groups there are and secondly what they do, who is involved in them, how well they feel they are achieving their aims, and whether they have a productive relationship, or any relationship at all, with the local public sector bodies (as discussed in Chapter Eight). It is change in this sector profile above all which will tell us later whether the community is getting stronger as a result of our intervention.

Neighbourhood partnership – an effective and accountable vehicle is needed to carry out the strategy (point 3). Since this must mobilise both a wide variety of community groups and input from all the public services, this would need to be some form of neighbourhood partnership. Many neighbourhoods already have some collective body either deriving from a previous regeneration scheme, a public service initiative, a community development project, a parish council or a voluntary and community sector umbrella group. All these will have done sterling work but may or may not have credibility with the residents and be capable of taking a dynamic lead in current conditions. One or several stakeholders, either from the service side or residents' side, may need to raise the question of whether to build on an existing body or start a new one. Any new grouping should be sure to involve pre-existing ones and respect and build on their track record. If a wholly new body is needed, there should be a clear development process with rapid reinforcement at each stage, as for example in the 'C2' model described in Chapter Six.

The *community practice initiative needs to be led* (point 4) by a co-ordinator who is not tied to a particular local interest, and/or by a small team. We have discussed the value that the community development tradition can bring to such leadership in terms of understanding how to nurture community groups, whilst stressing that what is required is a new breadth and a new openness to collaboration across public services. Who is fit for the task must be decided locally without preconceptions – talent may arise from unexpected quarters.

A major part of the leadership job is to locate and mobilise a *network of community practitioners* (point 5) across the neighbourhood. Some of these individuals will be easily identifiable by job titles but others may not, and may not think of themselves in these terms. There may be an existing network to build on – no existing network should be bypassed. The new or enhanced network may not be a finite number of members, and it may grow as word gets round and more workers become interested and realise this is an important aspect of their job. For some it will be central, for others marginal. For most there will be a particular angle linked to their other responsibilities – a concern with housing, health, welfare, young people, elderly or some other specialist focus. However much or little each member can contribute, these are the people who between them will help the community to transform itself. Organising this network, working out how to enhance members' community practice function, boosting their community practice skills, matching them up with groups which need help, facilitating cross referrals, monitoring their progress and creating a sense of combined achievement is a central part of the work of the intervention.

To obtain this wide cooperation it will be necessary to draw on, and perhaps to influence, the *community engagement strategies of the agencies and departments* to which these workers belong (point 6). Some of the agencies will have active strategies and immediately see the benefit of giving their workers the time to participate in the community practice network. Others may only have token policies and will need to be convinced that putting real energy behind them will be to the advantage of their agency. There may be partnerships at a higher geographical level, such as a local strategic partnership or a health and wellbeing board, where many agencies can be negotiated with together. A key point to get across is that however much cooperation is agreed at a high board level, it is practical cooperation in problem-solving at neighbourhood level that makes the difference, and workers need to be given the time and space to do this.

Once the initiative is under way, attention will inevitably need to be given to the conditions which enable people to participate more actively in community life, groups and networks, as discussed in Chapters Four and Five. One of the most fundamental is *space for community activities and meetings* (point 7). A serious strategy to strengthen communities will not leave this to chance. Many local authorities in the past have maintained a range of community centres and buildings to serve this purpose. Others have been more haphazard. When communities begin to organise themselves, getting space for activity, if not already available, is often a prime focus. In recent years some centres have closed for lack of local authority support. In other cases centres have been sold off to community groups, but not always with assurances of long-term viability or diverse access. Elsewhere regeneration schemes have provided new spaces, but others have withdrawn community facilities without replacing them. Some public sector institutions – schools, sports centres, fire stations – have found ways to make space cheaply available to community groups; others are more rigid. The landscape needs to be reviewed closely in the neighbourhood in question, and it is likely that improving access to usable space will form a key part of the development agenda in any area.

Equally fundamental will be ensuring adequate *income for community groups* (point 8). There is little doubt that income both for professionally run charities and community groups has declined since 2010, despite the intentions behind the big society concept. Our main concern is with community groups rather than professionally run charities but the dividing line is not always absolute. Small community groups do not necessarily need much money – their main input is their own activity – but they do need some, and if they are to grow they may need to fund, for example, a coordinator or secretary, use of premises and other basic costs. Larger groups, such as community associations, sports clubs and social clubs, like professionally run charities, will need proportionally more funds. Income will typically be assembled from a mixture of membership subscriptions, local fund-raising activities, grants, contracts and donations. All these are under greater pressure when the economy is in turmoil, but in disadvantaged areas they are not easy to come by at the best of times. The new community practice strategy will need to include, perhaps by means of a dedicated subgroup of the practitioner network, an incisive re-examination of the economic situation of the local community sector and what can be done to improve it. It is important that it be mapped separately from the professionally led voluntary sector – averaging income across the combined sector often masks a dearth of funding for community groups.

The detailed work with residents to be carried out by the practitioner network will focus centrally on bringing people together in *groups and networks* (points 9 and 10). The way that this can happen in a particular neighbourhood is unpredictable – there are an infinity of possible pathways – but the underlying patterns are similar. Depending on existing levels of activity, for some people it will be a matter of cooperating with their neighbours for the first time. For others it will involve expanding existing contacts or building on a long history of effort and achievement. Groups may need help individually, but once they are reasonably well established they can be further strengthened by taking part in sector networks to exchange information and help and, at times, to campaign jointly on a local issue.

All this requires some level of *financial resources* (point 11). We have made the case throughout this book that the major party of the necessary resource lies in existing aspects of the work of a wide range of local workers. But this would not cover the central cost of coordinating such an initiative. Providing resources for, and oversight of, community practice could suitably be shared, in their own interests, by local authorities, health authorities, social services, police, education and other agencies.

Restoring vision

The whole history of government policies on community involvement, reviewed in Chapter Two and referred to throughout this book, shows that local involvement is essential to the successful running of a modern state. Governments of all complexions have repeatedly felt it necessary to come back to community involvement in one way or another yet have rarely approached it in a universalistic, strategic way. It is often left to local government to make sense of a cocktail of initiatives and directives about community involvement from central government, arriving through different departments and schemes – and unceremoniously departing again with a tweak of policy.

Some local authorities and their partners have shown how it is possible to form coherent local community involvement strategies, and have in turn had significant influence on national policies. In the present climate, austerity has sharply narrowed these horizons and some policy makers have abandoned long-term vision. It urgently needs to be opened up again. In the long run, and even in the short term, stronger communities make for greater economy. But they do need some initial investment. Most useful in localities at the present time may be some form of Total Place calculation to map all the public funding going into an area and showing how a larger allocation to strengthening community life could yield cost-beneficial savings in other services, for example by improving health and education and reducing crime. Ultimately this needs to be demonstrated, as discussed in Chapter Eight, by bringing together in an evidence triangle: (i) the statistics regularly collected by the major services; (ii) evidence of growth in community activity and influence; and (iii) testimony of service managers and front-line workers that the growth in community activity and influence has been a key factor in improvements in each of the *social issues and services* (point 12).

As we said in Chapter One, what we mean by transformative neighbourhoods is not places which completely change their character, but neighbourhoods which make it easier for people to transform the conditions of their lives: to build wider friendship networks; to create new activities and facilities around them; to connect better with areas of economic opportunity; to overcome poverty and disadvantage; to create a more ecologically sustainable lifestyle; and to exercise a more meaningful local democracy. It is an ambitious prospect with many obstacles to overcome, but all the experience reviewed in this book shows that it can be achieved to one degree or another. The great challenge is to pull the best experience, methods and policies together to enable it to happen more often, in more places, so that it becomes a direction of travel for the whole society.

Notes

[1] Pratt et al (1999).

[2] Senge (1990).

[3] CLG (2011c).

[4] Banks et al (2003); Butcher et al (2007).

References

Abbott, J. (1996) *Sharing the city: Community participation in urban management*, London: Earthscan.

Allinson, C. (1978) *Young volunteers?*, London: Community Projects Foundation.

Amion Consulting (2010) *Evaluation of the National Strategy for Neighbourhood Renewal, Final Report*, London: Department for Communities and Local Government.

Animation and Research (1994) *Poverty 3, Developments and achievements, Central Unit Report, Fourth period*, Lille: EEIG Animation and Research, pp 160–1.

Arnstein, S. (1969) 'A ladder of citizen participation in the USA', *Journal of the American Institute of Planners*, vol 35, no 4, pp 216–24.

Atkinson, D. (2004) *Civil renewal: Mending the hole in the social ozone layer*, Studley, Warwickshire: Brewin Books.

Attwood, M. et al (2003) *Leading change: A guide to whole systems working*, Bristol: The Policy Press.

Audit Commission (1998) *A fruitful partnership: Effective partnership working*, London: Audit Commission.

Bailey, G. (2006) *Neighbourhood Support Fund evaluation*, London: Community Development Foundation.

Banks, S. et al (eds) (2003) *Managing community practice*, Bristol: The Policy Press.

Barr, A. and Hashagen, S. (2000) *ABCD Handbook*, London: Community Development Foundation.

Belfast City Council (2011) *Community development strategy*, Belfast: Belfast City Council, www.belfastcity.gov.uk/communitydevelopment.

Belbin, M. (2011) *A comprehensive review of Belbin team roles*, www.belbin.com

Bell, J. (1992) *Community development teamwork: measuring the impact*, London: Community Development Foundation.

Bichard, Sir Michael (2009) 'Local incentives and empowerment' in HM Treasury, *Operational efficiency programme, Final Report*, London: HM Treasury.

Boffey, D. (2012) 'Deprived areas hit hard by cuts in charity funds', London: *The Observer*, 4 March.

Bowen, M. and Keogh, H. (2011) *Key findings from Our Life's survey of community engagement practitioners*, Manchester: Our Life www.ourlife.org.uk (July).

Boyle, D. and Harris, M. (2009) *The challenge of co-production: How equal partnerships between professionals and the public are crucial to improving public services*, London: NESTA (National Endowment for Science, Technology and the Arts).

Butcher, H. et al (eds) (1993) *Community and public policy*, London: Pluto Press.

Butcher, H. et al (2007) *Critical community practice*, Bristol: The Policy Press.

Cabinet Office (2010) *Thriving third sector*, London: Office of the Third Sector and Sheffield: NAVCA.

Cameron, D. (2009) *The Big Society*, November 10, www.conservatives.com/News/Speeches/2009/11/David_Cameron_The_Big_Society.aspx

Campfens, H. (ed) (1997) *Community development around the world*, Toronto: University of Toronto Press.

CDF (1997a) *Regeneration and the community*, London: Community Development Foundation.

CDF (1997b) *Guidelines to the community involvement aspect of the SRB Challenge Fund*, London: Community Development Foundation.

Chamberlain, T. et al (2010) *Implementing outcomes based accountability in children's services: An overview of the process and impact*, Slough: NFER, www.nfer.ac.uk/nfer/publications.

Chanan, G. (1992) *Out of the shadows.* Dublin: European Foundation for the Improvement of Living and Working Conditions.

Chanan, G. (2003) *Searching for solid foundations*, London: ODPM (later CLG).

Chanan, G. (2004) *Measures of community*, London: Home Office and Community Development Foundation.

Chanan, G. and Miller, C. (2010) *Big Society and public services: Complementarity or erosion?* Available at www.pacesempowerment.co.uk.

Chanan, G. et al (2000) *The new community strategies: How to involve local people*, London: CDF.

Changes UK (2006) *Axis of influence*, www.changesuk.net

Christie, C. (Chair) (2011) *Report on the future delivery of public services,* www.scotland.gov.uk/Publications/2011/06/27154527

Clark, C. (2001) *A self assessment toolkit for partnerships,* Nottingham: Engage East Midlands.

CLG (Communities and Local Government) (2006) *Strong and prosperous communities*, Local Government White Paper, Cm 6939-1, London: CLG.

CLG (2008) *Communities in control*, White Paper, London: CLG.

CLG (2009) *Eco-towns, A supplement to Planning Policy Statement 1*, London: CLG.

CLG (2010) *Decentralisation and the Localism Bill: An essential guide* (December), www.communities.gov.uk/documents/localgovernment/pdf/1793908.pdf

CLG (2011a) *A plain English guide to the Localism Bill*, London: Department for Communities and Local Government;

CLG (2011b) *Community budgets prospectus*, London: CLG.

CLG (2011c) *Community spirit in England: A report on the 2009–10 citizenship survey*, London: CLG.

Community Development Challenge Group (2006) *The community development challenge*, London: CLG. Also available at www.pacesempowerment.co.uk

Community Development Foundation – see CDF.

Conn, E. (2011) *Community engagement in the social eco-system dance*, Birmingham: Third Sector Research Centre.

Connecting Communities (2012) C2, www.healthcomplexity.net

CPF (Community Projects Foundation) (1982) *Community development – towards a national perspective*, London: CPF (later CDF).

CPRE (Campaign for the Protection of Rural England) (2012) *How to shape where you live: A guide to neighbourhood planning*, London: CPRE in association with the National Association of Local Councils.

Crawley, J. and Watkin, R. (2011) *Crisis and contradiction: research into the current issues facing small voluntary and community organisations.*, South West Foundation (May) www.southwestfoundation.org.uk

Daft, R.L. (2007) *Understanding the theory and design of organizations*, London: Thomson Learning.

DETR (Department for Environment, Transport and the Regions) (1995, revised 1997) *Involving communities in urban and rural regeneration*, London: DETR (later CLG).

DETR (1997) *Effective partnerships: A handbook for members of SRB Challenge Fund Partnerships*, London: DETR.

DETR (1998a) *Modernising local government: Improving local services through Best Value*, London: DETR (later CLG).

DETR (1998b) *Single Regeneration Budget Bidding Guidance Round 5*, London: ODPM.

DETR (2000a) *Our towns and cities: The future*, Urban White Paper. London: DETR.

DETR (2000b) *Preparing community strategies: Government guidance to local authorities*, London: DETR.

Dickinson, S. and Prabhakar, M. (2009) *An analytical framework for community empowerment evaluations*, London: SQW Consulting and CLG.

Diers, J. (2004) *Neighbor power: Building community the Seattle way*, University of Washington Press.

DoE (Department of the Environment) (1995) *SRB Challenge Fund, Guidance Note 1*, London DoE (later CLG).

Duffy, B., Vince, J. and Page, L. (2008) *Searching for the impact of empowerment*, London: IpsosMORI.

Dwelly, T. (2005) *Delivering neighbourhood management: A practical guide*, National Neighbourhood Management Network, for the Neighbourhood Renewal Unit, Office of the Deputy Prime Minister.

Egan, J. (2004) *Skills for sustainable communities*, London: Office of the Deputy Prime Minister. Also available from the Royal Institute of British Architects.

European Funding Network (2012) *Unleashing the potential of civil society in the EU Programmes 2014–20*, London: National Council for Voluntary Organisations.

FCDL (Federation for Community Development Learning) / National Empowerment Partnership (2008) *Engaging and influencing decision-makers*, Sheffield: FCDL.

Fisher, B. (2011) *Community development in health: A literature review*, Health Empowerment Leverage Project, www.healthempowermentgroup.org.uk

Foot, J. and Hopkins, T. (2010) *A glass half full*, London: IDeA and LGA.

Francis, D. et al (1984) *A survey of community workers in the United Kingdom*, London: National Institute for Social Work.

Friedman, M. (1995) *From outcomes to budgets*, Washington: Centre for the Study of Social Policy, pp 4–5.

Gaffikin, F. and Morrissey, M. (2011) *Planning in divided cities: Collaborative shaping of contested space*, Chichester: Wiley-Blackwell.

Gawlinski, G. and Graessle, L. (1988). *Planning together: The art of effective teamwork*, London: Planning Together Associates.

Geyer, R. and Rihani, S. (2010) *Complexity and public policy*, Abingdon: Routledge.

Gilchrist, A. (1995). *Community development and networking*, London: Community Development Foundation.

Gilchrist, A. (2009) *The well-connected community: A networking approach to community development* (2nd edn), Bristol: The Policy Press.

Gilchrist, A. and Taylor, M. (2011) *The short guide to community development*, Bristol: The Policy Press.

Glen, A. et al (2004) *Survey of community development workers in the UK*, London: Community Development Foundation and Sheffield: Community Development Exchange.

Griffiths, S. (2012) 'Illustrative cost-benefit model', in Health Empowerment Leverage Project, *Empowering communities for health*, www.healthempowermentgroup.org.uk, Appendix B.

Groundwork (2009) *Groundwork Impact Report 2009*, Birmingham: Groundwork UK.

Handy, C. (1988) *Understanding voluntary organizations: How to make them function effectively*, Harmondsworth: Penguin.

Handy, C. (1993) *Understanding organizations*, Harmondsworth: Penguin.

Hayes, R. and Reason, J. (2009) *Voluntary but not amateur: A guide to the law for voluntary organisations and community groups*, London: Directory of Social Change.

Health Empowerment Leverage Project (2012) *Empowering communities for health*, www.healthempowermentgroup.org.uk

Heinberg, R. (2011) *The end of growth: Adapting to our new economic reality*, Forest Row: Clairview Books.

Henderson, P. and Thomas, D.N. (2012) *Skills in neighourhood work* (4th edn), London: Routledge.

HMG (Her Majesty's Government) (2011) *Open Public Services White Paper*, Cm 8145, www.cabinetoffice.gov.uk

HM Treasury (2009) *Putting the frontline first: Smarter government*, Cm 7753, London: HM Treasury.

Home Office (2004) *Firm foundations: The government's framework for community capacity building*, London: Home Office, Civil Renewal Unit.

Home Office (2008) *From the neighbourhood to the national: Policing our communities together*, Cm 7448, London: Home Office.

Home Office (2010) *Policing in the 21st century: Reconnecting police and the people*, Cm 7925 (July), London: Home Office.

Hudson, M. (2002) *Managing without profit: The art of managing third sector organizations*, London: Directory of Social Change.

Jeffrey, B. (1997), 'Dominant gatekeepers and unwanted voices amongst community participants in local government', *Scottish Journal of Community Work and Development*, vol 2.

Jones, R. and Gammel, E. (2009) *The art of consultation,* Biggleswade: Consultation Institute.

KPMG (1998) *Final evaluation of City Challenge: What works – emerging lessons for urban regeneration*, London: DETR (later CLG).

Ledwith, M. (2005) *Community development: A critical approach*, Bristol: The Policy Press.

Local Government Association (2010) *Place-based budgets: The future governance of local public services*, London: LGA.

MacFarlane, R. (1993) *Community involvement in City Challenge: A policy report*, London: National Council for Voluntary Organisations.

Marshall, T.F. et al (1997) *Local voluntary action surveys (LOVAS),* London: Home Office, Research and Statistics Directorate.

Miller, C. (2008) *Management: Towards high standards in community development*, London: Community Development Foundation.

Mintzberg, H. (1983) *Structure in fives: Designing effective organizations*, New Jersey: Prentice Hall.

Mitchell, J. et al (1979) *In and against the state* (expanded edn), London Edinburgh Weekend Return Group, London: Pluto Press.

Mouffe, C. (2005) *The democratic paradox*, London: Verso.

Mullins, L. J. (1989) *Management and organisational behaviour*, London: Pitman.

Murtagh, B. (2010) *Urban regeneration and community development*, Belfast: Northern Ireland Department for Social Development.

Neighbourhood Renewal Unit (2001a) *Community Empowerment Fund, Preliminary Guidance*, London: DTLR (later CLG).

Neighbourhood Renewal Unit (2001b) *Neighbourhood Renewal Community Chests*, London: DTLR (later CLG).

NEP (National Empowerment Partnership) (2009) *National empowerment partnership resources catalogue*, London: Community Development Foundation.

NESTA (2012) *People powered health co-production catalogue*. London: NESTA and New Economics Foundation, www.nesta.org.uk.

New Economics Foundation (2010) *Catalysts for community action and involvement*, London: Community Development Foundation.

NHS Commissioning Board (2012) *Clinical commissioning group authorisation: Draft guide for applicants*, April, Domain 2.

Northern Ireland – community development: www.communityplaces.info.

Northern Ireland Health and Social Care Board and Public Health Agency (2011) *Community development strategy for health and wellbeing*, Belfast: NIHSC/PHA.

ODPM (Office of the Deputy Prime Minister) (2005a) *Getting closer to communities*, Beacon Scheme, London: ODPM (later CLG)/IdEA.

ODPM (2005b) *The Safer and Stronger Communities Fund: The Neighbourhood Element. Implementation Guidance*, London: ODPM.

Office for Civil Society (2010a) *Building a stronger civil society: A strategy for voluntary and community groups, charities and social enterprises*, London: Cabinet Office, OCS.

Office for Civil Society (2010b) *Supporting a stronger civil society*, Consultation paper. London: Cabinet Office, OCS.

Pitchford, M., Archer, T. and Ramsden, S. (2009) *The duty to involve: Making it work*, London: Community Development Foundation.

Pratt, J., Gordon, P. and Plamping, D. (1999) *Working whole systems: Putting theory into practice in organisations*, London: Kings Fund.

Prendergast, J. (2008) *Disconnected citizens: Is community empowerment the solution?*, London: Social Market Foundation.

Putnam, R. (2000) *Bowling alone: The collapse and revival of american community*, New York: Simon and Schuster.

Rhodes, J., Tyler, P. and Brennan, A. (2007) *The Single Regeneration Budget, Final Evaluation*, Cambridge: University of Cambridge, Department of Land Economy.

Richardson, L. (2009) *Developing community empowerment measurement and monitoring*, Manchester: North West Together We Can Network.

Richardson, L. (2012) *Working in neighbourhoods, Active citizenship and localism: Lessons for policymakers and practitioners*, York: Joseph Rowntree Foundation.

Robson, B. et al (1994) *Assessing the impact of urban policy*, London: HMSO.

Rogers of Riverside, Lord (Chair) (1999) *Towards an Urban Renaissance, Report of the Urban Task Force* (Executive Summary), London: DETR (now ODPM).

Rowson, J. et al (2010) *Connected communities: How social networks power and sustain the Big Society*, London: Royal Society of Arts.

Sanderson, I. (2006) *Worklessness in deprived neighbourhoods: A review of evidence*, London: Department for Communities and Local Government.

Savage, V. et al (2009) *Public services and civil society working together*, London: Young Foundation.

Scotland – community development: www.scdc.org.uk and www. communitydevelopmentalliancescotland.org.

Scott, M. (2009) *Unseen, unequal, untapped, unleashed: The potential for community action at the grassroots*, London: Community Sector Coalition.

Sender, H. et al (2010) *Report on survey of community development practitioners and managers*, London: CDF.

Senge, P. (1990) *The fifth discipline: The art and practice of the learning organisation*, USA: Random House.

Skinner, S. (1997) *Building community strengths*, London: Community Development Foundation.

Social Exclusion Unit (2001) *A new commitment to Neighbourhood Renewal, National Strategy Action Plan*, London: Cabinet Office, SEU.

Soteri-Proctor, A. (2011) *Little Big Society: Micro-mapping of organisations operating below the radar*, Birmingham: Third Sector Research Centre, Working Paper 71.

Southwark, London Borough of (2000) *Community Development Audit 2000*, Appendix 1, Local Case Studies, Consort and Friary Development Project, London: Southwark Council.

SQW (2008) *Neighbourhood Management Pathfinders Final Evaluation*. London: Communities and Local Government.

Stuteley, H. and Hughes, S. (2011) *Transforming challenging neighbourhoods: Building partnership the C2 way*, University of Exeter: Peninsula School of Medicine and Dentistry, Health Complexity Group. The handbook was initially only available as part of C2 training.

Sustainable Development Commission (2010) *The future is local: Empowering communities to improve their neighbourhoods*, London: SDC.

Taylor, M. (2011) *Public policy in the community*, Basingstoke: Palgrave Macmillan.

Taylor, P. (2006) *Who are the capacity builders? (Summary report)*, London: Community Development Foundation.

Thapa, M. (2006) 'Refugee action', CDX Information Sheet, June, Sheffield: Community Development Exchange.

Thomson, H. et al (2006) 'Do urban regeneration programmes improve public health?', *Journal of Epidemiology and Community Health*, vol 60, no 2, pp 108–15.

Travers, T. (2011) *Engaging London's communities: The Big Society and localism*, London: London Councils and London School of Economics.

Tuckman, B. (1965) 'Developmental sequence in small groups', *Psychological Bulletin*, vol 63, no 6, pp 384–99.

Twelvetrees, A. (2008) *Community work* (4th edn), Basingstoke: Palgrave Macmillan.

Tyler, P. and Rhodes, J. (2007) *The Single Regeneration Budget: Final Evaluation*, Communities and Local Government, Urban Research Summary No 25.

Wales – community development: www.cdcymru.org.

Working for Change, the Irish Journal of Community Work (2010) vol 2, Editorial.

Index

A

Abbott, John   46
accountability   71, 97
Accrington   64
Achieving Better Community Development   138
ACRE – *see* Action for Communities in Rural England
Action for Communities in Rural England   89
activists   6
advocacy   57
Arnstein, Sherry   97
Ashton   51
Asian   126
asset-based   38, 84, 128
assets   31, 58
Association of Community Workers   22
Atkinson, Dick   99-100
Audit Commission   136, 143
austerity   2, 3, 5, 10, 86ff, 112
Axis of Influence   138

B

Bailey, Gavin   82
Balsall Heath   11, 99
Bangor, Wales   103
Banks, S.   8, 162
Barking and Dagenham   63
BASSAC   112
Belbin, M.   60
Belfast   80, 87-8
Bell, John   51
benefits   43, 46
best value   36, 136
Bichard, Michael   93-4
Big Local   114
big society   9, 10, 29, 30, 56, 77, 111ff, 157, 162, 169
Big Society Bank   113
Billericay   64
Birmingham   11, 100
black and minority ethnic   39. *See also* ethnicity
Blunkett, David   102
Blyth Valley   49-50
BME – *see* black and minority ethnic

Bradford   87, 100
Brazil   119
Brighton   63
Bromley by Bow, London   100
budgets   94. *See also* funding
business improvement districts   113
Business in the Community   118
Butcher, Hugh   8, 162

C

'C2'   52, 103ff
Cabinet Office   23, 145
Callaghan, Jim   18
Camden, London   62
Cameron, David   111
Campaigning   39,
capacity building   22, 103
capitalism   37, 41, 44, 46
carers   92
Castle Vale, Birmingham   100
CDF – *see* Community Development Foundation
CDP – *see* Community Development Project
charities   146, 169
Charity Commission   109
Chester   109
children   43, 72, 85, 126
China   47, 126
citizenship   8, 36, 42, 155
City Challenge   18-19, 20, 135
civil society   46
CLG – *see* Department for Communities and Local Government
Coalition Government   9, 29, 30, 78, 90, 102, 111ff, 136
communism   47
community   14 and *passim*
  community associations   55
  community budgets   114
  community centres   50, 58, 166, 169
  community chests   26,
  community cohesion   145
  community development   1, 2, 13, 30, 35 and *passim*
  Community Development Challenge   107, 140
  Community Development Exchange   22

Community Development Foundation 20, 21ff, 29, 51, 65, 81, 143, 154
community development national occupational standards 138
Community Development Project 17, 18, 22
Community Development Trust 62
Community Development Venture Fund 26
community empowerment 2, 25, 28, 119
Community Empowerment Fund 26
community engagement 1, 2, 9, 12, 13, 168 and *passim*
community groups 2, 6, 7, 9, 21, 49, 53, 70 and *passim*
Community Improvement Districts 113
community involvement 1, 2, 13, 17, 29, 31 and *passim*
community led planning 11, 89-90
communities of identity 81
communities of interest 81, 156
community organisers 30, 112
community practice 1, 9, 13 and *passim*
Community Projects Foundation 21,
community sector 55, 62, 93, 111, 145, 149, 165, 167
community work 1, 8, 9, 13, 36, 38
complexity 95, 164
compulsory competitive tendering 36, 135
Conn, Eileen 96
connectivity 80, 166. *See also* networks
Conservative Government 8, 9, 36, 134
constitution 108
consultation 1, 8, 54
contracts 135
co-ordination – see management
co-production 4, 37, 97, 148
Cornwall 63
cost benefits 153ff
costs 152
Council of Voluntary Service 62, 108
councillors – *see* local councillors
councils 5, 36. *See also* local authorities
Creswell, Whitwell and Clowne 64
crime 51, 89
culture 4,
cutbacks 5, 17, 84, 110

D

Daft, Richard L. 69
Dartmouth 52
democracy 1, 2, 3, 8, 35, 41, 44, 46, 57, 97 and *passim*
dentist 52, 66

Department for Communities and Local Government 28, 114, 143, 158
Department for Education and Skills 81
Department of Environment 22
deprivation 67
Development Trusts Association 112
devolution 28
Devon 52
disadvantage 1, 5, 10, 25, 35, 91-2, 149 and *passim*
disempowerment 5, 12. *See also* community empowerment
diversity 145
Duty to Involve 9

E

East Midlands 102
Eastern Europe 118
economy 5, 17, 56, 83, 169
eco-towns 90
education 2, 81
Egan, Sir John 78-80
elderly – *see* older people
Eldonians, Liverpool 100
employment 17, 18, 51, 66, 81, 85, 118, 159
empowerment – *see* community empowerment
Empowerment Unit 29, 144-5
Engage, East Midlands 102
England 2, 3, 10, 14, 30, 38, 62, 67, 77, 162 and *passim*
environment 2, 5, 47, 83, 90, 128, 152
equality 5, 12, 36, 145
estates 52, 118
ethnicity 4, 27, 145
EU – *see* European Union
Europe 32, 47, 61
European Union 19, 88, 90-1, 99, 167
evaluation 19, 53, 84, 133ff, 142
evidence 14, 23, 133ff, 149ff, 163, 170

F

faith organisations 26
Falmouth 11, 52
Federation for Community Development Learning 22, 138
fire and rescue service 103, 152
Firm Foundations 58-9, 139
floor targets 25, 27
Flourishing Neighbourhoods 118ff
Friedman, Mark 133-4, 139, 142
friendship 56, 92
front-line 29, 93, 148, 159, 161
funding 20ff, 40, 58-9, 161, 166, 169-70

G

Gaffikin 80
gate-keeping 71, 110
Gawlinski 111
GDP 84
gender 3-4, 43
Geyer, R. 95
Gilchrist, Alison 59, 109, 137-8
globalisation 86, 156
Graessle 111
Groundwork 90

H

Handy, Charles 69, 109
health 1, 2, 4, 5, 17, 37, 43, 44, 56, 66, 85, 102, 126ff and *passim*
Health and Wellbeing Boards 102, 168
Health Empowerment Leverage Project 52, 103, 153
Heath, Edward 18
HELP – *see* Health Empowerment Leverage Project
Henderson, Paul 109, 162
Heseltine, Michael 18, 135
highways – *see* transport
holistic 94, 165. *See also* whole systems
Home Office 55, 58, 61, 63
housing 1, 2, 4, 8, 17, 37, 50, 152
Huddersfield 64
Hughes, Susanne 103

I

In and Against the State 43
index of multiple deprivation 151
indicators 136, 143ff. *See also* measurement
inequality – *see* equality *and* poverty
influence 56, 66, 94, 97, 143ff, 148
innovation 37,
IpsosMORI 66
Ireland 138. *See also* Northern Ireland
isolation 8

J

job creation 83. *See also* employment
Joint Strategic Needs Assessment 151
Joseph Rowntree Foundation 87

L

Labour – *see* New Labour
ladder of involvement or participation 57, 97
LEADER programme 90

LEAP 138
leisure 4
Liberal Democrats 32
life expectancy 82, 89
Liverpool 100
Local Area Agreements 26, 30, 136, 144
local authorities 26, 30, 38, 62, 78 and *passim*
local councillors 36, 37, 45, 57
Local Government Association 35
Local Strategic Partnerships 25, 27, 28, 30, 136ff, 158, 168
localism 31, 112
Locality (organisation) 112
local umbrella groups 60, 62, 99, 167
London 62, 100, 113
LOVAS 55, 61, 63
LSPs – *see* Local Strategic Partnerships

M

MacFarlane, 18
MacMillan, Harold 17
Major, John 8, 18, 135
management 8, 29, 106-7, 126 and *passim*
Marxist 18
measurement 12, 45, 65, 142, 166
meeting space 58. *See also* community centres
Mintzberg, Henry 122
mobility 80
Morrissey 80
Mouffe, Chantal 40,
Murtagh, B. 83
mutual aid 56-7

N

NALC – *see* National Association for Local Councils
National Association for Local Councils 89
National Association for Neighbourhood Management – *see* neighbourhood management
national lottery 114
national occupational standards – *see* community development national occupational standards
National Standards for Community Engagement (Scotland) 138
National Strategy for Neighbourhood Renewal 29. *See also* Neighbourhood Renewal
national survey of charities and social enterprises 133, 149ff

national survey of third sector organisations –
see national survey of charities and social
enterprises
neighbourhood   1, 6, 10, 35, 77 and *passim*
  neighbourhood element   88
  neighbourhood management   24, 26, 88,
  100, 119
  neighbourhood partnership   4, 6, 14, 62,
  74, 101ff, 104, 167ff and *passim*
  Neighbourhood Renewal   9, 11, 23, 25, 26,
  27, 29, 30, 56, 84-6, 88
  Neighbourhood Support Fund   81
networks   7, 22, 58-9, 148, 166, 168
New Deal for Communities   66
New Economics Foundation   153
New Labour   9, 22, 23ff, 28, 29, 30, 32, 56,
  90, 102, 119, 133, 157
NHS   121, 130. *See also* health
Northern Ireland   2, 9, 22, 28, 29, 77, 112,
  138, 157
Northern Ireland Health and Social Care
  Board   82
Northern Ireland Public Health Agency   82
Northumberland   49

O

ODPM – *see* Office of the Deputy Prime
  Minister
Office for Civil Society   145, 147
Office of the Deputy Prime Minister   24,
  28, 51
Office for the Third Sector   145
older people   128
online centres   26
Open Services White Paper   112
OPM   50
organisational culture   69-72, 109
organisational development   81
organisation theory   49, 67, 69
outcomes   66, 80, 133ff, 139ff, 153, 157, 166

P

parishes   10, 28, 89-90
parks   52
participation – *see* community involvement
partnership – *see* neighbourhood partnership
patient and public involvement   1, 102
PCT – *see* Primary Care Trust
Pickles, Eric   112
philanthropy   3, 39, 55
place based budgets   35, 94
place survey   143. *See also* Total Place
planning   4

policing   1, 5, 8, 50, 52, 102-3, 152-3
Policy Action Teams   23
policy-making   35, 95, 155 and *passim*
poverty   5, 19, 36, 37, 44, 118, 141, 149, 170
Pratt, J.   110
Prendergast, J.   28
Prescott, John   78
Primary Care Trust   50, 52
private sector   4, 19, 29, 36, 134, 161
psychology   68, 108
public sector – *see* public services
public services   1, 36, 37, 42, 56, 84, 92 and
  passim

Q

quangos   29, 90

R

radicalism   18, 35, 37, 40, 44
recession   3. *See also* austerity
refugees   81
regeneration   17, 29, 30, 84-6, 99
Regional Empowerment Partnerships   145,
  158
regions   157ff
retrofitting   78
revolution   44, 46
Richardson, Liz   87
Rihani, S.   95
Robson, Brian   18
Royds, Bradford   100
Rubery, West Midlands   103
rural   5, 89-90. *See also* Community Led
  Planning
Rural Community Council   62
Russell, Cormac   128

S

safer and stronger communities   136
safety   85, 128, 136
Sanderson, I.   83
schools   4, 37
Scotland   2, 10, 22, 28, 29, 77, 112, 138, 157
Scottish Community Development Centre
  138
Seattle   11, 119
Senge, Peter   159
seven step model   105
Single Regeneration Budget   9, 11, 20ff, 30,
  32, 84-6, 88, 100, 135
Skills in Neighbourhood Work   109
Smallbury Down   126ff

social capital   23, 56, 90, 149
social enterprise   1, 55, 56, 112, 147
socialism   43
social return on investment   65, 153
social services   5, 37, 103
Soteri-Procter   54, 58
South Hams   52
Southwark   50-1
Soviet   47
sport   4, 56-7
SRB – *see* Single Regeneration Budget
SROI – *see* social return on investment
state   35, 39, 41, 43, 170
statistics – *see* measurement
strategy   4, 7, 15, 25, 49, 65, 77ff, 117, 155ff,
    161ff and *passim*
Structural Funds   90, 157
students   117
Stuteley, Hazel   103
subsidiarity   158
Sudanese   126
sustainability   78
Sustainable Communities Academy   80
Sustainable Development Commission   78-
    9, 90
systems   159. *See also* whole system

T

Tameside   51
targets   137
taxation   36
Taylor, Peter   39,
teamwork   89, 105ff, 159
tenants   4, 26
Thapa, Mani   81
Thatcher, Margaret   18
third sector   1, 62, 133, 145ff
Third Sector Research Centre   147
Thomas, David   109
Torbay   63
Total Place   29, 94, 114, 170
Townstal, Devon   52, 103
trade unions   46,
Trafford Hall   109
transformation   5, 10, 99, 170
transport   4, 80, 130
travellers   82
trustees   108
Tuckman, B.   69
Twelvetrees, Alan   106-7, 109

U

UK   2, 38, 39

umbrella group – *see* local umbrella group
unemployment – *see* employment
university   117
Urban Programme   18
Urban Task Force   23
Urban White Paper   24, 27, 28
US   11
USSR   47

V

values   108
VCS – *see* voluntary sector *and* community
    sector
villages   5, 10, 35, 61, 160
voluntary organisations – *see* voluntary sector
voluntary sector   1, 3, 6, 37, 38, 93, 111, 145,
    149, 167
volunteering   40, 57, 63, 66, 143 and *passim*

W

Wales   2, 10, 22, 28, 29, 77, 103, 112, 157
wards   124, 166. *See also* councillors
wealth   36. *See also* private sector
West Midlands   103
Westminster model   95
whole system   79, 94ff, 132. *See also* holistic
Wilson, Harold   17, 18, 21
Working Neighbourhoods   56
Wrexham   51, 60

Y

Young Volunteer Force Foundation   21-2
youth work   1, 37, 103